Remembering the Lotus-Born

Studies in Indian and Tibetan Buddhism

This series was conceived to provide a forum for publishing outstanding new contributions to scholarship on Indian and Tibetan Buddhism and also to make accessible seminal research not widely known outside a narrow specialist audience, including translations of appropriate monographs and collections of articles from other languages. The series strives to shed light on the Indic Buddhist traditions by exposing them to historical-critical inquiry, illuminating through contextualization and analysis these traditions' unique heritage and the significance of their contribution to the world's religious and philosophical achievements.

STUDIES IN INDIAN AND TIBETAN BUDDHISM

REMEMBERING THE LOTUS-BORN

Padmasambhava in the History of Tibet's Golden Age

Daniel A. Hirshberg

Wisdom

Wisdom Publications
199 Elm Street
Somerville, MA 02144 USA
wisdompubs.org

Library of Congress Cataloging-in-Publication Data
Names: Hirshberg, Daniel Alexander, author.
Title: Remembering the Lotus-Born : Padmasambhava in the history of Tibet's golden age / Daniel A. Hirshberg.
Description: Somerville, MA : Wisdom Publications, 2016. | Series: Studies in Indian and Tibetan Buddhism | Based on the author's thesis (doctoral—Harvard University, 2012) under title: Delivering the Lotus-Born: historiography in the Tibetan Renaissance. | Includes bibliographical references and index.
Identifiers: LCCN 2016000542| ISBN 9781614292319 (pbk. : alk. paper) | ISBN 1614292310 (pbk. : alk. paper)
Subjects: LCSH: Buddhism—Tibet Region—Historiography. | Padma Sambhava, approximately 717–approximately 762. | Ñaṅ-ral Ñi-ma-'od-zer, 1124–1192—Authorship. | Religious biography—History and criticism.
Classification: LCC BQ7578 .H57 2016 | DDC 294.3/92309—dc23
LC record available at http://lccn.loc.gov/2016000542

ISBN 978-1-61429-231-9 ebook ISBN 978-1-61429-246-3

20 19 18 17 16 5 4 3 2 1

Cover design by Gopa & Ted 2. Cover art: Padmasambhava, from a nineteenth-century thangka at Rubin Museum of Art. Author photo on page 239 is by Eve Kagan. Calligraphy by Daniel A. Hirshberg. Set in Diacritical Garamond Pro 10.5/13.

Wisdom Publications' books are printed on acid-free paper and meet the guidelines for permanence and durability of the Production Guidelines for Book Longevity of the Council on Library Resources.

This book was produced with environmental mindfulness.
For more information, please visit wisdompubs.org/wisdom-environment.

Printed in the United States of America.

MIX
Paper from responsible sources
FSC www.fsc.org FSC® C011935

Please visit fscus.org.

oṃ

āḥ

hūṃ

Contents

Preface

According to the Tibetan Buddhist tradition, the eighth-century tantric adept Padmasambhava is not bound by time or history. As the Second Buddha inseparable from the three exalted buddha bodies, he transcends past, present, and future. Padmasambhava, the "lotus-born," is not just a man who attained enlightenment in the past; he persists as the timeless continuity of ultimate truth, representing its potency and rendering it accessible for all those who seek to realize it. And yet Tibetans have long been fascinated by the conventional details of his life as well. Nearly a millennium of biographical materials informs the countless devotional liturgies to Guru Rinpoché, as he came to be known throughout the Himalaya. Celebrated under their own literary genre known as *katang* (*bka' thang*) and often ascribed to Padmasambhava himself, these "testaments" are understood to illuminate indisputably the historical activity of a man, albeit a uniquely accomplished one, who accepted an imperial invitation to Tibet in the eighth century.

For as long as Tibetans have had Buddhism, many have maintained a keen interest in the past and its representation in text. The imperial era, when Buddhism was introduced and established as the state religion, became a topic of intense interest even as the dust still settled from the empire's ninth-century collapse. Historical accounts were composed, compiled, and recovered over the centuries, and critically minded Tibetans noted and attempted to reconcile the many discrepancies in the records that recount this period, among them Padmasambhava's sojourn and the extent of his activities. Western scholars seeking to clarify the events of this era thus join nearly a millennium of critical historiography that seeks to clarify the influential persons and events of this era, although guided by the perspectives, methodologies, and objectives of our present context.

The following endeavor makes no attempt to point out the ultimate reality of Padmasambhava, philosophically or otherwise. And yet this inquiry is complementary in that it seeks to clarify his conventional identity, not just in his terminal representation as a historical person but as the enduring focus of an eminently human process of re/constructing and remembering the past—

a continuous practice that occurs only in the present. Therefore, like its Tibetan antecedents, may this too be a lamp that illuminates the face of the Lotus-Born.

I would like to acknowledge a series of educators and advisors who encouraged me to find my own path and taught me to trust in it. I would have met few of them if not for the generosity of my parents, James and Diane Hirshberg. Kevin Jennings, Cynthia Katz, and Sandy Stott at Concord Academy, and Jan Willis and Gene Klaaren at Wesleyan University, all helped shape my thinking, writing, and modes of inquiry. I would not have proceeded into a PhD without the training and support of Phil Stanley in the much-too-short-lived Nitartha/Shedra track at Naropa University. At different times, I also benefited from the instruction and direction of Craig Preston, Jules Levinson, and Jeffrey Hopkins as well as Godwin Samararatne, Chökyi Nyima Rinpoché, and Tulku Thondup Rinpoché. Susan Morgan is a lamp on the path that illuminates the way. Dzogchen Ponlop Rinpoché kindly bestows tools that pierce to the heart of my inquiry.

This book is a revision of my doctoral dissertation for the Committee on Inner Asian and Altaic Studies at Harvard University, which was funded by a Graduate Student Fellowship. I am indebted to my mentor and primary dissertation advisor, Leonard van der Kuijp, who upon first hearing of my interest in contrasting presentations of Padmasambhava suggested I have a look at Nyangrel's *Chos 'byung*. Both myself and my research were incalculably enriched by Leonard's breadth of knowledge, his willingness to share it, and his depth of kindness as a mentor. I would also like to thank my hosts while conducting research in Gangtok, Sikkim: it was delightful to be a perennial guest in the home of Séla Yeshé Dorjé and his family, and Acharya Lama Tshultshem Gyatso of the Namgyal Institute of Tibetology clarified many opaque colloquialisms in Nyangrel's biographies. The Harvard Graduate Student Council and the Fairbank Center for Chinese Studies funded travel to relevant sites in Tibet in 2011. Several photographs from this excursion are printed within, and Gyurme Dorje was kind enough to offer rare photographs of Nyangrel sites that remain inaccessible at present. My dissertation benefited from the critiques of my committee: Janet Gyatso, David Germano, and Robert Mayer especially, who remains a wellspring of valuable advice. Lewis Doney offered detailed notes on the dissertation and digitally exchanged several *bka' thang* manuscripts with me, and Adam Krug and Michael Sheehy provided valuable feedback on specific chapters of the final manuscript.

The process of revision was initiated during a postdoctoral fellowship in the Religious Studies Department at the University of California, Santa Barbara, where I enjoyed the warm collegiality of José Cabezón, Greg Hillis, and Vesna Wallace. It was foremost completed during a postdoctoral fellowship with the "Kingship and Religion in Tibet" project, funded by the Alexander von Humboldt Foundation and hosted at Ludwig Maximilian University of Munich. I am grateful to the leader of the research group, Brandon Dotson, for providing the time, space, and dialogue to complete a much-improved revision. In the final stages, I value the work of my editor, David Kittelstrom, my copyeditor Harmony DenRonden, and the production staff at Wisdom Publications. Most recently I have appreciated the welcome of my colleagues in the Department of Classics, Philosophy, and Religion at the University of Mary Washington in Fredericksburg, Virginia, where I finalized the manuscript for publication.

Having been hosted by many institutions, an equal number of unsung administrators have been invaluable for navigating so many distinct bureaucracies, ensuring that I arrived and often successfully departed: Mary Murray Coleman at Concord Academy; Giovannina Jobson of Naropa University; Margaret Lindsey and Lisa Simpson at Harvard University; Anna Balikci-Denjongpa at Tibetology; Shubra Agrawal at UCSB; Sandra Sucrow of LMU; and Cindy Toomey of UMW.

As the distances between these schools imply, over the time of this work my family has endured the upheaval of nearly annual cross-country if not intercontinental relocations, and I am deeply grateful for their extraordinary generosity, courage, and patience. With love and appreciation, this book is dedicated to our daughter, Milena, who is such a beaming source of joy and delight; to our sweet English setter, Bodha, who tolerated many kennels en route to residing on three continents; and to my wife, Eve Kagan, whose affection sustains me. She is my *mudrā*, my *sku zla*. The mere presence of her reminds me that anything is possible and it becomes so.

Publisher's Acknowledgment

THE PUBLISHER gratefully acknowledges the generous contribution of the Hershey Family Foundation toward the publication of this book.

Introduction

FOR TIBETANS there may be no individual more central to Tibetan history and the heart of Tibetan cultural identity than Padmasambhava, the "Lotus-Born" tantric guru of the eighth century. His vibrant biographical tradition, recovered as treasure texts from at least the twelfth century, apotheosizes Padmasambhava as the catalyst that successfully converted the animistic powers of Tibet's awesome natural landscape to Buddhism when all else had failed. At that time the emperor Tri Songdetsen (ca. 742–ca. 800) ruled over an empire so powerful that in 763 it sacked the capital of its neighbor and competitor, the great Tang dynasty, and the Tibetans briefly set their own proxy upon the throne of China. Having prevailed in these foreign conquests and established Tibet among the great regional powerhouses of the era, Tri Songdetsen sought to tame his domestic populace as well. While the earliest sources credit the coerced alignment of Tibet's clans as the voussoirs forming the arch of the Tibetan empire, post-imperial works often emphasize the interventions of a diverse and unruly taxonomy of spirits, ghosts, earthbound demons, and demigods that inhabited the features of the natural environment and roamed the landscape, interacting with its human inhabitants for good or ill.[1]

In Tibet seemingly minor environmental manipulations such as diverting a stream for irrigation or excavating earth to construct a foundation could provoke the wrath of these temperamental entities, thus Tibetans developed an array of rituals for placation, subjugation, exorcism, and so forth. As representatives of the indigenous religion, Tibet's earliest ritualists, known as Bön and Shen, primarily specialized in healing remedies for the living and funerary practices for the dead in reliance upon an array of apotropaic and divination technologies to facilitate both.[2] They would eventually be succeeded by Buddhist tantrikas who claimed to function as human interlocutors and emissaries to Tibet's nonhuman populations. Since digging a hole in the Tibetan

1. Dalton 2011, 59.

2. Dotson 2008, 43.

soil required propitiatory rites to placate agitated local spirits, then the introduction and promotion of a foreign religion could trigger a war. No detailed account can be reliably traced to the period of Tibet's conversion to Buddhism,[3] but subsequent reconstructions of this process in the centuries after the empire collapsed resolved upon a normative narrative: when Tri Songdetsen invites the ordained Indian abbot Śāntarakṣita to disseminate the Buddhist teachings, serve as court preceptor, and consecrate the ground for the construction of the first Tibetan monastery, environmental disasters assault the palaces and epidemics afflict people and animals alike. It is determined that the Tibetan spirits have risen in force to riot against these offenses, and the emperor has no choice but to delay his ambitions and regroup while the abbot is forced to fall back to a redoubt in Nepal. After the attacks launched by their adversaries subside, Tri Songdetsen compels Śāntarakṣita to return again, but the abbot admits that the abilities acquired through his exoteric Buddhist practice lack the firepower to challenge those they had provoked; only a fully enlightened master wielding the esoteric technologies of Buddhist tantra could overcome the host arrayed against them.

Śāntarakṣita thereby advises the emperor to employ the services of the world's most accomplished tantric adept, the one known as Padmasambhava, by inviting him to Tibet. Only he could subjugate and convert the rebellious malcontents that opposed Buddhism there. Emperor Tri Songdetsen dispatches messengers to the master's retreat in Nepal, and then Padmasambhava treks intrepidly through the Himalaya to the Tibetan plateau, battling Tibet's domestic divinities, subduing them with feats of martial thaumaturgy, converting them by force and binding them by oath to protect the Buddhist teachings as he blazes a path to the Tibetan court.

Whether authentically archaic or relatively late, all sources that describe the initial stages of Tibet's conversion to Buddhism in the eighth century generally agree up to this point, but the story then diverges into two contradictory narrative paths: one in which Padmasambhava establishes Buddhism and earns a most exalted status as "the Second Buddha" of the Tibetan people for perpetuity, and another where he soon departs ingloriously as a fleeting contributor and minor figure in Tibetan history. In the former, far more popular account, Tri Songdetsen, Śāntarakṣita, and Padmasambhava form a uniquely dynamic trio whose cooperation is essential to the establishment of Buddhism: Tri Songdetsen is the unwavering imperial patron who is determined to convert Tibet to Buddhism, invites both masters, sponsors the construction of the first monastery, Samyé Lhungidrupa, and initiates the great translation

3. Cantwell and Mayer 2007, 5–9.

project; Śāntarakṣita is the venerable conduit for the legitimate transmission of exoteric doctrine and monastic discipline; and Padmasambhava is the unconquerable master of tantric esoterica who single-handedly subdues the hostile demigods of the indigenous Tibetan landscape, prepares the ground for the construction and consecration of Samyé, and entrusts the most potent and prized soteriological technologies of Vajrayāna Buddhism to his Tibetan disciples. Padmasambhava enjoys an extended stay in Tibet, whereby he visits all the sacred sites, conceals countless texts and relics as consecrated "treasures" (*gter*) for later recovery, and departs after the death of Tri Songdetsen and the uncontested enthronement of his son, who pledges uninterrupted state support for Buddhism at the center of the Tibetan empire.

Even so, Tibetan Buddhists have emphasized for centuries that according to the ultimate, most authentic view, Padmasambhava never left Tibet. His physical presence (*sku*, "exalted form") pervades Tibet's sacred landscape interred as treasures still, and since the Buddhist teachings only became possible in Tibet by means of his original subjugations, all those instructions (*gsung*, "exalted speech") that reveal perfect buddha nature as the true essence of all sentient beings continuously resonate at the heart centers of the Tibetan people as the enlightened mind (*thugs*) of Padmasambhava. He is both cipher and simulacrum of the instructions he imparted, and therefore much more than a mere historical figure confined to time; he is the Precious Guru whose fundamental nature transcends time, revealing reality to all those who look to him. In fulfilling that function, Padmasambhava manifests in various aspects at the epicenters of countless ritual and meditative liturgies.

Dealing with questions of historiography, a significant issue is that the primacy of Padmasambhava's agency in Tibet's conversion is uniformly unattested in early sources. Scant evidence tethers his contributions to the thread of history, and what there is appears to have been amended amid the process of revisionary hagiography. Nevertheless, the story of Tibet's conversion to Buddhism starring Padmasambhava is the plot recounted by any Tibetan when asked about how Buddhism was definitively established there, and he even becomes an important source for contemporary Bön lineages, albeit with significant divergences in the narrative.[4] The ubiquity and significance of the Padmasambhava story is rivaled only by national myths identifying emperor Songtsen Gampo (d. ca. 649) as an emanation of Avalokiteśvara, and both

4. For an overview of Bön depictions of Padmasambhava and his incorporation into their origins, see Achard 2004, x–xi and xxvi–xxix. For a Bönpo synopsis of Padmasambhava's life by Jamyang Khyentsé Wangpo (1820–99), who was an advocate of Buddhist nonsectarianism and affiliated with Bön as well, see the translation in Zangpo 2002, 191–205.

were forged into more complete forms by many of the same twelfth-century treasure revealers. These two accounts are the twin foundation narratives of Tibetan cultural identity, the formative texts of the Tibetan people that persist in the present as a collective memory that bonds Tibetans by virtue of a common identity drawn from a correlate past. This function has become all the more critical as contemporary Tibetans continue to confront the pressure of Chinese administration in Tibet and the cultural diffusion of diaspora beyond it.

When Tibetans recount these stories they produce "forms of memory that are designed to stabilize a common identity,"[5] which may have been among the original impetuses that led to their elaboration as distinct syntheses in the twelfth century. At that time Tibetan culture was fractured more by forces from within than, as is the case today, by those from without. The unifying function of such shared "history" cannot be denied, even when analysis of early sources suggests that its ties to the actual occurrence of past events are tenuous. Historiographically savvy Tibetans recognized fundamental discrepancies between their sources as well, yet even in making such assessments, many scholars came to devalue ancient sources for those recovered in later centuries. Said to have been concealed during the imperium, these "treasures" were designated for later retrieval by karmically destined reincarnations of imperial-era figures.

In reliance upon the critical lenses of historiography and communicative memory, the social aspect of individual memory that highlights "the intermediary realm between individuals" and "grows out of intercourse between people,"[6] this book details the religious and textual innovations that produced the first complete revision of the story of Tibet's conversion to Buddhism at the apogee of the Tibetan empire, with Padmasambhava as its heroic protagonist. Since this narrative revises and reimagines the accounts of earlier sources, Tibetan and Western scholars alike have assumed that its first complete version, the *Copper Island Biography of Padmasambhava* (*Padma 'byung gnas kyi rnam thar zangs gling ma*), was revealed as an apocryphal treasure text. However, by reassessing this narrative across its available recensions and performing the first thorough investigation of its author, tradent, and/or revealer, Nyangrel Nyima Öser (1124–92), it becomes clear that the designation of the *Copper Island* as a treasure text obscures the complex of indigenous innovations that made its production possible. Rather than the wholesale invention or simple "revelation" of a new narrative, the *Copper Island* was the product of the

5. Assmann 2006, 11.

6. Assmann 2006, 3.

Tibetan assimilation and transformation of core Indian Buddhist literary traditions and religious concepts that coalesced in Nyangrel, who is celebrated as the first of the great Buddhist treasure revealers.

As a scion of the imperial Nyang clan and the heir to religious transmissions that would come to cohere as the Nyingma or "Old" school, Nyangrel continues to be renowned for his lineages of fierce deity-yoga praxis and the Great Perfection, the recovery of ancient texts and relics as treasure, and the first complete hagiography of Padmasambhava, but he also had a transformative role in promoting serial or "catenate" reincarnation lineages, the myths that establish Avalokiteśvara as the patron deity of Tibet, and with those myths the pervasive resonance of the *maṇi* mantra throughout the Himalaya. By drawing these latter three together in particular, Nyangrel devised "the clearest blueprint for the later Tibetan religiopolitical construction" that would be actualized and perfected by the Dalai Lamas.[7] All of these can be traced through Nyangrel, who in relying on the threads of inherited traditions, knit these elements into innovative literary tapestries that remain part of the fabric of Tibetan Buddhism and culture to the present. Nyangrel was a progenitor of some of the most definitive aspects of Tibetan Buddhism, yet these very innovations ensured that he would be eclipsed by later adepts who, in adopting his claims and methods, revealed new iterations of his scriptures and narratives.

In highlighting Nyangrel's contributions to Tibetan culture in general and the Padmasambhava narrative in particular, this book explores his roles in the employment and advancement of: the hagiographical construction of enlightened identity in chapter 1;[8] karmic causality and catenate reincarnation theory in chapter 2; the mode of exclusively material textual recovery, augmentation, and reintroduction known as *treasure* in chapter 3; and historiography in chapter 4 through analyzing *Honey Nectar, the Essence of Flowers: A History of Buddhism* (*Chos 'byung me tog snying po sbrang rtsi'i bcud*), which features all but the first five of Nyangrel's forty-chapter Padmasambhava narrative within it. In drawing together the conclusions of the previous chapters, chapter 5 then problematizes long-held assumptions concerning Nyangrel's Padmasambhava narrative, clarifies its transmission, and concludes with new theses concerning its composition, which has been a persistent source of intrigue throughout the history of Tibetan studies. It concludes with an investigation of the roles of both individual and collective memory in the introduction of this seminal text as well as its persistence to the present.

As is the case with so many grand narratives, this story is more of a cultural

7. Kapstein 2000, 162.

8. An early version of this chapter was published as Hirshberg 2009.

product forged by the confluence of collective memory and myth than a historical one drawn primarily from ancient textual witnesses. Academics first questioned its historicity nearly as soon as Tibetan studies dawned as a critical discipline, and more recent research demonstrates that while there is little reason to doubt that Padmasambhava was a historical person, his actual influence in imperial Tibet and his role in its conversion to Buddhism were likely quite limited. Nevertheless, some of his most definitive character traits are already attested in post-imperial literature, and it is illuminating to review his earliest extant depictions before shifting to consider his full-blown articulation as the Second Buddha who, in the eyes of the Tibetan people, is comparable to (if not an emanation or even a reincarnation of) the first one, Siddhārtha Gautama of India, Śākyamuni Buddha himself.

Padmasambhava in Early Sources

While Padmasambhava does appear in post-imperial manuscripts, some of which may preserve content that originated during the imperium, none can be definitively ascribed to the eighth century, and thus some have questioned whether Padmasambhava was a historical person at all. Regardless, the conflicting accounts of his time in Tibet have inspired surveys of the earliest extant sources in an attempt to distinguish whoever he might have been from what he became. Padmasambhava has yet to be found described in or cited as the author of a single Indic text, thus only early Tibetan materials can provide any insight into this inquiry.[9] The limited source material includes the epigraphic record carved into stone during the reigns of the emperors in the eighth and ninth centuries, and the ancient manuscripts recovered from grottoes near Dunhuang in Chinese Turkestan, most of which were produced in the two centuries after the collapse of the empire. Before proceeding to the written evidence, we might first consider Padmasambhava's background through investigating the place from which he so famously hails.

Padmasambhava is said to be from Uḍḍiyāna (also, Oḍḍiyāna, Udyāna/Oḍyāna, Uḍḍayana/Oḍḍayana; Tib. O/U rgyan; Ch. Wuzhangna), a place whose thick cloak of esoteric mystique is nearly matched by the confusion con-

9. Mayer 2011b refutes previous hypotheses that *'Phags pa thabs kyi zhags pa padma 'phreng gi don bsdus pa*, a text also recovered from Dunhuang as IOL Tib J 321, is the sole, verifiably ancient document attributed to Padmasambhava. With regard to Padmasambhava's historicity, however, Mayer 2015b, 346, softens this authorial absence by noting that "not a single name comes down to us today from Indic sources of any Mahāyoga *siddha* of the late eighth century, even though we know several influential ones must have existed at that time."

cerning its geographical location. While some Chinese sources and the scholarship focusing on them suggest its location to be on the east Indian coast in the area of Orissa and others look much farther northwest to the Silk Road oasis of Kashgar, recent consensus resolves upon a verdant alpine valley just north of Peshawar in the Swat region of present-day Pakistan.[10] It is thus restricted to a relatively limited area, estimated to be five thousand *li* or about sixty-five miles in circumference by the Chinese pilgrim Xuanzang, who visited in 631.[11] As its renown expanded in Tibetan sources, however, so too did its total area: by the fourteenth century the *Testament of Padmasambhava* (*Padma bka' thang*) eulogizes Uḍḍiyāna as a paradise spread over two-thirds of the world's total landmass.[12] With close proximity to both the Karakorum and Khyber passes as well as the wealth of the Silk Roads that flowed through them, this region flourished for centuries under the Buddhist empire of Gandhāra that enjoyed its apogee from the first to fifth centuries C.E. With merchants and commerce pouring into the realm, various strains of Indian Buddhism arrived as well, and monastic institutions of both the earlier and later Buddhist traditions benefited from significant patronage.

This Uḍḍiyāna was accessed only by steep passes and remained somewhat isolated from the developments of the larger populations in the valley beneath it.[13] When the Chinese Buddhist pilgrim Faxian (337–422) visited circa 400, he noted the presence of some five hundred monasteries exclusively in the tradition of the early Buddhist schools, but all of these had been destroyed by the time Xuanzang (602–64) returned in 631.[14] Mahāyāna Buddhism may have flourished following a devastating invasion that laid waste to those earlier establishments in the fifth century, but a new Silk Road that circumvented Peshawar became favored by the sixth century, such that the area continued its decline.[15] While Xuanzang notes that as many as eighteen thousand Buddhist monks formerly inhabited fourteen hundred monasteries in Uḍḍiyāna, only a smattering remained by the time of his survey, and very few could read Indic scriptures phonetically, never mind understand them.

10. The definitive discussion of Uḍḍiyāna in Swat is by Sanderson 2007, 265–69. Also see Davidson 2003, 209. Hodge 2003, 21 and 539–40n10, presents new hypotheses for its location in Kāñcī, one of which is that King Indrabhūti, Padmasambhava's adoptive father who returns with him to Uḍḍiyāna in his later hagiographical literature, is described as the ruler of Kāñcī in the *Biographies of the Eighty-Four Mahāsiddhas.*

11. Beal 1884, 119.

12. *Padma bka' thang*, 67.5–70.4.

13. Behrendt 2004, 23–24.

14. Beal 1884, 119n1.

15. Behrendt 2004, 25.

Nevertheless, Xuanzang describes the people of the region as devoted to Mahāyāna Buddhism and also reports that "they practice the art of using charms," magical incantations,[16] *dhāraṇī* if not the mantras of esoteric Buddhist practice that were hot technologies in India at the time of Xuanzang's travels. The Buddhist use of *dhāraṇī* may extend back to the time of the Buddha himself and is prevalent in both the early and later exoteric traditions, so in all likelihood they were introduced to Swat well before tantra developed in India, but this reference to incantation remains significant in that it may serve as one of very few indications suggesting the presence of Vajrayāna at any time in Swat's history. Another is a single rock sculpture from the region in which Anna Filigenzi discerns the severely abraded presence of what may have been a tantrika, perhaps even in Padmasambhava's common iconographical guise with the right hand raising a vajra and the left holding a skullcup.[17] In sum, however, Filigenzi admits that "the cultural blossoming [of Vajrayāna] has never been reflected in archaeological evidence in the territory of Swat," nor has any eighth-century textual evidence of tantric Buddhism been recovered from the area.[18] We know that the region was ruled by a series of Turkic Hindu-Ṣāhis throughout this period, however, and Uḍḍiyāna as Swat is foremost corroborated by the only extant inscription that mentions "Uḍyāna," which survives on the base of an eighth-century Gaṇeśa statue discovered nearby.[19]

Due to its association with Padmasambhava especially, Uḍḍiyāna came to be remembered as a mystical incubator of Vajrayāna in the Tibetan *imaginaire*, but the textual and archaeological record of Swat indicates that institutional Buddhism was in decline well before the eighth century, and there is no definitive evidence that esoteric Buddhism ever thrived there. Nevertheless, Kashmir, a hotbed of tantric innovation, was in relatively close proximity, and the decline of more conservative Buddhist institutions can introduce the opportunity for tantric Buddhism to flourish. Additionally, scriptures have not always survived even for well-established tantric sects, so it is certainly possible that Buddhist tantra persisted in Swat throughout this period. Whatever its location, Adam Krug aptly notes that scholars "appear to make the same move that emic tantric historiographers have made in placing Uḍḍiyāna, as the guarantor of authenticity in the tantric Buddhist world, in the closest proximity to their own disciplines as possible."[20] Regardless of whether Padmasambhava indeed

16. Beal 1884, 120.

17. Filigenzi 2003, 49.

18. Filigenzi 2003, 42.

19. Kuwayama 1991.

20. Adam Krug, personal communication, December 17, 2015.

originated from the Uḍḍiyāna of Swat or Orissa or elsewhere, he traveled to greater India and engaged the efflorescence of tantric Buddhism in the eighth century.

During his travels Padmasambhava would have discovered that northern India was already suffering its own tumultuous era with warring feudal states, decentralized authority, the decline of urban centers, and displaced populations in transit. Political and economic upheaval forced Buddhist centers to consolidate into larger institutions, and this era saw monastic universities like Nālandā and Odantapuri become international collectives as they magnetized Buddhist scholars and practitioners from greater Asia.[21] Among the most controversial topics on the peripheries of the esoteric curriculum were the recent Mahāyoga tantras, which employed antinomian and transgressive rhetoric concerning sex and violence, if not the advocation of their actualization in ritual practice. The novice Padmasambhava may have been a good candidate to enroll at one of these universities, but his lore presents him as ultimately eschewing the confines of institutionalization to tread the path of the *siddhas*, tantric exegetes who "operated on the margins of society, in the twilight zone between the forest and the fields, a place of potency and magic."[22] It was here that he is said to have perfected his abilities and gained such renown as a *vidyādhara*, a knowledge-holder or sorcerer, that his name would eventually reach the Tibetan court.

The earliest dateable sources for Padmasambhava would have been the inscriptions that survived uneffaced from Tibet's imperium, but these make no reference to the tantrika, even when the contributions of others from the era are commemorated. Padmasambhava is likewise absent from both the *Edict* and *Authoritative Exposition of Samyé Monastery* (*Bsam yas bka' gtsigs, Bsam yas bka' mchid*). This is especially notable in the latter since it narrates the calamities that obstructed the introduction of Buddhism and the construction of Samyé, the twin impetuses for his invitation. Admittedly, the *Authoritative Exposition* only refers to Buddhist "teachers of virtue" generically and fails to mention any by name, such that Śāntarakṣita is absent as well,[23] but the entire scope of extant epigraphic evidence, whether carved on stele or transcribed into surviving histories, offers no confirmation of Padmasambhava's presence in Tibet. Manuscripts dated to some time after the reign of Tri Songdetsen and likely after the end of the empire altogether are the only resources for early depictions of Padmasambhava.

As the empire collapsed and Tibet fragmented in the latter decades of the

21. Davidson 2005, 25–26 and 29.

22. Davidson 2005, 33.

23. Richardson 1998, 89–99.

ninth century, its texts were plundered and scattered such that very few remain extant today. While Tibetans have referred to the period between the end of the empire and the beginning of the later dissemination as "the dark period," this was due in part to the scarcity of resources available to them that could illuminate it. Only a relatively recent and remarkable discovery would provide some remedy for contemporary scholars. In addition to imperial-era inscriptions, what we now know of the empire is drawn almost exclusively from a cache of mostly tenth- and early eleventh-century Tibetan manuscripts discovered felicitously in China and subsequently hauled abroad by European scholars at the turn of the twentieth century. These were found in a former monastery cave at Magao near Dunhuang, a Silk Road town now in Gansu province, that came under the successive reigns of various powers throughout its history. Since Dunhuang was conquered by the Tibetans during Tri Songdetsen's campaign in 786, and since the Tibetan language persisted as a lingua franca in the region for some time thereafter, Tibetan documents were discovered among a diverse cache of manuscripts preserved there. These had survived untouched in a sealed cave library from the time this grotto was walled off circa 1010 to its discovery in 1900.[24]

While several manuscripts address Tri Songdetsen's reign, they are often generic, with little historical data concerning the establishment of Buddhism. The *Old Tibetan Chronicle* is one of the best resources for the history of the empire, yet it only provides a terse summary of these events:

> Seizing on the unsurpassed religion of the Buddha and practicing it, [Tri Songdetsen] built temples in the center and on all the borders. Having established the religion, everyone entered into compassion and was liberated from birth and death by calling their minds to it.[25]

Since so few of these early documents offer much detail, those that do are invaluable for gaining insight into how Buddhism was established in eighth-century Tibet. Foremost among these are fragments of a history that became known as the *Testimony of Ba* (*Dba'/Rba/Sba bzhed*) in later centuries. Whether the original elements of this autobiographical narrative stem from the time of its eighth-century narrator or shortly thereafter remains a topic of debate—it might even preserve older material from his ancestors[26]—but the

24. Dalton and van Schaik 2006, xxi; Dalton 2011, 8–10.

25. Translation following Dotson 2007, 26.

26. Kapstein (2000, 72) highlights text from the time of Tri Songdetsen's father, Tri Detsuktsen, that may be drawn from that period.

correspondence of these fragments to the earliest extant manuscripts of the complete narrative confirm the *Testimony of Ba*, or at least some textual components that became renowned as the *Testimony of Ba*, as the earliest extant narrative that details Tibet's conversion to Buddhism.[27]

As declared by its eponymous title, the *Testimony of Ba* alleges to be the first-person account of Ba Selnang Yeshé Wangpo (eighth century), one of the first seven Tibetans to be ordained as Buddhist monks and the original abbot of Samyé Monastery; thus the author claims to be a direct witness to these events. The Dunhuang fragments of this narrative only recount Śāntarakṣita's original invitation and temporary detainment in Lhasa—no mention of Padmasambhava is made whatsoever—but subsequent recensions flesh out the narrative. Following Wangdu and Diemberger's translation of the earliest extant version of the complete narrative (*Dba' bzhed*, eleventh–thirteenth centuries),[28] Śāntarakṣita recommends Padmasambhava to Tri Songdetsen:

> Once upon a time when the Transcendent Conqueror was dwelling in the world, there was no one among all the gods and *nāga* of Jambudvīpa who was not bound by the order of the Buddha. However, in this land of Tibet gods and *nāga* have escaped from control and seem to have prevented the emperor from practicing the sacred doctrine. At present nobody in Jambudvīpa possesses greater powers in the use of mantra than the master from Uḍḍiyāna called Padmasambhava. Last year calamities occurred such as the flood in Pangtang and the royal castle of Lhasa burned down, and the wicked gods and *nāga* have been hindering the emperor's practice of the doctrine. This master of mantra can perform the mirror-divination of the four great kings and make the relevant interpretation. If most of the wicked gods and *nāga* are subdued,

27. Based on their analysis of the Dunhuang fragments, van Schaik and Iwao (2008, 480) conclude that the *Testimony of Ba* is "the earliest extant Tibetan Buddhist history." Richardson (1998, 89–99) dubs the *Edict* and *Authoritative Exposition of Samyé* as the "first Tibetan *Chos 'byung*" or history of Buddhism, but these two documents offer almost nothing with regard to how Buddhism was established in Tibet. Instead, they preserve a declaration of state support in perpetuity in the former and some challenges to its establishment, a generic mention of "teachers of virtue," and a *précis* concerning religious law in the latter, but very little in the manner of detailing these events. For these reasons, van Schaik and Iwao seem justified in arguing that, given the presence of these fragments at Dunhuang, what we now know as the *Testimony of Ba* comprises the earliest extant history of Tibet's conversion to Buddhism, and these fragments certainly represent the earliest extant narration of these events in any detail.

28. Wangdu and Diemberger 2000, 8.

> bound by oath, and firmly instructed, the land will become peaceful. This master of mantra is capable of enabling the sacred doctrine to be practiced in the future.[29]

After his introductory audience at court, Padmasambhava proceeds to display various feats of magic mostly associated with water.[30] Perhaps because of these abilities, he is soon deported by the emperor, who at the suggestion of his imperial advisors comes to suspect that the spiritual master is a threat to his temporal authority. Following Matthew Kapstein, however, Robert Mayer argues that the real threat embodied by Padmasambhava was his promotion of Śaiva-influenced *kāpālika* practices, the modes of transgressive tantra often subsumed under Mahāyoga tantra in Tibetan doxographies that remained controversial among eighth-century Indian Buddhists and presumably their new Tibetan patrons as well. They would become revered forms of tantric Buddhist praxis over the coming centuries, however, which would help clarify why early negative depictions of Padmasambhava and his time in Tibet, such as the one below, soon gave way to his burgeoning apotheosis.[31] Again following Wangdu and Diemberger's translation:

> The ministers reported to Tri Songdetsen: "With his great magical powers this master might seize political power," therefore the emperor grew suspicious. He suspended the master's rituals and prevented them from being celebrated. These were the rituals for subduing the gods and *nāga* that were still to be repeated twice. The emperor presented the preceptor with many offerings and said: "Revered master! You let the holy doctrine come to the country of Tibet. You have already achieved what was in my mind; you bound by oath the gods and *nāga* and so on—that is enough. It is not necessary that the sand of Ngamshö be covered with meadows and that springs appear. It is enough that there is the river called Yarkyim in my own land. Master, please return to your homeland!"
>
> Master Padmasambhava replied, "I thought that in the land of Tibet the doctrine could be established very firmly, that the whole country of Tibet could be led to virtue and that it could become a

29. Translation following Wangdu and Diemberger 2000, 54.

30. Wangdu and Diemberger (2000, 13–14) bolster the case for Uḍḍiyāna as Swat in that Padmasambhava's primary thaumaturgical skillset appears to be an expertise in sophisticated irrigation technologies that were native to the area.

31. Mayer 2015b, 344, citing Kapstein 2000, 159, and Szánto 2013.

prosperous and happy land. However the emperor, being narrow-minded and greatly jealous, suspected that I might seize political power. I do not even desire universal political power, so how could I long for the political power of such a king?" When the master was leaving for India, the emperor circumambulated him three times and offered him a large quantity of gold dust in order to please him. "If I desire gold dust this is it!" He took a full sleeve of sand and this became gold dust. Still, in order to please the emperor he accepted a handful of gold dust and left for India.

After the restricted assembly had been summoned and a discussion held, it was declared, "If Padmasambhava is not killed, he will harm Tibet," so assassins were sent. While they were waiting at the gorge of Dongpam, the master said to his escort, "Someone will come to harm me tomorrow." While he was crossing the gorge of Dongpam, the archers nocked and drew their arrows. The master performed some *mudrā* and the twenty assassins were duly frozen like paintings, unable to speak and move, and he passed straight through them. Upon his arrival at the border of Mang-yul the master said, "If the gods, *nāga* and demons had been bound by oath three times, the emperor would enjoy long life, his descendants would have high political authority, the country of Tibet would avoid conflict, and the doctrine of the Buddha would flourish for a long time, so my mind is burdened with that which is still left unaccomplished. In the country of Tibet, approaching the final 500-year period of the doctrine, there will be no opposition from the non-Buddhists; instead there will be disputes among the Buddhists themselves. In the land of Tibet, there will still be a great fight."

He sent back his escort, gave them some mustard seed, and instructed them, "Give this to the people who wanted to shoot me with their arrows and they will be able to move again." As soon as they were given the mustard seed, the assassins at Dongpam who had been frozen like paintings were able to move and speak again. When the escort reported the events upon their return, the emperor felt great sorrow.[32]

So ends the earliest extant account of Padmasambhava's interaction with the Tibetan court and his role in the establishment of Buddhism in Tibet. Tri Songdetsen orders Padmasambhava escorted back to the border but,

32. Wangdu and Diemberger 2000, 58–59.

suspecting the worst from his imbroglio with such a powerful siddha, decides it best to not leave him alive and so scrambles a team of archer-assassins to pursue him. Meeting Padmasambhava at the border with bows drawn, the archers are paralyzed by his mystical gesture, and he safely passes back to Nepal, lamenting that later Tibetan Buddhists would descend into conflict and the Dharma would not last long. Having been quickly deported by imperial decree, Padmasambhava does not complete the rituals required to stabilize Buddhism in Tibet, does not consecrate Samyé Monastery, does not conceal a single treasure, and does not magnetize a retinue of core disciples for the transmission of the esoteric instructions. According to the *Testimony of Ba* account, it is unclear whether he ever taught Buddhism in Tibet. Robert Mayer suspects that Padmasambhava's deportation in the *Testimony of Ba* is a narrative consequence of imperial decrees, some of which are preserved in the *Two Volumes on Translation* (*Sgra sbyor bam po gnyis pa*), a manual (among other functions) for translating Sanskrit into Tibetan, completed in 814, that proscribes the translation and distribution of antinomian tantras in the decades after Tri Songdetsen's reign. Padmasambhava's invitation represents a rather brief trial period for these tantras in Tibet, though perhaps the terms of his employ as envisioned by Śāntarakṣita only required the ritual subjugation of obstructing forces rather than doctrinal instruction in Buddhist soteriology. The revocation of Padmasambhava's welcome, whether mythical or historical, may be considered a casualty of Tibet's failed experiment with the transgressive tantras of the day. As these tantras gained widespread popularity in subsequent centuries, Padmasambhava's original association with them necessitated his rehabilitation and re-membering as is forwarded by his hagiographies.[33]

Padmasambhava is cast only as a tangential figure in the *Testimony of Ba* rather than as its protagonist, a chance contributor perhaps but not the catalyst primarily responsible for Tibet's conversion and certainly not the Second Buddha. Given the inherently subjective nature of historical writing, the alleged author and narrator Ba Selnang Yeshé Wangpo seems to promote his own role as the ordained protagonist, so perhaps that of the foreign tantrika Padmasambhava was reciprocally diminished.[34] The wholesale omission of a key figure from benchmark events such as the consecration of Samyé would require a far more significant manipulation of the remaining narrative, however, and the

33. Robert Mayer, personal communication, March 9, 2015. Also see Mayer 2015a, 392, citing Ishikawa 1990, 4.

34. Uray (1968) emphasizes that an objective of many early Tibetan histories is to vaunt specific clans, so certain details counter to that purpose were likely omitted. For similar concerns regarding the *Testimony of Ba* in particular, see van der Kuijp 2013b, 162–63.

anxieties that inspired Padmasambhava's deportation retain a rather convincing plausibility. Tri Songdetsen's gradual introduction of Buddhism was no doubt intended to bolster his rule, but Padmasambhava's unique abilities and the awe they inspired could undermine the emperor's claim to singular authority, so deporting and perhaps even assassinating the tantrika may have seemed like a cogent course of action. Besides, Padmasambhava had already completed his original commission by subduing those who had instigated several calamities before, and the construction of Samyé could now progress unimpeded with or without his skill set. However the person of Padmasambhava is represented and perhaps manipulated within the *Testimony of Ba*, the fact remains that not a single early source corroborates his seminal role in the establishment of Buddhism in Tibet. This is part of what makes its counternarratives in the treasure literature so intriguing.

Several early references to Padmasambhava remain scattered among the manuscripts recovered near Dunhuang, but unlike the *Testimony of Ba* that contradicts so much of the later treasure accounts, they preserve numerous precedents for the character traits that would come to define Padmasambhava in later centuries. These manuscripts have been dated from the middle of the tenth century to the early eleventh century, though some were certainly sourced from "archetypal ancestors" or earlier materials. This being the case, some of their details could stem from the same era that Padmasambhava is said to have visited Tibet.[35] Other manuscripts may be tenth- or eleventh-century originals, but all mentions of Padmasambhava prior to Nyangrel are useful for tracing his apotheosis from a minor historical personage of ordinary human descent to the enlightened font of the most esoteric instructions.[36] Ranging from passing references in a list to brief narratives featuring him as a protagonist, these various details and episodic threads provide the only insights into the early development of his biographical tradition while revealing that much of who he became has its roots in this era that followed the collapse of the empire.

Given that the translation of the *Testimony of Ba* reproduced above represents a later exemplar, and that its Dunhuang fragments preserve no mention of Padmasambhava, its portrayal of his person and time in Tibet cannot be verified as authentically ancient. However, a well-studied depiction is preserved within a late tenth-century Dunhuang manuscript that details his mastery and

35. Cantwell and Mayer (2013, 24 and n12) argue that their critical edition of *A Noble Noose of Methods* reveals that the Dunhuang manuscript had at least two copyings prior to it. In a separate article, Mayer (2013a) explicitly clarifies the possibility of such a provenance.

36. Cantwell and Mayer 2013, 25.

transmission of the meditational deity Vajrakīla at Yangleshö in Nepal (near modern-day Pharping in the southwestern foothills of the Kathmandu Valley). Following Matthew Kapstein's translation:

> At first there was the journey from Yangleshö in Nepal to the temple of Nālandā in India in order to fetch the *Hundred Thousand Verse Tantra of Vajrakīla* (*Phur bu'i 'bum sde*): When the Nepali porters Śākyapur and Iso were hired and sent off, there was a tetrad of *sé* goddesses who, at about nightfall, killed everyone and stole their breath. Padmasambhava became short-tempered, made as if to steal their breath, and caught them as they were wondering where to flee. Then he put them in his hat and departed. Arriving at Nālandā, he opened his hat and an exceedingly pretty woman appeared in the flesh. When she vowed to be a protectress for the practice of Kīla, he empowered her as its protectress. Because the prognostications were fine, he laughed, offered up a whole handful of gold dust, and then brought forth the *Hundred Thousand Verse Tantra of Vajrakīla*. After arriving at Yangleshö in Nepal with it, he performed the practices belonging to all the classes of yoga from the general kriyā up through atiyoga. For the purposes of all the vehicles, he proclaimed each and every transmission of Kīla from the *Hundred Thousand Verse Tantra of Vajrakīla*, as is affirmed in all the secret tantras.
>
> In that way, having definitively established the transmissions concerning attainment, and having again escorted the *Hundred Thousand* back to Nepal, Master Sambhava then performed the rites of attainment in the Asura cave with the Newari Serpo, Indrashuguta, Prabesé, and others. And thus he performed the rites, impelling the four *sé* goddesses whose embodied forms had not passed away. He named them Great Sorceress of Outer Splendor, Miraculous Nourisher, Great Witch Bestowing Glory, and Life-Granting Conjuress. Having performed the great attainment for seven days, he manifestly beheld the visage of Vajrakumāra [an epithet of Vajrakīla].
>
> Having acquired the accomplishment of Kīla, concerning his attainment of the signs, Padmasambhava, having set a limitless forest ablaze, thrust the kīla at the flames. Śrīgupta, having struck it at the rock in the region of the frontier forest of India, broke the rock into four fragments and thus "thrust it at stone." The Newari Serpo thrust it at water and so reversed the water's course, thereby establishing Nepal itself as a mercantile center. Such were the miraculous abilities and powers that arose.

> In Tibet Master Sambhava explained it to Pagor Vairocana and Tsé Jñānasukha. Later Dré Tathāgata and Buna Ana heard it and practiced at the cave of Samyé Rock at Drakmar. Dré Tathāgata thrust it at fire. Buna thrust it at the Rock of Hepo. Then the glory of the Kīla came to Chim Śākya and Nanam Zhang Dorjé Nyen. Then it was explained to Jin Yeshé Tsek.
>
> The trio of Yeshé Tsek, Nyen Nyiwa Tsenbapel, and Demen Gyaltsen successfully practiced at Nyengong in Lhodrak. The Preceptor thrust the kīla, having set the rock of Bumthang ablaze . . .[37]

This brief episode already preserves several features that would come to define Padmasambhava throughout the later hagiographical literature. A special affinity for the practice of the deity Vajrakīla, his retreat at Yangleshö, the ritual subjugation of demigods, and his scattering of gold dust all become topoi of his core narrative.[38] Of particular significance to the present study is Padmasambhava's transmission of the Vajrakīla cycle to several disciples in the corridor from Bumthang in Bhutan to Lhodrak in southern Tibet, which was the exact range of Nyangrel's activities. Nyangrel was born, recovered most of his treasures, and established his hermitage in this area. Given the approximation of local geography, it seems appropriate to surmise that the author of this Vajrakīla text names sites that were familiar to him, thus it is not at all coincidental that Nyangrel was the first to introduce a complete hagiography of Padmasambhava: some of the earliest Padmasambhava lore apparently developed and circulated right in his neighborhood.

Another potentially early resource for Padmasambhava is among the very few non-treasure texts explicitly ascribed to him, *An Esoteric Instruction: The Garland of Views* (*Man ngag lta ba'i phreng ba*). Its early provenance has been attested by Samten Karmay and subsequent scholars via various modes of analysis and argumentation,[39] and its attribution to Padmasambhava seems at least somewhat viable, though it may simply reflect the spread of his mythology and the teachings associated with him.[40] Featuring an early version of

37. Pelliot tibétaine 44. Translation following Kapstein 2000, 158. For other studies and translations, see Bischoff and Hartman 1971; Takeuchi 2004; Cantwell and Mayer 2008a, 41–60; Akagi 2011; and a summary of all in Cantwell and Mayer 2013, 32n25.

38. See Kapstein 2000, 159 and 265n110; Dalton 2004, 762.

39. Dorje 1987, 69; Karmay 1988, 142–44; Davidson 2005, 153.

40. A prominent example with regard to the *Garland of Views* is its citation in only the later recensions of the *Testimony of Ba. Sba bzhed* S, 32; translated in Kapstein 2000, 157. Padmasambhava departs before bestowing any Dharma instructions in the earlier recension, *Dba' bzhed*.

the nine-vehicle doxography, the *Garland of Views* presents an early elucidation of the Great Perfection as a distinct category of soteriological theory and praxis, which is driven by the author's quotation of and commentary on several verses from the thirteenth chapter of the *Tantra of the Secret Quintessence* (*Rgyud gsang ba snying po, Guhyagarbhatantra*). While this seminal Nyingma mahāyoga tantra came under attack in subsequent centuries for the overtly sexual and ultraviolent rhetoric featured in some sections, the subsequent discovery of Sanskrit editions at Samyé and in Kathmandu silenced challenges to its Indic pedigree.[41] Such concerns for the continuity of Indic lineages implies a subtext of critique for the new and indigenous, and these verifications legitimated the *Tantra of the Secret Quintessence* and its attendant commentaries as well, even if some Tibetans would retain an ambivalence toward its content for centuries.[42] As further evidence of its antiquity, the *Garland of Views* and its attribution to Padmasambhava is cited in *Lamp for the Eye of Concentration* (*Bsam gten mig sgron*) by Nup Sangyé Yeshé (mid-ninth to mid-tenth centuries). If this latter text can indeed be attributed to its purported author, then it is possible that the source text and its attribution to Padmasambhava originated not long after his stay in Tibet.

Other early sources make fleeting mentions of Padmasambhava where he is described as the subjugator of seven *sinmo* demonesses, as the translator of a single treatise by Śāntarakṣita in the Tibetan canon, among the foreign scholars listed in the *Pangthangma* catalog (*Dkar chag 'pang thang ma*) of translations, and in a stanza of praise from another Dunhuang text attributed to Padmasambhava, *A Noble Noose of Methods*, that Nyangrel copied verbatim into the *Copper Island*.[43] As detailed in publications by Matthew Kapstein, Cathy Cantwell and Robert Mayer, and Jacob Dalton, even at this earliest stage of textual evidence concerning the Padmasambhava story, there is a rather remarkable degree of harmonization or consistency among the threads of his biography, many of which persisted for Nyangrel to gather under a single title. How he accomplished this is the primary inquiry of this book, which is driven by an investigation of Nyangrel himself.

41. For a complete translation, transcription, and analysis of *Man ngag lta ba'i phreng ba*, see Karmay 1988, 137–74. Thubten Jinpa's translation can be downloaded from tibetanclassics.org.

42. See Karmay 1998, 6–13.

43. Respectively, see Dalton 2004, 765, Tucci 1949, 88, and Cantwell and Mayer 2012, 92–94.

Lives and Times of the Dreadlocked Sovereign

Given that the emperors are said to have descended from the heavens, it is ironic to state that the collapse of the Tibetan empire was a godsend for Tibetan Buddhism, but in the light of retrospection it may be argued that this is precisely the case. The emperors sponsored and coordinated the translation of Indian Buddhist literature into Tibetan, a feat counted among the greatest translation endeavors ever accomplished in the history of the world,[44] yet with the collapse of Tibet's centralized administration, the erosion of its Buddhist institutions, and the plundering of its coffers, the flow of Indian teachers ebbed for a time, and the regulations imposed on the translation of Buddhist texts by the last Buddhist emperors dissolved, especially with regard to the translation of the tantras. Unchecked by such authorities during the subsequent "age of fragmentation," Buddhism in Tibet was free to become Tibetan Buddhism, one developed by the needs and interests of Tibetan Buddhists rather than one dictated by Indic precedent and imperial decree. In particular, the antinomian tendencies and esoteric technologies of some Buddhist tantras led to their ban under the emperors, but as can be the case with illicit products, the law seems to belie their popular demand. Translations of these Indian tantras spread throughout Tibet after the imperium but so did apocryphal mimicries and uniquely Tibetan syntheses such as the Great Perfection. As necessary steps in the process of indigenization, cultural preferences and creative ingenuity helped transform the foreign import of Indian Buddhist discourse and praxis into a genuinely Tibetan Buddhism.

The inception of a Tibetan renaissance in the late tenth century was initiated in part by a neoconservative backlash to the widespread propagation of tantric products that, regardless of origin, were uniformly presented as translations bequeathed as Tibet's imperial inheritance.[45] In order to distinguish authentic Indian source texts from Tibetan apocrypha, reintroduce conventional Buddhist ethics, revitalize institutional Buddhism, and establish a new orthodoxy, Indian masters were once again invited to Tibet by feudal rulers who sought to model themselves on the emperors of old. This resulted in the influx of contemporary esoteric Buddhist scriptures whose origins could at least be verified by Sanskrit originals, even if their Indic composition was

44. Kapstein 2006, 72.

45. Davidson (2005, 20–21) is careful to define this period as "a" renaissance rather than "the" Renaissance. He describes the rise of Tibet's neocons, the competition between Nyingma and Sarma scriptures, and the production of "gray texts" in response to burgeoning Tibetan demand in the eleventh century (Davidson 2005, 148–51).

original as well. Whether translated during the imperium or developed in the process of indigenization thereafter, the transmissions that traced their origins to the empire and the period that immediately followed it were in competition with a wave of new translations (*gsar 'gyur*) that formed the basis of new sects and monastic centers. This competition defined this renaissance period of Tibetan Buddhism, especially for those designated as proponents of the "old school of the early translations" (*snga 'gyur rnying ma*).

So it was that in 1124 Ngadak Nyangrel Nyima Öser was born into a dynamic religious context amid the tumult of widespread political instability. By his time several imperial-era clans had reasserted their influence and authority through consolidating power and patronizing Buddhism once again. While Nyangrel hailed from the imperial Nyang clan (archaic: Myang) and proudly maintained its tantric transmissions, by his time his immediate family lived under modest circumstances and limited prestige. Such diminished status was in stark contrast to when, as one of Tibet's Buddhist aristocratic families, the Nyang clan populated the inner circles of the emperors for generations, rising to prominence and prosperity in lockstep with the Buddhist empire. As evidenced by their ancient tombs, the Nyang clan hailed from the region that still shares their name to the west of Lhasa.[46] The *Old Tibetan Chronicle* records that the sixth-century emperor Namri Löntsen rewarded the Nyang clan with estates and vassals for their role in delivering him into power, and that two clan representatives were henceforth "attached to the emperor's side" as well as the court.[47] While one influential ancestor was purged during the reign of Songtsen Gampo, a ninth-century stele commemorates the service of Nyang Tingezin (ca. 760–ca. 815) to the emperor Tri Desongtsen (r. ca. 798–ca. 800 and ca. 802–ca. 815), who rewards him with lands to the east of Lhasa.[48]

Nyangrel's father, Nyangtön Chökyi Khorlo, settled with a small retinue of disciples far from those areas into a much quieter life in Lhodrak, southern Tibet, quite far from the eponymous lands of their ancestors and safely

The indigenous composition of tantras was not always automatically problematic and delegitimizing, but Indic precedent eventually became the primary means of scriptural authentication during the renaissance and thereafter. Rongzom Chökyi Sangpo (1012–88) defended Tibetan scriptural compositions by equating accomplished authors with the Buddha himself and suggested that doubting the authenticity of their tantras carried the same severe karmic consequences as doubting the Buddha's own scriptures. See Wangchuk 2002, 282–85.

46. For a survey of the Nyang region and its imperial-era Nyang-clan tombs, see Hazod in Dotson 2009, 178–80.

47. Beckwith 1977, *Old Tibetan Chronicle* 19–23, transcribed on 189–90, translated on 207–8.

48. Richardson 1985, 43–45; also see Scherrer-Schaub 2002, 265. For clarification on the reigns after the abdication of Tri Songdetsen, see Dotson 2007.

distanced from the recurrent battles that ravaged the old symbols of power to the north. Due to a dispute between at least two resurgent Buddhist communities, the circumambulatory path and several temples of Samyé Monastery were set to the torch in 1106, less than twenty years before Nyangrel was born, and the Jokhang temple in Lhasa burned to the ground under similar circumstances in 1160. Such events fulfill Padmasambhava's parting prophecy in the *Testimony of Ba* (perhaps serving as further evidence of its interpolation during this period), where he laments that instead of "opposition from the non-Buddhists, there will be disputes among the Buddhists themselves," and "in the country of Tibet there will still be a great fight."[49] A dramatic depiction is recorded by one of Nyangrel's contemporaries, Lama Shang (1122–93), who recounts the arrival of his guru, Gomtsul, at the tragic scene after the arson of the Jokhang, Tibet's most sacred shrine:

> All of the members of the religious community were fighting. As when a lion's insides are eaten by worms, the Jokhang was destroyed from within . . . Nothing remained but ruins and smoke . . . When Gomtsul arrived at the ruins of the temple, there were tears in the eyes of the Jowo Śākyamuni statue. Light rays issued from its heart and dissolved into the teacher's heart.[50]

Given that the area had descended into factional violence and total anarchy such that not even the Jowo was safe, Gomtsul entrusted the taming of Lhasa and its environs to his disciple, Lama Shang, who soon took up the task with great gusto. In addition to his deployment of martial thaumaturgy to sway battles in his favor, Lama Shang exerted his will throughout the region by conscripting monks to serve several martial functions: soldiers who marched against those who opposed him, peacekeepers between warring factions, armed escorts for merchants and pilgrims on the roadways of central Tibet, and enforcers for the rule of law that he imposed throughout the region. Among other signs of Lama Shang's success in these endeavors, in 1175 and 1187 he built two major monastic institutions as citadels and barracks at strategic locations outside the city,[51] recognizing that the conflicts in Lhasa necessitated such fortifications through the end of the twelfth century. This was too late for Nyangrel, however, as his limited peregrinations in search of the

49. Wangdu and Diemberger 2000, 59.

50. Translation following Yamamoto 2009, 87.

51. On the deployment of martial monks, see Yamamoto 2009, 214 and 216; on the construction of these two monasteries, see Yamamoto 2009, 89.

treasures seem to have concluded before Lama Shang's intervention bore fruit, and he settled into his hermitage safely insulated from the instability that persisted north of the Tamshöl gorge throughout most of his life.

Whereas Nyangrel's biographies only hint at the disorder of his era, noting his struggles with hunger and a demand for his performance of fierce rites for hire, he embeds a vivid prophecy for the time of treasure recovery in the *Copper Island.* Across the spectrum of later sources such as treasure materials, "prophecies" by eighth-century figures such as Padmasambhava most often describe the era of their authorship or interpolation rather than that of their alleged prophesizers. While this prophecy in the *Copper Island* defines both the destined treasure revealer and the circumstances he would awaken within, they may be Nyangrel's most direct reflections on himself and his twelfth-century climate. According to the earliest recension of the text, with regard to the character of Tri Songdetsen's treasure-revealing reincarnation (i.e., Nyangrel), Padmasambhava attests:

> Vigorously exerting himself in great discriminative awareness and compassion, he will have pure samaya and little mental agitation. He will be vast and quiet. He will not cast praise and blame toward others in his peaceful mind. He will be of swift intelligence and continuously attentive. He will be fair-skinned and good-natured. Being born as such a person, once the king himself comes to possess all the instructions I have given now, he will sever the continuity [of karma and rebirth] by means of that life.[52]

Later recensions accrue additional compliments; there can be no doubt that the text was manipulated. However much of this can be attributed to Nyangrel, the choices here highlight those personal qualities that Nyangrel would have found most positive in himself, which are uniformly laudatory and somewhat generic. More illuminating is the description of Nyangrel's era:

> Concerning the time when the treasures will emerge, people will eat spoiled food and dung. They will suppress the wheel of doctrine and destroy the hermitages. They will sell religious instructions as commodities and count the dead by the thousands. Donning coarse

52. Translation following the earliest extant recensions as preserved in *Zangs gling ma* H, 82b5–83a3, and *Me tog snying po* M, 256.3.4–257.1.1; K, 354.21–355.5. For the latest recension, cf. *Zangs gling ma* A, 138.4–139.1 and its translation in Kunsang 1993, 139.

garments of goat hair, they will quarrel with family and wear iron mail into action.

Venerable elders will act as army generals, and monks will take up swords. Fortifications will be erected at sacred sites, and solitary retreats will be built as citadels in the center of towns. Practitioners of mantra will use dorjés to inflict injury in battle and lace foul food with poison. Warriors will take aim with catapults. Easterners will take up bows. Leaders will renege on their promises of safe passage. Tibet will descend into chaos like a hundred fragmented pieces of armor. Fathers and sons will argue. Siblings and parents will quarrel. Malevolent entities such as *tsen* and *nöchin* will summon warrior spirits. Bandits will conquer and control the treacherous roads.

At that time ghosts and *gongpo* demons will enter the hearts of all. *Tedrang* ghosts will enter the hearts of children. *Senmo* will enter the hearts of women. By provoking all the eight classes of gods and demons of appearance and existence, disease, famine, and a turbulent age will ensue. At that time the three inabilities will occur:

1. The earth will not be able to hold precious treasures, so doctrinal and wealth treasures will come forth.
2. The Dharma protectors will not be able to guard the caches of precious gold and silver entrusted to them, so the sangha's wealth will be stolen.
3. Dharma practitioners will not be able to practice sādhanas, so each will sell the profound instructions as merchandise to unaccomplished individuals, and they will wish to explain to individuals that which they have not understood and in which they have no experience.[53]

Apparently the situation was quite dire in twelfth-century Tibet. While it may be tempting to read this prophecy as relying on the flourish of hyperbole, there is little reason to doubt that it could accurately record Nyangrel's view of the unstable time in which he lived. It depicts a period of decentralized administration, lawlessness, anarchy, poverty, violence, and the denigration of the Buddhist teachings, all of which is corroborated by Lama Shang's detailed

53. Translation based on its earliest recension in *Me tog snying po* M, 256.2.4–256.3.2 and *Zangs gling ma* H, 81b.4–82b.3. Cf. its latest recension as translated by Kunsang 1993, 138–39, and Davidson 2005, 214. An excerpt that clearly parallels much of its form and context is found in *Maṇi bka' 'bum*, 1:192–93, translated in Kapstein 2000, 150.

accounts of the period.[54] There is a consensus among sources that it indeed was a time when authoritative religious figures like Lama Shang became military leaders commanding armies of monk-combatants, and mantrins—including Nyangrel himself, according to his biographies—profited from the performance of apotropaic and martial rituals in response to surging demand from a nervous populace threatened by countless dangers.[55]

As specified in the set of three inabilities, all of this signifies the descent of an especially degenerate age where the Three Jewels are threatened at three distinct levels, beginning with the fundamental ground of Tibet itself. Just as Padmasambhava inters all the treasures to subjugate and consecrate Tibet as a land of Dharma in the *Copper Island*, the rampant negativity of this era so inverts his original intent—the earth, demigods, and people are so poisoned, perverse, and corrupted—that the soil will purge itself of all that is enriching, proper, and immaculate. Being omniscient and practically omnipotent, this must all be part of Padmasambhava's master plan, however, and these most infelicitous occurrences are simultaneously auspicious, because that purging results in the treasures' ascent for recovery, their emergence as salvific interventions for a tumultuous age. Even the Dharma protectors are rendered impotent, helpless to uphold their sworn oaths to protect the sangha and its resources, and esoteric instructions are bartered in the streets by the unscrupulous and unrealized. Such dangerous and endarkened circumstances help explain why Nyangrel elected to operate within a circumscribed area throughout his life, rarely venturing beyond it.

According to both of his biographies, Nyangrel lived his life sheltered within a long gorge cut by the Tamshöl River, and he built his Mawochok hermitage in a relatively desolate, unclaimed adjacency beyond the interest of whatever powers were in the vicinity. His biographies do not record any interactions or exchanges with local political entities or patrons, and except for a mysterious nun who greets him and points out the geomantic features of the site, Nyangrel stakes his claim to Mawochok alone and uncontested.

While paths along the Tamshöl served as a pilgrimage route from central Tibet to Bhutan, it seems that it was a relatively quiet zone safely removed from the conflicts to the north, and Nyangrel limited his explorations almost exclusively to this area (see plate 2). Such a narrow range of activity may very well reflect a pronounced concern with travel farther abroad. His biographies never mention a pilgrimage to Lhasa, perhaps because of the risks incurred on those prominent routes, never mind the conflicts endemic to the valley

54. See Kapstein 2000, 264n63.

55. *Gsal ba'i me long*, 331.

Figure 1. Mawochok hermitage prior to the Cultural Revolution, fronted by the massive reliquaries of Nyangrel and Namkhapel. "Mawochok Monastery in the Lhodrak region," photograph by Hugh E. Richardson, 1950 (detail). Copyright Pitt Rivers Museum, University of Oxford, 2001.59.4.17.1.

itself; nor do they describe him as venturing farther north than Samyé Monastery or farther south than Bumthang in search of treasures. These mark the most distant poles of Nyangrel's recorded wanderings, but the densest cluster of Nyangrel's treasure caches were secured within the Tamshöl corridor. Despite such modest environs, Nyangrel conceived a far more significant role for himself based as much on the circumstances of his present as the unique insights he envisioned of Tibet's past.

Paralleling the life of the Buddha, Nyangrel's biographies record that from the moment of conception, his parents experienced dreams and signs that confirmed their child as a *tulku* (*sprul sku*, *nirmāṇakāya*) or magically emanated reincarnation. Being tantric adepts themselves, perhaps they encouraged their son to recognize such qualities within himself, and he is said to have recalled his "preincarnations" by the age of ten. Additional recollections result in the sequencing of an exact catenate or unbroken series of lives beginning with none other than emperor Tri Songdetsen himself. Of all of his preincarnations, the emperor is uniquely consequential for Nyangrel, for it is within that life that the karmic seeds were planted both for his enlightenment and for the enlightened activity by which he would become renowned: treasure recovery. Given the turbulence of central Tibet since the collapse of the empire, there was a popular nostalgia for the imperial era defined by centralized authority, safety, prosperity, and glory. While the feudal lords sought to mimic the emperors by sponsoring Buddhism and regaining some semblance of the old imperium within their limited dominion, no evidence suggests that Nyangrel held any such political aspirations. For him this nostalgia manifests as the direct memory of empire in personal recollections of his previous life as Tri Songdetsen. While this is a consistently defining feature throughout both of his biographies, and while these recollections form the legitimating basis of his life's work as a treasure revealer, this claim must be accompanied by a degree of skepticism, given the antiquity of the texts and the clear evidence of their manipulation. It is impossible to know whether Nyangrel had these experiences, whether he orally recounted or invented their occurrence as recorded in his biographies, or whether he, like Padmasambhava, is so much an amalgamation of later authors that the person is lost to time—but such can be said of any historical figure. If we are to assert anything about the historical person, Nyangrel, it is that he relied on the conviction of his past life as Tri Songdetsen to recover the treasures.

When discussing the *jātaka* or past lives of the Buddha, Donald Lopez is quite right in underscoring that "our task is not to account for its fact but for its fiction and its function," its literary construction and diverse modes of application. These are two foci at the center of the present inquiry as well, but in Nyangrel's case it is more difficult to summarily dismiss his recollections "not as a case of memory but as the mythology of memory."[56] While we will see that Nyangrel's preincarnation list and its narratives also evolved with the help of many hands, his *Copper Island* is in many respects a vehicle for the prophecy concerning Tri Songdetsen's eventual reincarnation as an enlightened treasure revealer. Moreover, Nyangrel's status as the reincarnation of Tri Songdetsen is the most repeated claim throughout both biographies where his first-person accounts repeatedly suggest that he remembered his life as Tri Songdetsen in the eighth century in the exact same way that he remembered the details of his present life in the twelfth.

Memory itself is a peculiar form of thought. Discursively articulated by worded commentary and perfumed with emotion, the phantoms and echoes of direct perceptual experience are taken to be accurately representative of the past. While necessarily limited and subjective as a basis, memory can be confirmed, denied, or confused by consensus so long as there are others who

56. Lopez 1992, 24.

claim witness to the same events. Being nearly four centuries removed from the imperium, Nyangrel's claim circumvents this possibility and elevates his perspective as virtually unchallengeable—unless he meets another who claims both reincarnate descent from the empire and clear memories of it. His biographies report that Nyangrel met at least one other individual with a similar degree of realization and insight into an imperial-era preincarnation, in this case the translator Vairocana, but this person's primary function within the account is to corroborate Nyangrel's status as the reincarnation of Tri Songdetsen. Inhabiting such a position of mnemonic authority, Nyangrel not only gained exalted status as an enlightened, magically emanated reincarnation, but I suspect he also seized a unique form of editorial license in his revision of Tibet's conversion to Buddhism. He claims to be—and seems to believe himself to have been—a direct witness to those events as a personal disciple of Padmasambhava. Attempting to psychologize a twelfth-century Tibetan would inevitably devolve into tautology, whether cynical or apologetic, and provide more insight into the present analyst than the patient. Alternatively, it may be argued that these memories are the inventions and interjections of Nyangrel's biographers and subsequent interpolators in the transmission of their documents: adepts tracing the catenate sequence of their preincarnations becomes one of the most recurrent and definitive tropes of Tibetan biographical writing, but we shall see in chapter 2 that Nyangrel's articulation of catenate reincarnation was both revolutionary and rudimentary, thereby lending credence to the assertion that his claim preceded its normalization in literature. With so limited an array of exemplars for textual criticism and comparative analysis, a degree of skepticism remains necessary: it cannot be proven with total certainty that Nyangrel was the architect of his construction as depicted in his biographies. Nevertheless, the evidence we do have suggests that Nyangrel remembered his past lives, and that these memories were fact for Nyangrel and not fiction.

There are therefore two aspects of memory to be explored in this volume: Nyangrel's individual memory of his past and its representations, which include his past life as Tri Songdetsen; and the collective memory of the Tibetan people, Nyangrel included, that centers on the role of Padmasambhava in Tibet's conversion to Buddhism. I will argue that Nyangrel's personal recollections of his past life as Tri Songdetsen represent the culmination of a popular nostalgia for the stability and glory of the Tibetan empire in the twelfth century, and that it was the confluence of this acutely personal inspiration with a broader social yearning for the resurgence of Tibet's golden age that enabled Nyangrel to revise the historical record of the Tibetan people.

Tradition, Text, Traditional Texts, and Textual Traditions

The garuḍa eagle has a long and complex mythology. In the Indian epic *Mahābhārata,* the garuḍa independently fights free from its egg and bursts into flame, scorching space to the extent that the gods mistake it for Agni, the god of fire.[57] This depiction of the garuḍa later fused with indigenous Tibetan conceptions of a mythical bird with similar characteristics: associated with the element of fire, the *khyung* or *khanding* (*khyung, mkha' lding*) eagle is born completely formed and ready to fly upon its first breath.[58] The garuḍa may thus serve as an apt metaphor for tradition in a religious context, which is often presented as timeless, synchronic, perfect, and fully developed from the moment of inception, thereby obscuring the diachronic processes of its development.

Any tradition takes time to become resolved and refined into normative consistency: it is in fact a dynamic, ever-changing product defined by creativity, trial and error, critique, and apologetic defenses of it. From a contemporary critical perspective, the construction of tradition may be seen as an eminently human process rather than a miraculous and spontaneous emergence from the divine, which is one reason why its diachronic traces are so often excised from origin narratives. By its synchronic form, tradition may reflect something of the perfected and the eternal; it serves as a simulacrum, a manifestation of the divine in the world. This function is necessary, especially in religions such as Tibetan Buddhism that place a high value on the soteriological potential of faith. One well-known Tibetan parable is that of the old woman who asks her merchant son to return from India with a relic of the Buddha. Having been immersed in business, he only remembers his mother's request upon nearing home, so he extracts a tooth from the jaw of a dead dog, wraps it in silk, and presents it to his mother. She places the tooth on her shrine, reveres it as an authentic relic, and thereby attains enlightenment.[59] Thus in a Tibetan Buddhist context the authenticity of the object is ultimately irrelevant. While relics are certainly attested to be imbued with special properties, only faith can fully actualize that potential: without it a tooth remains a tooth. Tradition constructs itself as an orthodoxy by which these properties and potentialities are authoritatively identified, defined, and resolved as real, which establishes a foundation for faith and, in Buddhist contexts, for enlightenment itself.

Since Tibetan Buddhism is founded on the Mahāyāna ideal to benefit

57. Van Buitenen 1973, 78.

58. See Dowman 1973, 52–54. For additional details on garuḍa, see Cantwell and Mayer 2015, 161–62.

59. For one version of this parable, see Patrul 2011, 173–74.

beings, those who aspire to it may implement a full array of skillful means in pursuit of that ideal. Actions that would be considered negative in an ordinary context, from simple prevarications to the production of elaborate apocrypha, may be necessary to effect benefit. Needless to say, it can be quite difficult to discern selfless agents from those contaminated by self-interest when their actions appear identical to the observer, and there are many emic rationales for synchronic presentations of tradition and the selective refinement of texts over time that is required to present them as such. These need not be problematic from a critical perspective either, unless analysis allows a blaze of resolved synchrony to obscure the diachronic process of development itself. A major objective of the present study is to reassess three core elements of Tibetan Buddhism that have been obscured by their later traditions: catenate reincarnation, treasure recovery, and the Padmasambhava narrative. In relying on Nyangrel and his textual production as a case study, it becomes possible to destabilize normative assumptions of synchrony, whether traditional or critical, with regard to these three elements by demonstrating that normative presentations are only the most recent and refined examples of them.

While there have been many studies on various aspects of the Tibetan treasures, the convenient rubrics and resolved definitions of later traditions have too often come to define nearly a millennium of treasure recovery in Tibet.[60] According to more normative syntheses compiled by the eighteenth century, the treasures signify texts and relics that were concealed by Padmasambhava to be recovered by the reincarnations of his disciples in the centuries thereafter. The tripartite rubric of earth treasures (*sa gter*), exalted-mind treasures (*dgongs gter*), and pure vision teachings (*dag snang*) eventually became the standard typology, though downloading immaterial exalted-mind treasures from the expanse of enlightened awareness became the preferred and most popular method of revelation. The earliest iterations of the Buddhist treasures bear little resemblance to the normative treasure tradition they would become, however, and Foucault's deconstruction of tradition is precisely relevant to the task at hand:

> These pre-existing forms of continuity, all these syntheses that are accepted without question, must remain in suspense. They must not be rejected definitively of course, but the tranquillity with which they are accepted must be disturbed; we must show that they do not come about of themselves, but are always the result of

60. Davidson (2005, 213, and 2006, 125) was the first to raise these concerns.

> a construction the rules of which must be known, and the justifications of which must be scrutinized.[61]

Not since the first publications on the treasures in the nineteenth century has scholarship simply accepted these normative syntheses, but a late twentieth-century drive to advance the conversation beyond the question of in/authenticity inadvertently resulted in a reification of the treasure tradition that emerged concurrently with the critical deconstruction of it. The justifications or legitimation strategies of normative treasure traditions were indeed scrutinized, which was necessary and fruitful by providing far greater insight into their construction, but this focus has resulted in a tranquility like Foucault forewarned, whereby normative treasure rubrics have become normative in more general scholarship concerning the treasures as well. That the treasures are presented as synchronic by representatives of the tradition is expected, but the adoption of that presentation in scholarship has resulted in the superimposition of very late syntheses and rubrics onto the practices that preceded them, thereby obscuring the diachronic process by which the treasures *became* a tradition. As Foucault suggests, tradition by no means needs to be rejected entirely: it serves important functions, and in this case the progression of the academic conversation beyond in/authenticity was quite skillful precisely because it allowed the treasures to remain cohesive as an object of analysis, "in suspense" and appreciated for its literary and cultural contributions.

On the other hand, Foucault recommends caution in allowing that there is even "a tradition" to be found. This critical point is well taken, and all the more so in a Buddhist context, where all conceptual designations are empty of real existence and negated by analysis, yet both perspectives agree that such conventions remain useful as rhetorical conveniences, as relative truths rather than observable realities. In this respect I will introduce a terminological dichotomy to differentiate two artificial but nevertheless useful poles: the treasures before tradition and the normative tradition of the treasures. The former concludes with the first formal attempt at their codification in the thirteenth century, which is the focal range of the present inquiry; the latter begins by the eighteenth century when a relatively high degree of consistency pervades what has been commonly identified as "the treasure tradition." Again, the mention of a treasure tradition is not meant to suggest that a single, unified entity ever existed on the ground, but it does recognize a certain degree of consistency, coherence, and general agreement exemplified by normative treasure recovery practices and rubrics. Through analyzing the biographies and recov-

61. Foucault 1972, 25.

eries of Nyangrel in particular, it becomes clear that he would identify few correlates between his modes of textual production and the array of rubrics and definitions that would come to define treasure revelation in subsequent centuries. A similar caution must be applied when approaching other elements of Tibetan Buddhism that are now normative if not definitive. Recollection of prior incarnations and catenate reincarnation had yet to become standardized and ubiquitous tropes in the twelfth and thirteenth centuries; rather, this represents a critical period in their development as such, so we must again proceed carefully to undermine the reflexive imputation of now familiar claims and concepts on literature that preceded their widespread popularization.

The philological analysis of Tibetan literature is both complicated and elucidated by the rather amazing fluidity of its textual reproduction and publication practices. Books are deeply venerated in Tibet, and scriptures are considered sacred relics, yet Tibetans over the centuries have displayed an equal enthusiasm for altering them! Aside from updating orthography as well as introducing new spelling errors and variants, Tibetans involved in textual reproduction commonly inscribe commentary and corrections between the lines, interpolate and append excerpts from other documents, expand sections with fresh content, extrapolate swaths without citation into distinct documents often with distinct purposes, and even redact the words of original authors revered as omniscient and enlightened.

Unlike xylographs, where at least one hard copy is preserved for as long as the carved blocks remain, the reproduction of manuscripts tends to smooth most irregularities like sands in the ebb and flow of recensional tides. The alterations evident in one manuscript may be invisibly integrated into a copy that follows: errors are corrected, others introduced, and new inclusions from distinct documents are incorporated, as may be the interlinear notes and marginalia of various readers. Without several versions to compare, it thus becomes difficult but certainly not impossible to retrace the transformation of Tibetan manuscripts over time. While much detail is lost, evidence of some textual manipulations remains. I thus rely on textual criticism and comparative analysis of all available versions as the primary methodologies to cull evidence and propose theses, beginning with the compilation and transmission of Nyangrel's two biographies. These inform my analysis of his inception of the first complete narrative of Tri Songdetsen and Padmasambhava, now known as the *Copper Island* and replicated within a *History of Buddhism* also attributed to him, that became the emic history of Tibet's golden age.

1. Karmic Foreshadowing on the Path of Fruition

In Buddhist life-writing, as in Buddhist life, the karmic process by which actions produce corresponding results drives the narrative of human experience. This process is necessarily simplified in biography, since the full complexity of actual causality cannot be replicated or effectively condensed into a literary form. Instead, the objective is to present a clear and coherent plot or path for the reader: like a single stone dropped into a still pond, one action or event results in ripples setting off toward the shores in a clear progression of cause and effect. A classic Buddhist example is when Prince Siddhārtha Gautama, the Buddha-to-be, having been thoroughly sheltered by the pleasures of his palace life, first encounters the so-called "four sights" of an elderly man, an invalid, a corpse, and an ascetic. In recognizing that life is defined by old age, sickness, and death, he renounces his ignorant existence to discover a path to enlightenment that would ultimately transcend it. Causality in real life is rarely so simple, however: rather than a march of perfectly distinct ripples, life is more analogous to a vast rainstorm spattering the surface of an endless ocean of awareness. It is no wonder then that only the fully omniscient buddhas are said to truly understand the intricacies of karma, the awesome complexity of cause and effect that produces "the world and its inhabitants," every moment of experience and every atom of its content.

While Tibet had its share of enlightened authors who might claim such omniscience, for biography (or any history for that matter) to be effective as a form of literature, it cannot account for the infinitely vast array of data that represents a moment of real time; biography is necessarily selective so as to make sense of a life that is to be reconstructed and reformulated for the written page, and all the more so in the controlled, often idealized format of hagiography that might evade the complexity of worldly entanglements or omit less saintly elements of character. Analysis of this selective process sometimes betrays that the narrative product tells us more about the author than its subject, but postponing a more elaborate discussion of this until the next chapter, it is important to recognize that in Buddhist biographical writing, this simplification of causality is among the most prominent narrative devices. By incorporating Buddhism's fundamental truth of karma, Buddhist biographies progress in stages from clearly rendered causes to their projected results such that a karmic foreshadowing permeates these narratives as harbingers of the enlightened activities to come.

Like much of Tibetan literature, Tibetan religious biographies take Indic literary traditions as their basis. By according with the biographical traditions of the Buddha in particular, Tibetan biographers sought to retain the same legitimacy, both soteriologically for their subject and textually for their document, while incorporating the tantric tendencies of their tradition. Thus enhanced by the multivalent potency of tantric symbolism, these infallible machinations of karmic process legitimate the protagonist as an authentic adept. Loaded with vivid imagery, the dreams and designations, signs and visions, imbue mundane events with profound significance, thereby indicating the true nature of relative phenomena while confirming the attainment of those who recognize it. Tantric hermeneutics empower the reader to extract the genuine significance of these events just as those who witnessed them, with proper interpretations revealing the implicit prophesies and ultimate meanings embedded within the narrative. In sum, karmic process manifested as tantric symbols is among the most prominent literary devices for the construction of enlightened identity in Tibetan Buddhist life-writing. It not only grounds the accomplishment of the protagonist in causality but also leads the reader along the narrative path of fruition to its ultimate end of "complete liberation" (*rnam par thar pa*), which is a literal translation of the Tibetan term for the biography genre.

Among the earliest and most elaborate examples of indigenous Tibetan life-writing are the two biographies of Nyangrel Nyima Öser (1124–92), who is renowned as the first of the great Buddhist treasure revealers not because he was the first Tibetan Buddhist to employ this mode of textual and relic recovery—he certainly was not—but he appears to have been more prolific and influential than those that preceded him, thus he retains this mantle of recognition. Another reason may very well be that the details of his life in the twelfth century are preserved within his two exquisitely detailed biographies, titled the *Clear Mirror* and the *Stainless Proclamations*, which are the earliest complete accounts of a Buddhist treasure revealer. The statements contained in the latter are "stainless" because Nyangrel is alleged to have provided much of the testimony himself, and both biographies feature first-person episodes that are said to be recorded verbatim from the mouth of the master to his retinue. Indeed, according to the colophons of both biographies, much of their core data was compiled by direct disciples within a generation of his death, a reasonable claim, though both texts clearly contain numerous insertions by later contributors. As shall be thoroughly analyzed in the next chapter, foremost among these later contaminants are the brief accounts of Nyangrel's preincarnations that are to be distinguished from the far more elaborate and complete narratives of his life, the "primary biography" of the *Clear Mirror* and the *Stainless Proclamations*, which will serve as the fraternal twin bases of the present discussion.

Due to the inclusion of these first-person statements, it has been suggested that these are autobiographies, but this is not the case in the most literal characterization of the genre: Nyangrel did not write any part of these texts himself. The colophon of the *Clear Mirror* names another author, and while the *Stainless Proclamations* explicitly claims to record Nyangrel's oral narration of his own life, he did not write it.[62] His first-person statements often conclude with final honorific verbs that are rarely used in reference to oneself, which corroborates the compositional process of the biographies as attested in the colophons: as much as possible, direct disciples reproduced Nyangrel's first-person testimony, and these honorific verbs denote their reverential authorship.[63] As such, the *Clear Mirror* and the *Stainless Proclamations* may transcribe some first-person testimony, but they are not autobiographies.

These two biographies are the main sources for recent portraits of the master, yet in light of the many divergences between them, it appears that little of Nyangrel's past can be confirmed. A close comparison of the two reveals that only the broad generalities and basic facts concur; the fine details that drive the narrative of his life vary between the biographies to the degree that they compete rather than complement each other. Only his most recent biographers have had access to both texts, but they selectively weave distinct episodes from each biography into a coherent narrative that renders such issues in the record invisible.[64] A critical approach to the sources provides a more complete introduction to the information available on Nyangrel.

62. *Dri ma med pa*, 163: "The great sovereign spoke this to his wife, his heirs, and his five great cherished disciples."

63. Both biographies display orality, most especially in the completion of an inordinate number of phrases with a third-case particle (*gyis*, or appended *pas*) or a fifth-case particle (*nas*). These finish the phrase with a long –s sound, which signifies the quoting of another source or the telling of a tale, thereby implying "as has been said." These particles should not always be rendered with their standard grammatical value: they signify an oral continuative instead of an agentive, ergative, or ablative particle. This is reflected in my translations.

64. In fact, I have only found one source that reproduces details that are unique to the *Stainless Proclamations*, such as Nyangrel's treasure recovery at Mutik Shelgyi Pamagong and his miraculous visit to the Śītavana charnel ground near Bodhgaya, India, which is Dudjom Rinpoche's *Rnying ma'i chos 'byung*, written in 1962 and translated as the *Nyingma School of Tibetan Buddhism* (Dudjom Rinpoche 1991, 757). Given that Dudjom Rinpoche was the one who brought the *Stainless Proclamations* to light, it is not surprising that he included its details in his short biography of Nyangrel. The mystery is how the *Stainless Proclamations* persisted for as many as

While performing text-critical analyses of primary sources, this chapter deliberately avoids attempting to disentangle the historical from the hagiographical: it is difficult if not impossible to discern whatever may have actually occurred from fictional or symbolic embellishments. Besides, with divergent sources stemming from such similar provenance, one biography cannot be elevated above the other as more historically accurate, and we find ourselves no closer to the man himself. Corroboration between the sources seems to support a stronger claim toward historicity, but we must concede that in many respects, the historical Nyangrel is lost to time. Yet even if we take the biographies to be only suggestive of the historical person, they still provide clear insights into who Nyangrel was, his context, and his products. Accepting this, my object in this chapter is not to attempt to historically verify the available information on the early life and adolescence of Nyangrel but rather to interrogate it with an eye toward the narrative construction of his adult identity as an enlightened adept. By focusing on the literary devices used by his biographers, we will see how they promote Nyangrel's status as a buddha incarnate and establish the karmic pretext to legitimate his later activities, which were foremost expressed through his recovery of the treasures.

Just as Nyangrel's biographies follow a coherent narrative structure from his birth through his death, the discussion below follows the chronological progression of Nyangrel's final lifetime. Beginning with his parents' dreams at the time of conception, it progresses through his childhood training and concludes with the series of tantric empowerments that precipitate his adult life. Thus this chapter focuses on the episodes that function as karmic indicators of how his life will unfold. Episodes from one biography are neither conflated with nor presented in exclusion of those of the other. Redundant episodes with unique details are presented contiguously and analyzed independently.

Oneiric Conception

The identities of Nyangrel's parents are corroborated in his biographical traditions, where both their common and initiatory or secret names are provided. His father was Nyangtön Chökyi Khorlo, a lay guru with the title "the Nyang teacher" (*Nyang ston*) who continued the unbroken tantric transmissions of his clan. Far less is known of his mother, Jomo Yeshé Drön, though *jomo* often denotes a woman of royal lineage. Perhaps she also hailed from one

---

eight centuries before being included in Kaḥthok's *Eight Instructions* and consulted by Dudjom for his 1962 publication.

of the imperial clans, received the title upon marrying into Nyang, or received it posthumously in recognition of her son's Dharmic achievements. Any one of these is difficult to confirm given that so little of the parents' own stories remains outside the biographies of their son. It appears that their greatest impact was in producing him.

The sexual relationship, chemistry, and potency the parents share is somewhat tempered by symbolism and euphemism but can nevertheless be exposed quite explicitly through interpreting the terms provided. While each symbol has a range of meanings and there may very well be additional, equally valid interpretations, some appear especially relevant to this context. To begin, the *Clear Mirror* introduces Nyangrel's mother as "the female *mudrā*," or religious consort, of his father, thus passion and sexual intercourse in their relationship as husband and wife is a religious practice, a means to enlightenment.[65] This sets the basis for their invitation of a *nirmāṇakāya*, or *tulku*, the magically emanated reincarnation or embodied form of a buddha, through conception.

Their secret names detail this purpose even more. Given that tantra relies on symbolism to link mundane appearances with their exalted aspects, tantric initiatory names point out the ultimate potential and true nature of the saṃsāric individuals they designate. Only the *Stainless Proclamations* provides the secret name of Nyangrel's father: Dorjé Wangchuk Tsal (Rdo rje dbang phyug rtsal), "dynamic expression of the powerful lord vajra," where the significance of each of these terms should be considered individually.

As a ritual implement depicted in the hands of countless deities, the dorjé, or *vajra* in Sanskrit, is one of the most ubiquitous symbols of tantric Buddhism. It is most commonly formed by two metal sets of three, five, or nine prongs that extend out in opposite directions from an orb and converge into two tips. Its symbology textually begins with Indra's lightning bolt, which when striking the earth in the *Ṛg Veda* was said to produce diamonds, or as the Tibetan literally renders it, "the lord of stones" (*rdo rje*). In exoteric Buddhist interpretations, the vajra functions as a scepter, where it is often paired with a bell such that this dichotomy unites the vajra, skillful means (*thabs*, *upāya*), with its counterpart, discriminative awareness (*shes rab*, *prajñā*), the two being ultimately indifferentiable. These are also considered to be masculine and feminine aspects respectively, so in tantric applications the vajra and bell are often

65. White 2003, 82–83, notes that for the Nāth siddhas, *mudrā* explicitly refers to the vulva as the seal that enables the urethral suction of female discharge into the body of the male practitioner, thereby resulting in the attainment of "fluid gnosis." While sexual yoga or *karmamudrā* was imported to Tibet, I do not know to what degree this seminal soteriology was promulgated or practiced.

sexualized: *dorjé* in tantric "twilight language" is a euphemism for the phallus. Wangchuk (*dbang phyug*) literally translates as "having much power" and so nominalized may be rendered "powerful lord." Tsal (*rtsal*), "dynamic expression," has the sense that the individual arises impersonally, objectively, selflessly as the play of luminosity, the manifest aspect of ultimate reality; s/he is merely a refraction of enlightened awareness in human form. In sum then, for Nyangtön Chökyi Khorlo or Dorjé Wangchuk Tsal, the "dynamic expression of the powerful lord vajra," sexual potency is a defining characteristic.

His wife's secret name testifies that each is the ideal counterpart for the other. Nyangrel's two biographies nearly agree on his mother's initiatory name with the exception of one dyad. Whereas the *Clear Mirror* names her Pema Dewa Tsal (Pad ma bde ba rtsal), "dynamic expression of the blissful lotus," the *Stainless Proclamations* reads Pema Wangchen Tsal (Padma dbang chen rtsal), "dynamic expression of the great powerful lotus," which in addition to the evocative literal translation is an epithet for Hayagrīva, the fierce "horse-necked" deity who will become her son's tutelary deity, or *yidam*.[66] Here his

66. There is a tendency, even in the relatively short time of translation from Tibetan to English, to reify a familiar translation without reconsidering the semantic connotations of the selection. Many translations for specific terms are already accepted as normative based on their consistent usage and ubiquity, but their implications in English warrant further discussion. One such term is "wrathful" (*khro bo*) for the deities that appear in monstrous aspects. Likely derived from Catholic notions of *irae caelestes*, "divine wrath," it presents a certain overarchingly powerful appeal. This term, however, connotes a sense of vengeance and emotional content, both of which contradict the nature of these buddhas according to the tradition. All buddhas, however they manifest, are free from the passions by definition; likewise, vengeance gained through wrath is furthest from their *modus operandi*, which is attested to be the selfless benefit of beings. The manifestation of buddha activity takes whatever form is necessary as determined by the context and the needs of beings. In the context of these buddhas, "wrath" as the translation of *khro bo* signifies a misapplication of biblical notions of a God defined by emotive experience, from affectionate to vengeful, which is incongruent with Buddhist notions of identitylessness, the quelling of emotions, and thus the absence of emotional reactivity. As such, "fierce" is a more appropriate translation than "wrathful."

This term describes the appearance and activity of such deities without straying into emotional imputations and, most importantly, not into notions of anger-based revenge. Fierceness might be considered a neutral emotional state of intense potentiality that does not preclude the imminent threat of violence. It is a state of severe provocation certainly, but in response to the needs of beings in this context as opposed to some kind of individual gain. In the case of these buddhas, it is necessarily pervaded by the realization of emptiness, enlightened awareness, which transcends the cognitive state of animals and most humans as well. As a corresponding antonym, "pacifistic" may be preferable to "peaceful" for *zhi ba*: the former describes a state of being whereas the latter is commonly used as a quaint adjective to describe the scenery. In Tibetan contexts these terms may predominantly refer to the guise of these deities, but in their translation and attendant assimilation to the West, they have too often been misunderstood as a means to distinguish the character and not just the appearance of diverse buddhas.

mother's initiatory name indicates that Nyangrel literally is the son born from Hayagrīva, whereby it subtly interjects some prophetic foreshadowing of his tantric affiliations and introduces an additional semantic shift not present in the variant. Nevertheless, its complementarity with his father's initiatory name remains the same.

The first term is the key: lotus is a euphemism for the vulva in tantric symbolism, thus Pema is the female counterpart to Dorjé, and the *Stainless Proclamations* juxtaposes Nyangrel's parents with gendered constructions of the same name: Dorjé to Pema; Wangchuk to Wangchen; and the shared Tsal, which is often appended to secret initiatory names and is identical in word and meaning here. Given that their tantric names emphasize the "great power" of their genitalia, Nyangrel's parents are defined by their reproductive potential; their primary purpose within the biographies is to conceive together their destined son.

As is typical when comparing these two biographies, even when the general context of an event concurs, their details often diverge, which becomes evident beginning with the accounts of Nyangrel's conception. Both emphasize that his mother had an auspicious dream at that time, yet the symbols and experiences described therein are distinct, and even the exact place of conception differs. The *Clear Mirror* recounts that Nyangrel was conceived when his parents copulated within the local religious center:

> Ngadak Nyang Nyima Öser was conceived within the body of the great secret mother, Pema Dechen Tsal, who was the spouse and spiritual consort of his father, Nyangtön Chökyi Khorlo, at Jöpaser hermitage in the male earth-rabbit year (1099 [*sic*]).[67] Concerning the signs of a magically emanated reincarnation, in his mother's dream countless white lions dissolved into her body, and a five-pronged golden dorjé arose into the sky before implanting into her womb. She swallowed an outer ocean in one gulp. By purging that

67. This is an error based on an incorrect rendering of the year's element. Nyangrel was born in 1124 according to the *Clear Mirror*, so the year of conception was 1123, the water-rabbit year of the second *rabjung* and not the earth-rabbit year as stated here. The error is repeated in *Gsal ba'i me long* B, 108.2.

Also, Tashi Topgyal Wangpodé (1550–1607), identified as a reincarnation in the line of Rikzin Gödem (1337–1408) and Ngari Paṇchen Pema Wangyal (1487–1543), is reported to have recovered treasures from the golden stūpa at Lhodrak Jöpa (Lho brag 'jod pa), which is likely the Jöpa Sergyi Gönpa ('Jod pa ser [gser] gyi dgon pa) described as Nyangrel's place of conception here in the *Clear Mirror*. See Boord's expanded and revised version of his 1993 chapter 1: http://www.khordong-byangter.org/teaching.html.

> out again, she was filled with the three-thousand-fold universe. She consumed a galaxy into her belly and having mounted the sun and moon circled the four continents. A retinue of ladies tossed flowers, prostrated, and circumambulated her. Many light rays beamed into her body, which was blissful and vibrating, and her radiance intensified—such were the signs that numerously arose. When she told her husband they were very happy, and he replied, "This is a sign that the one to arrive is the magical emanation of a bodhisattva who will benefit transmigrators." Having said that they paid homage and performed preventative healing rituals.[68]

Like many Tibetan biographical structures, this account of conception is modeled on the hagiographies of Śākyamuni Buddha, several of which were translated during the dynastic period, and thus whose lore, if not the texts themselves, were available to Nyangrel and his biographers. This becomes especially evident in the close correlates with certain details in hagiographies like Aśvaghoṣa's *Buddhacarita* that record the dream and experience of Siddhārtha's mother at the time of his conception:

> Before she conceived she saw in a dream
> a white elephant king
> entering her body, yet she did not
> thereby feel any pain.[69]

We thus find the white elephant of the Buddha's famous biography echoed in Nyangrel's as white lions. Both evoke regality, albeit with inverted time signatures: Prince Siddhārtha is prophesied to become either a wheel-turning monarch (*cakravartin*) or a Buddha in the future, whereas Nyangrel is the enlightened reincarnation of a past emperor and separated from any immediate political authority based on that status. Nevertheless, the intent of this replication is clear: it suffuses Nyangrel's conception with the arrival of a magically emanated reincarnation and aligns the significance of his birth with that of the Buddha's, thereby foreshadowing Nyangrel's enlightenment and functioning as a basis for the legitimation of his subsequent activities. Such alignment soon becomes standard in Tibetan Buddhist hagiography.

When a protagonist is to attain enlightenment not just in Tibetan but Buddhist hagiographical writing in general, the life of the Buddha remains the

68. *Gsal ba'i me long*, 324.3–325.2.

69. Olivelle 2008, 3.

foremost exemplar, the foundation upon which new layers of culturally specific contexts, language, symbols, and so forth are drawn in reconstructing a narrative path to enlightenment. As for the Tibetan iterations of this process, Nyangrel's biographies employ details, topoi, and episodic structures from the life of the Buddha, but they also elaborate and expand them through the inclusion of vivid tantric imagery to enrich the narrative.

After the white lions enter the body of Nyangrel's mother, a golden dorjé is implanted in her womb, which seems to represent an oneiric reenvisioning of intercourse and conception: again referencing her husband's secret name and phallus, the golden dorjé is also the seed that inseminates her. Tantric language and its attendant symbolic imagery thereby imbues a relatively ordinary event, in this case conception, with its ultimate significance, transfiguring the mundane elements of intercourse into Dharmic symbols rich with meaning. The one conceived will be a buddha, thus the symbolic values are more true than the mundane trivialities of these events as ascertained though ordinary perception. They augur for the reader the extraordinary qualities of the child to be born to them.

While the biographies share the same episodic framework, the *Stainless Proclamations* diverges from the *Clear Mirror*'s account of conception at the outset since Nyangrel's parents are practicing together in a municipal court residence rather than a remote hermitage. The intended symbolism of the mother's dream is perhaps even more apparent, though the details of the parents' practice are veiled by tantric terminology as well.

> The two, having opened the maṇḍala of Pema Wangchen at the court of Tsenchö town, when they were abiding in approach and accomplishment, in the night on the tenth day of the fifth month of a rabbit year (1123), there arose four extraordinary women in the mother's dream. A red, thousand-petaled lotus with anthers in the shape of a precious jewel was placed on the crown of the mother's head and dissolved into her, whereby the ladies circumambulated her three times. Having strewn four handfuls of multicolored flowers, they declared, "This is the Dharma king, the last existence of the bodhisattva. By means of this birth he will not return. He will become a buddha. There is no doubt that those transmigrators who see, hear, or remember him will become liberated." Then they dissolved like a rainbow in the sky and departed. The next morning she prostrated to her husband upon awakening.[70]

70. *Dri ma med pa*, 85.2–86.2.

Compared to the somewhat more explicit imagery of conception in the *Clear Mirror*, at first glance this account is quite modest, yet while Pema Wangchen indicates a *sādhana*, or tantric liturgy, of Hayagrīva ("approach and accomplishment" are the two stages of deity yoga meditation), there remains the veiled reading of the passage as well. As in the discussion of the mother's name above, it is difficult to ignore that she is the "dynamic expression" of the deity and maṇḍala they are practicing; this is a direct reference to her secret name, Pema Wangchen Tsal. Rather than euphemistic symbols conveyed through dream, the sex here is made explicit in describing their "opening the maṇḍala of the great powerful lotus." While the parents are indeed practicing the sādhana of the fierce tutelary deity, Hayagrīva, they are also consummating their relationship as husband and wife in conceiving together their prophesied son.

The imagery indicates that the one conceived within her will be like a wish-fulfilling jewel satisfying the needs of beings as explicitly confirmed by the ethereal ladies. While a lotus is the throne of all the buddhas, a red lotus specifies the padma buddha family, the fierce emanation of which is, once again, Hayagrīva. References to red phenomena recur as signs throughout the *Stainless Proclamations*, reiterating Nyangrel's affiliation with Padmasambhava, Hayagrīva, and the deities of that family.[71] With Nyangtön Chökyi Khorlo also having an auspicious dream on the same night, the *Stainless Proclamations* intensifies the time of conception:

> After hearing about her dream, he replied: "I also had a dream in which four extraordinary men arose. Bearing a white conch with 108 petals spiraling to the right, they said, 'This is the white conch of the Dharma. If it is blown, the sound of the Great Vehicle doctrine will resound. Whoever hears it will become a liberator of transmigrators and a subjugator of wrong views.' They gave it to me, and I was very pleased. Upon blowing it, 108 melodious and beautiful languages arose from within the 108 petals of the conch, and the sound of my conch was heard in all the lands of the world. This I dreamed. It is a sign that the heir to be born to us will be a magically emanated reincarnation, which is paramount we keep very secret." Having spoken thus, they were very happy.[72]

71. See the red yogin (emanation of Padmasambhava) at *Dri ma med pa*, 93.6; red mass of light dissolves into his heart center at 105.6; vision of Yeshé Tsogyal with a red cloak at 106.2; red bird at 107.3, and so forth.

72. *Dri ma med pa*, 86.2–87.1.

Numerous adjectives specify the significance of the conch, and the father distills the meaning of the dream, so its symbolic indications are apparent. Of particular note is the symmetry between the dreams of the mother and father, where each encounters four "extraordinary" beings who correspond to the gender of the dreamer and bestow on each a single symbolic item.[73] Given the emphasis on the esoteric derived from the symbolism of the red lotus in the mother's dream, it is important to juxtapose it against the white conch received by the father: on the one hand, these clearly correspond to the red ovum essence or *thiklé* (*thig le*, *bindu*) derived from the mother and the seminal white essence derived from the father, which are said to abide at the lower and upper poles of every individual's energetic subtle body until the time of death. More specific to the hermeneutic provided by the text, however, these two gifts may also symbolize Tibetan Buddhism's synthesis of the esoteric Vajrayāna with the exoteric Mahāyāna, since the red lotus specifies the family's tantric affiliations and yet the conch resounds with the doctrine of the Great Vehicle. One prevalent theme here and throughout Nyangrel's biographies is that, despite the fact that he exclusively practices the supreme vehicle of Vajrayāna and never demonstrates an affinity for or knowledge of sūtra, the conch functions as a harbinger that Nyangrel will master and propound the Mahāyāna as much as the Vajrayāna. This accords with common presentations of Tibetan Buddhism where the Vajrayāna is often (but not always) considered a set of esoteric technologies located within the larger rubric of the Mahāyāna more than a category of soteriological theory and praxis that can be thoroughly isolated from it.

Having oneirically confirmed that the son to be born to them symbolically bears all the promise of the Buddha, the two biographies diverge into variant contexts for rearing the destined son.

The Arrival of the Nirmāṇakāya

In continuing to draw from Indic literary traditions, while both biographies specify that Nyangrel was born in the same month as the historical Buddha, Siddhārtha Gautama,[74] the *Clear Mirror* provides little additional information

73. While lotuses are closely associated with the feminine and their counterparts are usually a vajra or dorjé, conches are often associated with the masculine but can signify either gender in Hinduism (Beer 2003, 9–10).

74. Olivelle 2008, 1:9, 5: ". . . as Pushya turned propitious . . ."

aside from the specific date and a set of extraordinary environmental signs at the time of Nyangrel's birth:

> When she was completing the ninth month and starting the tenth, he was born in the constellation *puṣya* during a female wood-dragon year (1124). Various wondrous signs such as rainbow-colored tents, lights, sounds, earthquakes, and so forth numerously occurred.[75]

Once again these signs accord with the birth of the Buddha according to his biographical traditions and become standard in Tibetan biographies when describing the delivery of the magically emanated buddha body of an enlightened adept, which again demonstrates an authorial awareness of the tradition exemplified by works like *Buddhacarita*:

> At his birth the earth,
> pegged down by the mountain king,
> shook like a ship tossed around by the wind;
> and from a cloudless sky fell a shower filled with lotuses blue and red,
> and with the scent of sandalwood.[76]

Given the discrepancy and contemporary debate concerning the dates of Nyangrel's birth and death, it is significant that the *Clear Mirror*'s inclusion of the element specifies 1124 as the year of his birth; the *Stainless Proclamations* only remarks that it was a dragon year, thereby failing to identify the twelve-year cycle of his birth and leading to some confusion later (for a complete discussion, see the appendix). Despite such issues, what the *Stainless Proclamations* lacks in date specificity, it adds in style:

> In the following year on the eighth day of the eighth month of a dragon year, just as the sun rose in the constellation *puṣya*, a son was born. Furthermore, he was untainted by saṃsāric defects and, as for the marks of the lotus buddha family, his body was white with a ruddy complexion. As for the signs that he would not be born again in existence, there was a finger-tall protuberance at the crown of his head. As for the signs of having completed all the qualities of the Great Vehicle, the hairs of his head extended down in [dread?] locks. As for the signs that he had perfected all the qualities of the

75. *Gsal ba'i me long*, 325.3–4.

76. Olivelle 2008, 5.

> exalted form of all the ones gone to bliss, his body had a white *oṃ* mole on his forehead. As for the signs that he had perfected the sixty melodies of a buddha's exalted speech, there was a red birthmark at his throat center in the shape of *āḥ*. As for the signs that he had mastered exalted mind, the meaning of birthlessness, there was a black birthmark in the shape of *hūṃ* at his heart center. As for the signs that he had perfected the five paths and ten grounds, there were eight-spoked Dharma wheels on his feet. As for the signs that he was victorious over all māra demons and obstacles, he had four fanged teeth. So he was born with these eight great marks on his body.[77]

Just as *Buddhacarita* tallies "the signs on the body of this illustrious one,"[78] Nyangrel is also born with an array of signs and marks that prophesize and prove his status as a magically emanated reincarnation, but as would be expected, only some of these signs are direct correlates to the Buddha's whereas others are more idiosyncratic. Among the eight signs inventoried here, only the protuberance at the crown of his head, the Dharma wheels on his feet, and the four fangs are counted among those found on all buddhas as "the signs of a great man" according to sūtra and the biographies of the Buddha.

These signs and the condition of rebirth within their final lifetime signifies that individuals like Siddhārtha and Nyangrel are on the verge of enlightenment; their only tether to saṃsāra is the karmic residue that propels them to effect the vast benefit of beings, though even aspects of this statement are controversial. Indeed, the issue of whether the Buddha (and later, by extension, any buddha) is born enlightened or becomes so continues to provoke animated argumentation on the debate courtyards of Tibetan monasteries and in academic circles as well.[79] Underscoring the paradox, these interpretations of Nyangrel's birth specify that he has indeed completed the path and is perfected already, and yet later empowerments are still required to provide further "maturation." Nevertheless, the various marks on his body have manifested as confirmation of that perfection in physical form, resulting in a rather striking appearance in the *Stainless Proclamations* that, according to his parents, necessitates that he be sequestered from public view. Following his birth they withdraw with their child into a closed retreat, where he will spend the first six years of his life and complete the initial stages of his studies in private.

77. *Dri ma med pa*, 87.1–88.2.

78. Olivelle 2008, 13.

79. See Silk 2003, passim.

Despite being such prominent figures during Nyangrel's childhood, the importance of his parents ebbs quite soon thereafter. Nyangrel is the protagonist of his own biographies of course, so it is appropriate that the narratives reduce the roles of the parents as the child matures and becomes more independent. The more immediate circumstances that quite literally birthed him become secondary to the karmic thrust from his past lives. While his father also functions as his first guru and thereby fulfills an additional role of primary importance throughout his youth, his mother is solely defined by bearing him and disappears from the biographies thereafter.

Empowerment and Experience

As the biographies progress into Nyangrel's early childhood, the auspicious signs and omens that attended his conception and birth are confirmed by his development of extraordinary personal qualities. Whereas contemporary studies of child prodigies may gesture toward the origin of a peculiar affinity but can rarely account for their spectacular abilities, a Buddhist context (whether literary or lived) requires karmic preconditioning as an explanatory basis. With the basic concept of reincarnation now popularly known in the West, previous lifetimes of study and practice may be blithely forwarded in lieu of a scientific explanation for preternatural talent, but this is standard in Buddhist contexts, where all manifest effects are necessarily linked to causes in the past, even if only an omniscient buddha can directly discern their correlation.

When causes accumulated in previous lives meet requisite conditions in the present, their expression becomes possible. The *Stainless Proclamations* attributes Nyangrel's extraordinary capacity for learning to the special environment created in the seclusion of retreat, where, free from the distractions that would inevitably arrive once people beheld his unusual appearance, the boy could focus on his studies: "Since they were able to keep him secret, he learned how to read and so forth. Because of that, he became learned in everything without obstruction and came to know it as in an instant."[80] The child appears to have emerged from strict retreat in his seventh year, but the *Stainless Proclamations* maintains that the parents were able to keep their child hidden until the age of nine and attributes his unusual scholastic abilities to individualized instruction. While the *Clear Mirror* concurs that Nyangrel was a gifted child, it attributes his aptitude to a peculiar familiarity with a more distant past:

80. *Dri ma med pa*, 89.1.

> In dependence on having diligently studied many times [in former births], from the age of two or three he knew how to read and so forth without requiring any study. Without studying he also knew the tantras and liturgies of the three, Viśuddha Heruka, Vajrakīla, and Yamāntaka. There arose a zeal for meditation, accomplishment, and general Buddhist conduct. No one could decide whether he was a magically emanated reincarnation or what.[81]

While the *Stainless Proclamations* relies on physical signs on Nyangrel's body to confirm his sanctity as a magically emanated reincarnation, the *Clear Mirror* introduces other evidence in their stead. His knowledge of various key tantras is compelling as proof for prior lives of intensive practice, and the selection of tantras recollected here is not at all random: Viśuddha Heruka, Vajrakīla, and Yamāntaka are among those attested to have been continuously transmitted by the Nyang clan since the empire, and they will become three of the eight fierce deities that Nyangrel will propagate in his most extensive treasure collection, the *Eight Instructions: Gathering of the Ones Gone to Bliss*. In sum, Nyangrel's affinity and natural aptitude for Buddhism during his childhood, particularly with regard to the esoteric Vajrayāna, are evident in the account provided in the *Stainless Proclamations*.

Within the *Clear Mirror*, such aptitude serves as a preliminary corroboration of the mother's dream: the son born to them is indeed a magically emanated reincarnation, and further confirmation arrives at the age of seven, when Nyangrel has the first of many auspicious dreams and visions. Both biographies punctuate his life with the apparition of various divine and semi-divine beings who bestow instructions, encourage practice, and provide companionship and support in lonely times.

> When he reached age seven, the people in the area celebrated with much dancing and playing, but he was unhappy. With thoughts of compassion for transmigrators, he took off for the snows of Jötselé. While staying there for one day, he was visited in a dream by four women—white, yellow, red, and green. In one melodious voice they called to him, "Son of the lineage arising from learning, we are your friends. You are the lord of the secret mantra, the oral transmissions, and the treasures: please open the doors to the treasures of the sacred doctrine. Care for those whose karma is ripe, the fortunate students. We and you transcend meeting and parting." Having

81. *Gsal ba'i me long*, 325.4–6.

> spoken thus, they faded into the sky. Upon waking, he saw magical apparitions. Then, after returning inside himself, he practiced.[82]

This episode is the first mention of treasures in the *Clear Mirror*'s primary biography and the first indication that his future manifestation as a teacher will specifically be as a treasure revealer in the company of his disciples. By contrast, whether ostracized for his own preternatural aptitude for Buddhism or concealed in retreat because of his appearance, the biographies present a childhood defined by isolation. There is no record of him having any siblings, thus the beings that make themselves apparent to him are his only companions, offering comfort through the consolation of an illustrious future.

While the *Stainless Proclamations* provides few details of Nyangrel's training in his late childhood and teenage years, the *Clear Mirror* presents a more continuous narrative, punctuating this period with several visionary episodes. These are presented as defining moments for the young yogin, and they compel his father to bestow key empowerments, thus maturing him on the path of tantra as he develops both physically and soteriologically. The first occurs in a dream not long after his encounter with the ladies above:

> When I had reached the age of eight, I dreamed one night that the sky was filled with rainbows and one of the rainbow strands descended and pierced the earth. In the center of that spot was the one called Bhagavan Śākyamuni in the guise of an ordained one amid a large sangha of monks. I went forward to meet him, and after strewing flowers, I requested teachings. At this point I dreamed that Śākyamuni taught the doctrine through the door of symbolic language: "Precisely when mistaken: that's luminosity!" (*zhib par log na gsal*?). When I awoke the sun was already up, and since it had risen high, my body was sweating. My bedding had become damp, and I was dazed and disoriented, as though drunk and about to black out. This state endured for a month. I told my father, Nyangtön Chökyi Khorlo, and he said, "It was a good dream but there may be obstacles," so he bestowed the empowerment of the tutelary deity.[83]

The mere mention of Śākyamuni, ordination, and monastic Buddhism is

82. *Gsal ba'i me long*, 325.6–326.4.

83. *Gsal ba'i me long*, 326.4–327.3. For another translation, see Kunsang 1990, xi. Also reproduced in Phillips 2004, 119n39 and Dudjom 1991, 755.

one of exceedingly few references to anything resembling the Lesser Vehicle in the biographies, as Nyangrel remains focused on Vajrayāna practice throughout. The one cryptic line of actual instruction only further distances the episode from an exoteric context as this phrase finds few referents in sūtra and instead points toward Vajrayāna meditation technologies and the subtle inversion required to directly perceive luminosity-emptiness as the ultimate nature of apparent phenomena in the moment of their arising. Likewise, the dream results in Nyangrel's induction into the maṇḍala of his meditational deity, so the Hīnayāna imagery is concluded by tantric reinforcement.

A couple of years later, Nyangrel has the first of a series of encounters with the tantrika Padmasambhava that would occur throughout his life. In this dream, Nyangrel receives the four empowerments and rests in the three experiences of bliss, clarity, and nonthought, which demonstrates a high degree of meditative accomplishment, all the more so since he is only ten years old.

> In a dream one night when I had reached the age of ten, men, women, and a vast cavalry filled the sky, the earth, and all the space between. After raising parasols, victory banners, and flags aloft, a symphony of music from small ritual drums and cymbals, flutes, bells, large drums and cymbals, and so forth echoed through the mountains. At the center of that assembly was the one called Master Padmasambhava. The master mounted a white horse, and four ladies lifted its four hooves. Having venerated him, I wept, and as devotion arose naturally, the four ladies raised their hooves with a thunderous roar, and Padmasambhava arrived before me bearing a jeweled vase filled with *amṛta* nectar. In an instant he completely bestowed the four empowerments on me with a single word, and the three experiences dawned in me. The sky was rent, the earth shook, and the mountains trembled. Pristine awareness roared like fire, like water churning, like wind howling. When I awoke, dawn had broken and my body was filled with bliss; light and the appearances of the three experiences were there as before.[84]

Energized by this dream and its subsequent attainment, "he ran to the summits of Jögang and all the windswept mountains and performed for a few days the various accumulations of conduct. Everyone said he was insane or stupid."[85] Nyangrel meets detractors and skeptics throughout his life, but

84. *Gsal ba'i me long*, 327.4–328.4.

85. *Gsal ba'i me long*, 328.5–6.

his father continues to train him despite such criticism, and various indications of accomplishment such as clairvoyance develop in the child. Continuing from above:

> The higher perceptions dawned exclusively. He recognized his past and future lives. He also knew the lifespans of all [his father's] students and retinue as well as their good and bad qualities. He asked his father, Nyangtön Chökyi Khorlo, about those signs, and his father said, "The signs and auspicious connections are good." Then the venerable father bestowed an empowerment for the singular form of heroic Hayagrīva.[86]

Once again Nyangrel's father bestows empowerment following an auspicious dream and the particular empowerment is far from random: it precisely corresponds to the content of Nyangrel's dream. The dream and subsequent empowerment reinforces the connection between Nyangrel and Padmasambhava and foreshadows his treasure activity as the reincarnation of emperor Tri Songdetsen. Hayagrīva then becomes the focus of Nyangrel's practice.

Following several years of solitary retreat in a mountain hermitage, Nyangrel displays various signs of accomplishment that are apparent to people throughout the area. Signs function as evidence, provided through the medium of public testimony, that an individual has attained the stages of realization attempted through a specific practice, thereby demonstrating that the practitioner has meditated successfully. Since the primary objective in deity yoga is for the meditator to relinquish contaminated conceptions of self and with them the fundamental dichotomies maintained through dualistic thought, the meditator recognizes his or her own "identity" and every aspect of experience to be the deity that is enlightened awareness itself. When all phenomena are recognized as the apparent aspects of the deity, as the manifest display of enlightened awareness, and when the conception of self is so thoroughly undermined that there is nothing other than this awareness, the tradition asserts that a manipulation of phenomena deemed "miraculous" by ordinary beings becomes possible. Such signs are dismissed within a conventional worldview founded on the basic laws of the physical world, but according to Tibetan Buddhism such complacent dismissal is a symptom of ignorance. Such laws function as artificial constructs that confine one within the prison of saṃsāra. Signs are not miraculous but super-*natural*: they demonstrate reality while undermining the narrow-minded assumption of illusory limita-

86. *Gsal ba'i me long*, 328.6–329.2.

tions, the seemingly unimpeachable rules of the relative world. They fill the pages of Tibetan biographies as vivid evidence of transcendence, as freedom from saṃsāra and the ignorance that defines it. The *Clear Mirror* includes an extended description of signs that occur at the conclusion of a six-year retreat in Nyangrel's teenage years:

> Between the ages of thirteen and nineteen, by accumulating seven *dré* of consecrated mustard seeds through the practice of Hayagrīva's fierce mantra at Jöpuma in the snowy land, many additional signs of accomplishment appeared. After water in the vase boiled and fire blazed on the *torma*, his home in the south was illuminated by firelight. The snows at Tselé melted and accumulated at Jölung as a lake in the shape of a horse's head. His copper *kīla*-dagger neighed three times, and the sound was heard all over his home area. Many merchants behind the snowy peaks had not heard it, however, so those who did named the hill Deaf Pass. Moreover, he had a vision that his tutelary deity, the singular form of heroic Hayagrīva, actually resided in the opening at the crown of his head. The retinue of deities started dancing, and the sound of *phaṭ* was heard. The local gods and *nāgas* also prostrated and promised to do whatever he commanded. The steam of his breath shimmered into rainbows. Flames flared up from the saliva he spat on the ground, and it was said that people's clothes and so forth became scorched when coming into contact with it. Additionally, Jöpu rock has many body impressions and footprints.[87]

The Tibetan for Hayagrīva, Tamdrin (*rta mgrin*), literally translates as "horse neck," and this deity is depicted with a horse's head emerging from his crown, so the signs associated with the accomplishment of Hayagrīva are often equine in nature. Likewise, since practitioners of Hayagrīva visualize themselves as inseparable from this fierce blazing deity, the sound of the fierce mantric syllable *phaṭ*, heat, and flame are concomitant products of accomplishment. These signs and others demonstrate that external phenomena have taken on a certain malleability. In some cases this is quite literal, as when Nyangrel impresses his body and feet into solid rock. In others the nature of a substance is thoroughly transmogrified, as when his spit scorches clothing. Important throughout is that these signs are clearly witnessed by others, authenticating Nyangrel as a realized adept, spreading faith among the populace, and given his young age

87. *Gsal ba'i me long*, 329.2–330.3.

here, establishing him as a tantric wunderkind while highlighting his connection to these practices in former lifetimes.

In addition to confirming an adept's realization, signs prove that the particular practice is ideally suited for that practitioner: the deity harmonizes with the secret nature of the person such that meditation on the deity actualizes the enlightened potential of the individual, thus resulting in attainment. Signs prove that the empowerment previously bestowed was karmically potent and soteriologically effective; they obliquely serve as evidence that authenticates the one who bestowed the empowerment as well. Since this was none other than Nyangrel's father in these biographies, it provides additional clout to the continuity and strength of his family lineage as well as its transmissions.

The *Stainless Proclamations* offers few details concerning Nyangrel's training in his teenage years. Rather than promoting a natural preponderance for Viśuddha Heruka, Vajrakīla, and Yamāntaka from the age of two or three as in the *Clear Mirror*, the *Stainless Proclamations* only states that he did not receive the empowerments and instructions for these three cycles until he was fifteen. Additionally, he also received Great Perfection transmissions at that time, the fourth of the four "soul-doctrines of the forefathers" (*yab mes kyi bla chos*), representing the rarefied, most profound practices of his lineage that allegedly had been transmitted unbroken from his imperial-era ancestors through his father to him.[88]

While the death of Nyangrel's father is not mentioned in either biography, it seems reasonable to deduce that he died when Nyangrel was in his late teens. His final activities in both biographies are the transmissions just described, though Nyangtön Chökyi Khorlo is mentioned once more in the *Clear Mirror* to introduce "the way in which the sovereign [Nyangrel] trained his mind in the doctrines of the oral transmissions."[89] Here the father is eulogized as an accomplished practitioner of several tantric cycles whose continuity survived unbroken from the imperium, with the implication being that he transmitted all of these to his son. But still there remains no explicit indication that he himself had passed. Nyangtön Chökyi Khorlo may have been somewhat older or in poor health even when his son was born. In an attempt to interpret the various signs that appeared at that time, the *Stainless Proclamations* recounts that members of the local populace speculated that Nyangtön Chökyi Khorlo had died and that these were the "signs of his nirvāṇa," or death.[90] In any case, his father was by far the most significant figure in Nyangrel's life and yet dis-

88. *Dri ma med pa*, 90.4.

89. *Gsal ba'i me long*, 348.4.

90. *Dri ma med pa*, 88.4.

appears from both biographies after bestowing these empowerments. By the time Nyangrel reaches the age of twenty-one, he has sought out and received instructions from other teachers for the first time, a development that may have been necessitated by the death of his father and root guru. From this point in the biographies Nyangrel moves from preparing for his destiny to inheriting it, from establishing the karmic potential for his activity to manifesting it, from ensuring the preservation of the treasures in his former lives to recovering them in his present one. As Nyangrel ventures out from the tutelage of his father to receive the instructions and aid of other teachers, including contemporary treasure revealers, he begins to fulfill everything that his biographies have thus far foretold.

Claiming His Karmic Inheritance

The karmic theory implemented throughout Nyangrel's primary biographies is quite simple: causes produce results of a similar nature—a barley seed, when met with the necessary conditions, produces a barley sprout. In these biographies the activities of his former incarnation, Emperor Tri Songdetsen, ripen into the lifetime of the fully enlightened treasure revealer Nyangrel. The primary causes for that final life were thus planted in a former one, and the current life is, on the one hand, merely their fruition. On the other hand, these dreams, signs, and visions are causal in that they inspire his path and catalyze key developments—such as empowerments—upon it. Appropriate to its tantric context, this karmic theory is not especially complex. Absent is the sophisticated interplay of causes, conditions, and effects so minutely outlined in Abhidharma literature. After the collapse of the empire, Nyangrel's antecedents were non-institutional, non-monastic tantrikas, and by the twelfth century they appear to have had little knowledge of nor interest in the complexities of Buddhist scholasticism. Nevertheless the karmic worldview informs tantric Buddhism as well, so a respect for Buddhist fundamentals of karmic cause and effect necessarily drives the narratives. The literary construction of Nyangrel's life employs the topos of karma to spell out his destiny as a magically emanated reincarnation.

The two primary biographies are the best sources for the historical Nyangrel and yet the variance between them is such that it is impossible to confirm the majority of their data; little evidence of the historical person remains. Nyangrel's youth as presented in his two biographies correspond on the names of his parents, the general location of his birth and upbringing, and his preponderance for specific lineages of the Vajrayāna transmitted through his father. Both also demonstrate the pervasive influence of the Buddha's biographical traditions, giving parallel yet variant descriptions of his parents' dreams at the time of conception, extraordinary signs concurrent with his birth, and his visionary experiences during childhood. The variants suggest that such details are likely idiosyncratic reformulations of standard Buddhist tropes rather than events that actually occurred in his life. Thus, while vividly compelling in a literary sense, the conflicting minutiae of Nyangrel's primary biographies are historically problematic.

Nyangrel is now more a figure of memory than history. It is difficult to distinguish the personal qualities of the historical man from the details and episodes layered over their subject by subsequent biographers that have informed the popular remembrance of him.[91] However, given the repetition of his dates, the various texts still attributed to him, and their mode of production as treasure, among other details, even the most critically minded among contemporary scholars must allow that some enduring qualities of Nyangrel were drawn from history and not mere legend alone. We may discern three intricately codependent elements that repeatedly define Nyangrel both within his biographies and in his subsequent renown:

1. His claim to recollect the complete sequence of his past lives beginning with emperor Tri Songdetsen
2. His recovery of allegedly imperial-era texts and relics called "treasure"
3. His devotion to the tantrika Padmasambhava, whom he claims to personally remember as the guru of his imperial preincarnation, as the concealer of countless treasures, and as the catalyst responsible for the successful establishment of Buddhism in Tibet

Having compared Nyangrel's two primary biographies and detailed their variants with regard to his early life, these three defining characteristics, each of which is consistently and repeatedly attested among all sources relating to Nyangrel, may be forwarded as the most historical qualities of the man. They define Nyangrel throughout both of his biographies in particular and, along with several literary products forged in direct reliance on them, are the focus of analysis for the remainder of this book.

91. See Assmann 1997, 1–2, for his discussion of Moses as "a figure of memory but not of history," as contrasted against the Egyptian king Akhenaten, who is "a figure of history but not of memory."

2. Reincarnation and the Return of the Sovereign

THROUGH THE EMERGENCE of the Fourteenth Dalai Lama on the world stage as a Tibetan cultural hero, international peace advocate, and pop icon, reincarnation has become one of the most renowned and definitive aspects of Tibetan Buddhism, yet relatively little has been clarified concerning the Tibetan assimilation and transformation of this prominent Indian concept. While the singular descents of premier institutional reincarnates like the Dalai Lamas and Karmapas have been rightly complicated by academic inquiries into their histories as well as more inclusive assessments of their presents, especially with regard to the selection process and its discarded candidates,[92] a significant gap has persisted in our knowledge of reincarnation prior to its institutionalization in Tibet.

The Karmapa hierarchs and their disciples are correctly credited with developing catenate reincarnation into a viable system of inheritance that would have wide-ranging significance: with the aura of enlightened authority and esoteric power, reincarnate lamas have gained access to and often patronage from Mongol khans, Chinese emperors, and American presidents, yet to date there has been little insight into how reincarnation developed from the singular identifications of the eleventh century into the institutionalized series

92. Concerning their past, the history of the Dalai Lamas is complicated by the fact that the Third Dalai Lama Sönam Gyatso (1543–88) was actually the first to receive the title—only then were his two predecessors identified and appropriated into that reincarnate sequence, so the line of Dalai Lamas extends from 1578 although the tradition dates its origins to "the First Dalai Lama" Gendun Drup (1391–1474). Even this earlier origin does not contest the Karmapas as the oldest institutional line, but research into its earliest representatives demonstrates that there was a significant gap between the death of the "First Karmapa" and the recognition of the Second, and it took several incarnations before the sequence of prophecy, death, and recognition became normalized (see Manson 2009, 31–32).

Concerning their present, there exists an ongoing feud between rival factions of the Karma Kagyü school such that three incarnations of the Seventeenth Karmapa have been recognized, but since much of the property in dispute now lies in Sikkim, a northeast state of India, no faction has been allowed to recover that inheritance, and the main monastery (Rumtek) remains under armed Indian guard.

of reincarnations that gained prominence from the fourteenth century. This chapter attempts to bridge this gap by clarifying some early links in the chain of serial reincarnations in general, and by detailing Nyangrel's previously unattributed yet critical role in this development in particular. As we shall see, his innovations concerning catenate reincarnation were critical to the conception of his past and were intended to secure the legacy of his future, not as an inexhaustible series of lives for the benefit of beings but as the prophesied treasure revealer who, having attained enlightenment in that final lifetime, would not reincarnate again.

In the era that followed the ninth-century fragmentation of the Tibetan empire, we find the first identifications of Tibetans as the reincarnations of deceased adepts. One of the earliest biographies of the proto-Nyingma luminary Rongzom Chökyi Sangpo (1012–88?) states that he was the reincarnation of a certain Tralo Ringmo who visited Kham, and although their meeting is historically tenuous, Atiśa (d. 1054), the Bengali adept credited with instigating the new translation period, is said to have recognized Rongzom as the reincarnation of another Indian master, Kṛṣṇapāda the great.[93] We might recognize certain parallels with the avatars or human incarnations of Hindu gods, but these are distinct from the Tibetan process of reincarnation, where one adept dies to be found reborn as another. Rather than drawing the celestial into the tangible and the eternal into the ephemeral for a single human life, Tibetan reincarnations are human-to-human series united by the continuity of enlightened awareness. There is scant indication that the recognition of reincarnations originated in India,[94] and little precedent for the distinctly Tibetan tradition of intentional reincarnation—whereby prophecy serves as guarantor for the continuity of a single unbroken series, a catenate sequence of lifetimes—that became a catalyst for the revitalization of institutional Buddhism during the new translation period.

While some Kadampas had identified themselves as reincarnations of recently deceased masters, and the biographies of Atiśa's foremost disciple, Dromtön (1005–64), would be manipulated to include a sequence of preincarnations by the thirteenth century,[95] reincarnation claims were being pro-

93. Almogi (2002, 70) notes that this is from one of the earliest biographies of Rongzom, which was written by his disciple, Yöl Genyen Dorjé Wangchuk (Yol Dge bsnyen Rdo rje dbang phyug), and it is almost identical to his short biography in the *Blue Annals* (see Roerich 1949, 160–61).

94. Van der Kuijp 2005, 28.

95. One issue in the chronology of catenate reincarnation is the dating of *Sbrom ston rgyal ba'i 'byung gnas kyi skyes rabs*, which contains a sequence of catenate preincarnations for Dromtön.

posed among a specialized class of adepts by the middle of the twelfth century. Buddhist treasure revealers claimed to recollect the lives of imperial-era pre-incarnations as they relied on the karma and memory of those past lives to aid their recoveries of buried texts and relics. Having received teachings and perhaps even possessed these materials previously, treasure revealers awaken centuries later to reclaim, reintroduce, and redistribute these sacred items. Since Buddhist treasures are so often presented as products of the imperium, reincarnate claims to imperial-era personages eventually became normative within the tradition itself.

Perhaps due to the distribution of his elaborate biographical tradition as much as by his revealed products, foremost among the early Buddhist treasure revealers is Nyangrel, whose Nyang clan enjoyed imperial favor in former times, as we have seen, but was reduced to more modest circumstances following the collapse of the empire.[96] While their wealth and influence may have diminished, Nyangrel's father claimed to preserve the unbroken tantric transmissions of the Nyang clan that he passed to his son when signs proved that he was ripe for them. As detailed in the previous chapter, such signs were remarkably forthcoming, thus Nyangrel's parents are said to have recognized their son as a magically emanated reincarnation as soon as he was conceived.

Nyangrel's two biographies, the *Clear Mirror* and the *Stainless Proclamations*, provide a range of insights into the development of catenate reincarnation in general and how it was conceived and employed by early Buddhist treasure revealers in particular. While his biographies record that other contemporaries also claimed reincarnate descent from renowned figures of the imperial apogee,[97] they demonstrate that Nyangrel was among the first Tibetans who attested to recall an unbroken sequence of lifetimes in support of that claim. It is unlikely, however, that Nyangrel introduced the other critical innovation that produced catenate reincarnates like the Karmapas and Dalai

---

Kapstein (2003, 775) contends that this text was likely redacted in the thirteenth century, though it contains some eleventh- and twelfth-century elements, and van der Kuijp (2005, 29) concludes that the earliest biographies of Dromtön contained no references to a series of preincarnations, thus these were not conceived by Dromtön himself but were devised posthumously by later redactors, some of whom likely were contemporaries of Nyangrel's biographers. Cf. Jinpa 2008, 28.

96. This favor was literally inscribed for perpetuity on the Sha (*zhwa*) temple pillar in which the minister Nyang Tingezin is rewarded with lands and title for his service to Tri Detsuktsen. This is transcribed and translated in Richardson 1985, 43–63. For a narrative account of the Nyang clan's population of imperial inner circles from the time of Songtsen Gampo, see Richardson 1998, 140–48.

97. See below for the claims of Nyangrel's guru Nyönpa Dönden.

Lamas, which is the promise and prophecy of future lives. The development of perpetual reincarnation lines is the culmination of an evolution that may extend back to the historical Buddha himself.

Foundations of Catenate Reincarnation

The Buddha's preincarnation narratives (*skyes rabs*, Skt. *jātaka*) were finely carved into the gates of Bhārhut and Sāñcī by the second century B.C.E., thus they rank among the earliest Buddhist narratives. These were subsequently gathered into textual collections to which additional preincarnations were added over time.[98] Pāli collections now include more than five hundred stories, though Sanskrit collections and the Tibetan translations based on them are more modest in number.[99] When Āryaśūra compiled his *Jātakamālā*, or *Garland of Lives*, in the middle of the first millennium C.E., he organized the Buddha's preincarnations thematically and almost atemporally:[100] internally each preincarnation narrative begins with birth and ends with death, but any sense of order, sequence, or linear chronological progression is absent within the total collection. They are not threaded karmically or temporally; causality and time are not used as methods to link these narratives. Thus the Buddha's preincarnations could have occurred in any order and at almost any time, which reflects their composition and compilation by multiple contributors rather than their emergence as a finite document by a single author.

Since Nyangrel conceived of his preincarnations as a karmically determined catenate sequence, a better comparator may be one of the earliest Mahāyāna scriptures, the *Samādhi of Direct Encounter with the Buddhas of the Present Sūtra*, which was translated into Chinese in 179 C.E. and into Tibetan circa 800.[101] In it Bhadrapāla is foremost among eight lay bodhisattvas and a retinue of five hundred devotees who request Śākyamuni Buddha for instruction in this *samādhi*, or meditation practice, at Rājagṛha. While teaching it, the

98. Khoroche 1989, xiv.

99. Khoroche 1989, xiv.

100. Some attempt was made to organize these preincarnation narratives according to which of the six perfections was featured within them. For an exact accounting of this organization, as well as where it breaks down, see Khoroche 1989, xii.

101. Tib: *Da ltar gyi sangs rgyas mngon sum du bzhugs pa'i ting nge 'dzin gyi mdo*, Skt. *Praty utpannabuddhasaṃmukhāvasthitasamādhisūtra*. For a complete translation from the Tibetan with reference to remaining Sanskrit fragments and Chinese editions, see Harrison 1990, which describes its extant versions and their transmission beginning on xv. Harrison 1978 provides a critical edition of the Tibetan.

Buddha confides that the sūtra will disappear after his death but be reintroduced by the reincarnations of those present in the "last five hundred years" of this world.[102] Paul Harrison notes the rather remarkable correlation between this origin narrative and that of the Tibetan treasures,[103] but Robert Mayer recognizes a more striking correspondence to Nyangrel in particular: aside from establishing a precedent for the reintroduction of scriptures as treasure, Nyangrel's *Copper Island Biography of Padmasambhava* overlaps the context of the sūtra such that Padmasambhava appears to be substituted for the Buddha, Tri Songdetsen for Bhadrapāla, and the host of later treasure revealers for the remainder of the retinue. Moreover, there is some semblance of regular reincarnation sequences in the sūtra, as the Buddha prophesizes that his audience will "[meet] together in all their rebirths" and they will "have [met] together throughout the one kalpa."[104] This remains vague compared to the explicit catenation attested by Nyangrel a thousand years later, but these correlates to treasure recovery, reincarnation, and the fundamental dynamic of Padmasambhava and Tri Songdetsen as guru and disciple indicates that the *Samādhi of the Direct Encounter with the Buddhas of the Present Sūtra* may have influenced Nyangrel at least as much as the compendia of the Buddha's preincarnations.[105]

As evidenced by the inclusion of the sūtra in the ninth-century *Denkarma* catalog and the *Garland of Lives* in the slightly later *Pangthangma* catalog, Indic scriptures and narratives concerning reincarnation became available in Tibet by means of the great imperial translation projects.[106] But it has also been suggested that the concept of reincarnation was popular in Tibet prior to the translation of these Indic sources. Although the transmission of the text is notoriously complex, the *Testimony of Ba* preserves an early indigenous narrative where a child dies and a pearl, painted red and placed in the mouth of her corpse, is discovered in the mouth of a baby boy. This implies that a notion of continuity from one life to the next was already prevalent in pre-Buddhist Tibetan religion, even if it shared few features with the universal, karmically driven system imported later.[107] As such, this episode in the *Testimony of Ba* may serve as another example where the spread of Buddhism was aided by

102. Harrison 1990, xxix.

103. Harrison 1990, xvii n6; Harrison 2003, 124–25.

104. Harrison 1990, 105–6.

105. Mayer, personal communication, April 4, 2012. For his analysis of referents to treasure within the sūtra and other sources, see Mayer 1994, 533–44.

106. For the sūtra in *Ldan dkar ma*, see Lalou 1953, 321. For *Jātakamālā* in *'Pang thang ma*, see Halkias 2004, 72.

107. For a translation of the entire episode, see Wangdu and Diemberger 2000, 15. For an

some natural alignments with local correlates, but Tibetan Buddhists would continue to develop the concept of reincarnation well beyond its Indic and indigenous precedents.

Much is known about the translation and transmission of Indic Buddhist texts to Tibet during the imperium, yet very little is known about the preservation of Tibetan texts during the "age of fragmentation" that followed its dissolution. As in India, memorization and oral recitation were stalwart pedagogies of the monastic curriculum, but narratives may have spread well beyond the walls of Tibetan institutions because of their didactic content and entertainment value. Persevering in the form of orally recounted stories, the Jātakas may have been passed extratextually in the popular sphere following the collapse of institutional Buddhism in Tibet. There can be little doubt that Nyangrel was familiar with the Buddha's preincarnation narratives, and yet, as was his talent, he envisioned innovations that furthered that tradition as well.

Early Catenation of Preincarnations

Establishing the provenance of Nyangrel's preincarnation narratives proves to be a more complex task than the texts initially suggest. It has been assumed that Nyangrel's earliest biographies contain the earliest iterations of these narratives, but a thorough comparison with a third source demonstrates that Nyangrel's conception and recollection of catenate preincarnations must be distinguished from the vignettes that narrate them.

My analysis focuses on Nyangrel's two biographies and, in addition, a biography of Guru Chökyi Wangchuk, or Guru Chöwang (1212–70), who claimed to be Nyangrel's reincarnation. With the inclusion of first-person testimony, spoken by the masters themselves and recorded by direct disciples, elements of all three texts have endured as many as six or seven centuries of transmission. Unfortunately, there remain very few manuscripts that can help clarify how their recensions were carried out. While there are two available versions of the *Clear Mirror* with a third held captive in the Potala Palace collection, we presently have only one version of the *Stainless Proclamations* and one of Guru Chöwang's *Eight Pronouncements*.[108] Unlike Nyangrel's biogra-

---

analysis of it, see Kapstein 2000, 43–44 and 224n38, which cites Blondeau 1997, 213. Also see Blondeau 1997, 203–4.

108. Despite so many centuries of transmission, only the *Stainless Proclamations* (*Dri ma med pa*) was ever xylographed, and even this was in the late nineteenth or early twentieth century. All extant editions of both biographies have been transmitted within collections pertaining to Nyangrel's cycle of deity yoga known as the *Eight Instructions* (*Bka' brgyad*), where the Gangtok

phies, where the preincarnation narratives precede the accounts of his life, the *Eight Pronouncements* is primarily framed as a question-and-answer session between Guru Chöwang and Padmasambhava, and the majority of its content concerns Guru Chöwang's preincarnations. The primary biography of his life exists under a separate title (the *Eight Chapters*) within the same compendium of biographical materials.[109]

Even when comparing parallel narratives between these three sources, it is very difficult to establish a clear line of transmission based on a more microscopic approach to textual criticism alone. Orthography and other precise analyses of internal evidence are indeed useful but weave a web of competing hypotheses that simply cannot be disentangled without additional manuscripts. I thus rely on a more macroscopic approach to content, drawing hypotheses based on thematic consistencies throughout the texts while incorporating evidence drawn from textual criticism as well. My hypotheses may change should additional manuscripts come to light, but as for the texts available now, the following is clear.

A striking feature of Nyangrel's two biographies and Guru Chöwang's compendium of biographical materials is that they share parallel preincarnation narratives, the brief accounts of past lives, while retaining distinct primary biographies for their respective protagonists.[110] This variation is expected for

---

edition in thirteen volumes is the only one that preserves an example of the *Stainless Proclamations*. As stated in its edition notice, this collection was "reproduced from the sole known surviving set of prints from the Kaḥ-thog blocks from the library of H. H. Dudjom Rinpoche" (1904–87). The two available editions of the *Clear Mirror* (*Gsal ba'i me long*) were reproduced from manuscripts, one within the thirteen-volume *Eight Instructions* from Tsamdrak (Tshams brag), and the other from a biographical collection of *Eight Instructions* lineage holders. A third currently inaccessible manuscript of the *Clear Mirror* is also contained within a volume of *Eight Instructions* texts according to the Potala's *Rnying ma'i gsung 'bum dkar chag*, 109. Last, the table of contents for the incomplete Dalhousie *Eight Instructions* lists a *Rnam thar dri med* in three folios and a *Rnam thar gsal ba'i me long* in seventy-two, but both are missing. Given its brevity, it seems unlikely that the former could represent a fragment of the complete biography, but the latter was almost certainly a version of the *Clear Mirror* biography of Nyangrel.

For the biography of an early Bönpo treasure revealer, Shenchen Luga (eleventh century), see Martin 2001. For another set of early indigenous auto/biographical materials in translation, see Yamamoto 2009 on Lama Shang (1122–93). For an extraordinarily rich account of this figure and his era in Lhasa, see Sørensen 2007.

109. "*Skabs brgyad ma*," in *Gu ru chos dbang gi rang rnam dang zhal gdams*, I: 1–53.

110. Phillips (2004, 166–68) notes this three-way alignment and highlights some discrepancies, but he assumes that, since Guru Chöwang postdates Nyangrel, Guru Chöwang's biography must have drawn the preincarnation narratives from Nyangrel's. Some of the details he presents as evidence of sharing are also mistaken, however, such as the secret initiatory name of Nyangrel's mother: Guru Chöwang's biography introduces a variant (Padma bde byed rtsal) that differs from those given in Nyangrel's biographies (Padma bde ba rtsal; Padma dbang chen

Guru Chöwang, since his is a different life, but as introduced in the previous chapter, a comparison of Nyangrel's two primary biographies reveals that these works are distinct from each other as well. While some of the more generic details concur, the primary biographies of the *Clear Mirror* and the *Stainless Proclamations* differ with regard to essential information such as Nyangrel's second treasure recovery site and the number of his spiritual heirs.[111] In fact, the episodes vary throughout, from the signs at his birth to his activities before death, and a thorough analysis reveals that Nyangrel's primary biographies do not share any text. No redactor ever attempted to integrate Nyangrel's biographies, and they remain distinct despite seven centuries of transmission. This is all the more unusual in that Tibetan biographers and historians commonly insert lines and even whole episodes from available documents to compile their new narratives, resulting in more complete presentations of the person, period, and events. The negative implications of plagiarism are absent in Tibetan literature; such borrowing, most often without citation, is ubiquitous and accepted. As such, Tibetan historians may be more accurately defined as "tradents" rather than authors—as compilers of established knowledge rather than creators of new content.[112] The tradent of the *Clear Mirror* admits just this as his methodology in the colophon:

> É ma ho!
> My mind understood yet did not appreciate
> the vast sky treasury of biographies
> concerning the exalted body, speech, mind, qualities, and activity
> of the final birth of the Dharma king, the precious sovereign
> [Nyangrel].

---

rtsal). Other evidence presented by Phillips is circumstantial. Based on a thorough comparative analysis of these sources, I argue the opposite of Phillips' assumption: the shared preincarnation narratives were incorporated into Nyangrel's biographies from Guru Chöwang's.

111. His second recovery is at Khomting temple (*'Kho 'thing lha khang*) in the *Clear Mirror* (*Gsal ba'i me long*, 340–42); it is at Mutik Shelgyi Pamagong (*Mu tig shel gyi spa ma gong*) in the *Stainless Proclamations* (*Dri ma med pa*, 99–100). The *Stainless Proclamations* counts five primary spiritual heirs (*Dri ma med pa*, 4 and 110–11) whereas the *Clear Mirror* only lists four (*Gsal ba'i me long*, 353), both of which exclude his son and primary heir Namkhapel. In the *Clear Mirror*, Nyangrel entrusts his library but perhaps all of his material possessions in general to his son (*Gsal ba'i me long*, 363.6), but the *Stainless Proclamations* never mentions his son by name among his bequests. However, he does appear in the introduction and colophon as among those who heard Nyangrel tell the story of his life and helped compile the biography based on that testimony.

112. Mayer 2010b citing Jaffee 2007, 17–37.

> Since the biographies requested by the four cherished heirs
> exist in many varied sizes,
> and since confusion produces doubt and makes realization difficult,
> this biography does not contradict the others but comprises all of them
> so that his life may be known by all. May all be happy and healthy![113]

He used all available resources to compile an authoritative version of Nyangrel's life, yet its divergence with the *Stainless Proclamations* indicates that this text could not have been one of his sources.

The congruence of the preincarnation narratives contrasted with the incongruence of the primary biographies indicates that the *Clear Mirror* and the *Stainless Proclamations* were composed and transmitted independently. If the authors or redactors of one total biography, the complete text as we know it today, had access to the other, why would they completely ignore its primary biography, rich in relevant content, just to copy the brief accounts of his preincarnations? It appears that the *Clear Mirror* and the *Stainless Proclamations* originally comprised only Nyangrel's primary biographies, the narratives of his life, to which other components such as the preincarnation narratives were added over time. This would then require the existence of a third source, one that narrated Nyangrel's past lives without contradicting or significantly supplementing either of his primary biographies, that served as the original source of the preincarnation narratives for both of them. This source is now preserved as a series of redundant episodes—variant editions of the same account—within Guru Chöwang's *Eight Pronouncements*.[114]

Guru Chöwang was an important disciple of Nyangrel's second son and chosen heir, Namkhapel (1169?–1235?), who likely died when Guru Chöwang was in his twenties. Not long after the death of Namkhapel, Guru Chöwang announced that he was Nyangrel's reincarnation. This was attested through his recollection of their shared preincarnations, which Guru Chöwang repeatedly describes with an array of variants in the *Eight Pronouncements*. Most important among their details are the lists of teachings and transmissions received, as they establish a connection to virtually every textual cycle Nyangrel recovered as treasure in his life, the most influential of which were then found in new iterations by Guru Chöwang. Since Guru Chöwang's legitimacy rested on his claim that he was Nyangrel's reincarnation, the narration of their shared preincarnations would indeed be compelling evidence in support of this claim, yet while Nyangrel most certainly recounted his past lives as a catenate sequence,

113. *Gsal ba'i me long*, 381.2–4.

114. For a detailed analysis see Hirshberg forthcoming.

his primary biographies provide much reason to doubt that he elucidated them in any detail or that he had any intention to incarnate again.

One Primary Preincarnation

With first-person testimony in both of his primary biographies, Nyangrel repeatedly states that he remembered a catenate sequence of lifetimes. His tallies correspond to the total number of preincarnation narratives that precede each of his primary biographies, yet he does not enumerate, name, or summarize this complete series in either.[115] Instead, Nyangrel merely states the total number of lives recalled while emphasizing the very first of them.

Each biography provides its own accounts of Nyangrel's recollections, but both describe his first pilgrimage to Samyé Monastery as especially provocative. According to the *Clear Mirror* alone, Nyangrel's memories of his preincarnations are initially instigated by meditative attainment during solitary retreat, first at the age of ten and later at the inception of his treasure career as a young adult.[116] Some time thereafter, "when he arrived at the mouth of the Tsangpo River by Samyé, he recalled his prior births."[117] He subsequently enters retreat in the caves at Samyé Chimpu, where he beseeches Padmasambhava to dispel the hindrances of doubt, comes "face-to-face" with the guru, and thereby recollects thirteen preincarnations.[118] Similarly, Nyangrel is en route to his third major treasure recovery in the *Stainless Proclamations* when, "after arriving at Samyé, he went to the valley of the main temple and instantaneously recollected fifteen prior births, like a reflection dawning in a mirror."[119] Enumeration is but one of several inconsistencies that helps distinguish these narratives, suggesting distinct lines of transmission and redaction, which will be considered in full below. Of immediate interest here is the site that stirs Nyangrel's memory.

While not stated explicitly in either biography, the location is significant since Samyé is Tibet's first monastery. Commissioned by Tri Songdetsen in the late eighth century, the site remains to this day the physical manifestation of the emperor's devotion and commitment to Buddhism. As *un lieu de*

115. *Dri ma med pa*, 100–101; *Gsal ba'i me long*, 348.

116. *Gsal ba'i me long*, 329 and 335 respectively.

117. *Gsal ba'i me long*, 348.1–2.

118. *Gsal ba'i me long*, 348.2–3.

119. *Dri ma med pa*, 100.6.

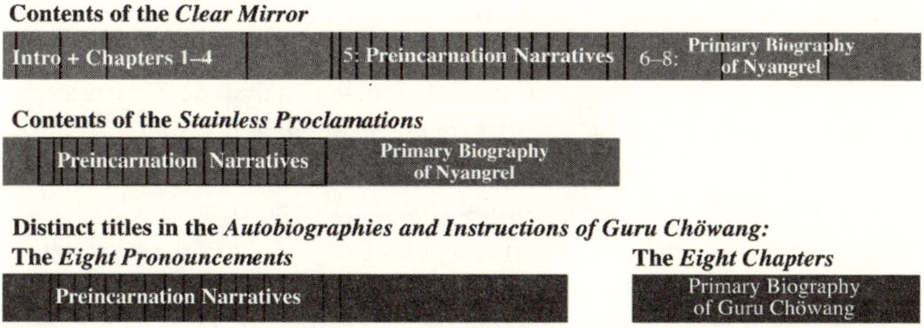

Figure 2. Graphic of the structure and divisions of the biographies. All of the preincarnation narratives in the *Clear Mirror* are contained in chapter 5, whereas each life, including Nyangrel's, is counted as a chapter in the *Stainless Proclamations*. The *Eight Pronouncements* contains assorted lists and narratives of Guru Chöwang's preincarnations, whereas the *Eight Chapters* concerns Guru Chöwang's life alone and exists as a distinct title within the compendium.

mémoire Samyé functions as a mnemonic device for Nyangrel, not only provoking the memory of his life as Tri Songdetsen but each of the lives that link them together in a catenate sequence as well. In both of his primary biographies, these brief statements of remembrance appear in place of the memories themselves; rather than the names, summaries, or narratives of those preincarnations, we find mention only of a nondescript series. The only preincarnation Nyangrel remembers with any detail within his primary biographies, and the only individual for whom he is designated a magically emanated reincarnation, is the emperor Tri Songdetsen, who as a primary disciple of Padmasambhava was charged with recovering the treasures in his future life, according to later treasure lore that stems from Nyangrel.

While the *Stainless Proclamations* allows a certain ambiguity to the identity of this original incarnation, the *Clear Mirror* specifies the identity unequivocally throughout. Nyangrel is recognized as the reincarnation of Tri Songdetsen at birth, and this is then reiterated throughout the text by various authoritative figures.[120] In one visionary episode, Padmasambhava directly addresses him as Divine Flower of Brahma, an epithet reserved for Tri Songdetsen.[121] Nyangrel later confides details of his life as this great emperor four times, each of which is preceded by a phrase such as, "Previously, when I was Tri Songdetsen . . ."[122] The authors of the *Clear Mirror*'s primary biography repeatedly

120. *Gsal ba'i me long*, 325.4.

121. *Gsal ba'i me long*, 346.5.

122. *Gsal ba'i me long*, 335, 363, 368, 372.

ensure that the identity of Nyangrel's preincarnation is clear. It is none other than Tri Songdetsen, and no other incarnation is described or named. The *Stainless Proclamations* is vague by comparison, but analysis demonstrates that the preincarnation can be none other than Tri Songdetsen as well.

According to the *Stainless Proclamations*, from the age of seven Nyangrel "came to be renowned as a magically emanated reincarnation. He was also named Ngadak Nyangrel."[123] The title *ngadak* (*mnga' bdag*), "the sovereign," is commonly used in reference to the emperors, most especially Tri Songdetsen but also the ninth-century emperor Tri Tsukdetsen (d. 838), who is often recounted in post-imperial histories by the epithet Ralpachen. This is significant since the latter is now counted among Nyangrel's preincarnations, thereby making it somewhat more difficult to ascertain which emperor is referenced by the title, if not both. One episode in the *Stainless Proclamations* provides more detail but remains inexplicit. At a tantric feast, one of Nyangrel's gurus, "the crazy one" Nyönpa Dönden, describes their karmic connection by declaring that in a previous life Nyangrel was "the king of the borderlands" and that the guru was "the translator Lotsā[wa]."[124] Tri Songdetsen is renowned for sacking Chang'an, the capital of Tang China that lay not far beyond the eastern limits of the Tibetan territories, yet it is Ralpachen who is credited with expanding the empire, as documented by several favorable treaties won from the Chinese and inscribed on stele, so thus far the ambiguity remains. Likewise several translators from the imperial period were renowned, though none was more vaunted—especially among the heirs of Nyingma—than Vairocana. Like Tri Songdetsen, Vairocana is counted among the cabal of twenty-five core disciples of Padmasambhava, and he is credited in several of Nyangrel's treasure colophons. If Nyönpa Dönden indeed refers to Vairocana as his former incarnation, then "the king of the borderlands" must specify Tri Songdetsen as that of Nyangrel. From this evidence alone it seems unlikely that Nyangrel named Ralpachen as a preincarnation, and there is additional support for this thesis as well.

Both this emperor and Nyangrel gained the nickname "Ralpachen," "the long-locked one," specifically because it was a distinguishing physical attribute. As we read previously in the *Stainless Proclamations*, Nyangrel is described as being born with long hair, which would seem to be the perfect opportunity to link this imperial preincarnation to his final emanation. The karmic bond between them would be so strong that Nyangrel was born with the defining physical feature of his predecessor, and yet no such correlation is made.

123. *Dri ma med pa*, 90.3.

124. *Dri ma med pa*, 91.5. For a translation of this entire episode, see Davidson 2005, 330.

While the *Stainless Proclamations* directly addresses the significance of the child's long locks, they are only a sign that he had "completed all the qualities of the Great Vehicle."[125] It is as if the authors of the *Stainless Proclamations* were unaware of the correlation, which is precisely what I take to be the case: Nyangrel's original biographers did not make such correlations because they neither knew nor reproduced the details of his preincarnation series.

Finally, the primacy of the treasures in Nyangrel's legacy underscores the karmic impact of Tri Songdetsen on Nyangrel's life. It is the activities of that first life, not Ralpachen's, that establishes the causal basis for Nyangrel to recover the treasures, thus the preincarnation designated as "the sovereign" must be Tri Songdetsen. Having been empowered and entrusted to recover these treasures in that past life, Nyangrel awakens more than three centuries later to fulfill the cycle, impelled by the inevitability of that karmic process. Tri Songdetsen is the preincarnation that is essential to legitimating Nyangrel's life, which is defined by his recovery of the treasures, and he is the only one named in Nyangrel's primary biographies.

In sum, based on what are presented as his own statements within his primary biographies, Nyangrel conceived of a catenate sequence of lifetimes that gloriously began with Tri Songdetsen and gloriously concluded with himself, Nyangrel, the enlightened treasure revealer. By this preincarnation alone, Nyangrel appears among the earliest Tibetans to implement the rhetoric of impending karmic destiny as legitimation for radical religious activity, which in his case was the reintroduction of scriptures through the mode of treasure recovery that was becoming increasingly popular and controversial at that time. There is little evidence, however, that he described the lives between them in any detail. Altogether this indicates that Guru Chöwang elaborated on a series that Nyangrel had only implied, and that the preincarnation narratives devised by Guru Chöwang were redacted into Nyangrel's biographies in subsequent centuries.

Only Nyangrel's first and final lifetimes, Tri Songdetsen and Nyangrel, the direct cause and its concluding result, are described in his primary biographies whereas the spectrum of lives between them remains merely implied. This set also excludes any lives that precede Tri Songdetsen or succeed Nyangrel; the lives before Tri Songdetsen appear to be less consequential while any after Nyangrel would lack a karmic basis. During Nyangrel's life, such narratives were not necessary to promote his primary project of recovering the treasures. Perhaps the final tally of lives was added later to accord with the preincarnation narratives: a few strokes of the pen would inject a number to fill the gap

125. *Dri ma med pa*, 87.

between Tri Songdetsen and Nyangrel, but Nyangrel's *Copper Island Biography of Padmasambhava* as well as his *Essence of Flowers* history, which reproduces most of it, record Padmasambhava as telling Tri Songdetsen that he will recover the treasures in the last of his seventeen lives, thereby prophesizing his final birth as Nyangrel. Given the corroboration between his historical narratives and his first-person testimony presented within his biographies, Nyangrel may very well have conceived this number himself and so deserves credit for what may be the first catenate reincarnation series attested in Tibet, but he also bears the blame for not checking his math: between the death of Tri Songdetsen and the birth of Nyangrel, their fourteen or fifteen incarnations endure an average lifespan of only twenty-two years. Since untimely deaths would have been considered inauspicious and incongruent, the number is therefore problematic. Nyangrel's biographical traditions embed an additional aspect of karmic harmonization by asserting that both Tri Songdetsen and Nyangrel lived for sixty-nine years, an unintended consequence of which is that these lives between them must be abbreviated in duration.[126] Perhaps the final tally was indeed born of inspiration more than calculation, and this average is a consequence of devising a definite sequence between his preeminent preincarnation and himself, which appears to have been quite unprecedented.

Nyangrel's innovations in catenate reincarnation theory share some correspondences and some divergences with the preincarnations of emperor Songsten Gampo (d. ca. 649) as presented in the *Maṇi Kambum*, another cycle for which Nyangrel is an acclaimed contributor that focuses on this emperor as the Great Compassionate One, Avalokiteśvara. With the *Maṇi Kambum*'s notoriously fluid construction, the process of its authorship/tradency/revelation is even more convoluted and opaque than most treasures, although traditional accounts identify a trio of twelfth-century figures who contributed to early iterations of the compendium. The siddha Ngödrup, Nyangrel, and Jetsun

126. Most accounts of the emperor would contradict a lifespan of sixty-nine years. While some sources suggest 797 for the death of Tri Songdetsen (see, for example, Wangdu and Diemberger 2000, 92–93n359), more recent work on early sources indicates 800 (Dotson 2007, 10–13). Since Nyangrel was born in 1124, this affords 324 years between the death of his first incarnation and the birth of his last. Given the fourteen lives between them in the *Stainless Proclamations* and fifteen in the *Clear Mirror*, the average lifetime for each would be about twenty-three years of age in the former and twenty-one or twenty-two in the latter. According to the preincarnation narratives, however, each individual lives a full life of virtuous activity that was uninterrupted by an untimely death. The total enumeration of the series is thus problematic: there are far too many incarnations for the time allotted.

Shākya Sangpo are each said to have compiled distinct sections, and yet the preincarnation section is not attributed to any of them.[127]

In reviewing the details of the *Maṇi Kambum*'s preincarnation series, while Songtsen Gampo like Nyangrel is presented as the final rebirth in his continuum, those that precede Songtsen Gampo tend to rely on a buddha's formulaic prophesizing of an explicitly catenated rebirth, providing the name, parents, and locale of the very next incarnation near the conclusion of most vignettes.[128] On three occasions, however, the incarnation makes the prophecy him- or herself and thus prefigures the normative processes of identification relied on for institutionalized reincarnation lines in later centuries.[129] Nyangrel's preincarnations (which I argue were devised by Guru Chöwang and his disciples) proceed without the precision of omniscience; biodata is only provided to introduce each incarnation and his narrative. Likewise, several of Nyangrel's / Guru Chöwang's preincarnations are eminently historical or at least tied to definite historical personages, whereas those of Songtsen Gampo are of the world and yet often exult beyond saṃsāric trivialities. In some instances it is questionable just how human his preincarnations really are: the first one described is a five-year-old girl who, preceded by an array of wondrous signs, manifests out of the expanse of space to an impoverished couple. The husband then discerns that "the nature of the girl was born from the state of emptiness,"[130] which is quite distinct from the grounded karmic and historical precedent afforded by Tri Songdetsen. In sum, while some elements of the *Maṇi Kambum* undoubtedly passed through Nyangrel and became one of his four or five premier Dharmic bequests, and while his innovations in reincarnation theory certainly came to influence the preincarnations of Songtsen Gampo that would become transmitted within it, it is unclear whether Nyangrel introduced these preincarnations, contributed to them directly, or merely inspired later contributors to this seminal collection to adopt his innovations.

Whereas the Buddha's *jātaka* are organized thematically and almost atemporally, Nyangrel recalls his past lives as a chronological progression of incarnations in real historical time. This was a crucial link that led to catenate reincarnation lineages, but Nyangrel did not employ the other essential component, which is the projection of future lives beyond his own. Although both biographies include Nyangrel's preincarnation narratives and the *Clear Mirror*

127. See Sørensen 1994, 8–9 and 642–43.

128. *Maṇi bka' 'bum*, 1: 293.2, 297.2, 301.2, 307.5, 311.4: *khyod skye ba 'di'i 'og rol du . . .*

129. *Maṇi bka' 'bum*, 1: 291.2, 328.4, 334.2: *bdag skye ba 'di'i 'og rol du . . .*

130. *Maṇi bka' 'bum*, 1: 289–90.

alleges to preserve his testimony ruminating on the possibility of his return, the text was manipulated to enhance Guru Chöwang's claim as Nyangrel's reincarnation. While Nyangrel still remains an enlightened treasure revealer in accordance with his renown, which is essential to Guru Chöwang's self-legitimation, this claim effectively displaces Nyangrel from the prophecy and with it his prestige as the final incarnation in the series. Guru Chöwang thus becomes the seventeenth incarnation of Tri Songdetsen, the foremost enlightened treasure revealer, who is prophesized by Padmasambhava in narratives attributed to Nyangrel. As such, these three biographies may preserve a literary frontline between two opposing inheritance models, patrilineal and reincarnate, that were meeting on the ideological battleground of late-renaissance Tibet. Guru Chöwang's claim relied on the recollection of the precise sequence and details of their shared former lifetimes. In dictating a series of short preincarnation narratives, Guru Chöwang filled in the details for the lives that appear to have been merely suggested, framed, or enumerated by Nyangrel.[131]

Nyangrel (and Others) on the Possibility of His Return

For Nyangrel, enlightenment ends the cycle of rebirth, as in the biographies of the Buddha. This is essential not only to legitimating Nyangrel's treasure recoveries during his lifetime but to securing his legacy thereafter. The *Stainless Proclamations* relates that he will depart for the western buddha realm of Dewachen (Sukhāvatī) at death, and this is corroborated in the biography of his son, Namkhapel. These accounts are consistent in asserting that Nyangrel never intended to reincarnate and that he bequeathed his lineages and possessions to his son and foremost heir. The primary biography of the *Clear Mirror* also contains many similar indications, and yet its final chapter is notable for its determination to advance the possibility of an alternative.

The *Clear Mirror*'s final chapter is divided into three sections: the first describes the last year of Nyangrel's life and presents his final instructions and testaments; the second section reproduces Padmasambhava's prophecies for Nyangrel's magical emanations; and the third depicts the circumstances of his death and funeral.[132] The first section is mostly consistent with other state-

131. Phillips (2004, 173) suggests the possibility of a rivalry between Namkhapel and Guru Chöwang. For an overview of the contents of these preincarnation narratives as well as their effect on Guru Chöwang's claim, see Hirshberg forthcoming.

132. Respectively, each section begins at *Gsal ba'i me long*, 362.2/ B, 144.3; 372.3/ B, 154.1; 377.3/ B, 158.6.

ments throughout the *Clear Mirror*'s primary biography: Nyangrel's final birth is acknowledged and lamented by his disciples; it is prophesized by Padmasambhava in a memory from Nyangrel's life as Tri Songdetsen; and it is reiterated by Nyangrel himself. He also repeatedly identifies the western buddha realm as his next destination, yet despite all this there is an effort to soften the finality of a final existence so as to introduce the possibility of a return.

Adding an element of ambiguity in the first section of the final chapter, Nyangrel announces, "Because I am the great Dharma king's final birth, now I need not be reborn. Nevertheless, the magical emanations (*sprul pa*) of exalted body, speech, and mind are inconceivable."[133] So even though Nyangrel has transcended cyclic existence and rebirth, he suggests that anything is possible in enlightenment. This is similar to the notion that Śākyamuni Buddha has attained complete cessation, the exhaustion of all karmic activity and manifestation, yet he may still respond to the prayers of devotees and project magical emanations that appear in the meditative visions of adepts, both of which may be karmically tied to the perceiving subject more than their enlightened object. Siddhārtha's declaration that this was his last rebirth is not challenged or diminished, however; it is fundamental to the Buddhist tradition, and I believe it was equally fundamental to Nyangrel's conception of his own life and legacy. Nyangrel saw himself as the conclusion of a profound karmic arc that began with Tri Songdetsen and ended with his enlightenment as the greatest treasure revealer of his age.

At work here is an important distinction between magically emanated reincarnations (*sprul pa'i sku*) and magical emanations (*sprul pa*).[134] The *Stainless Proclamations* is consistent in identifying Nyangrel as a magically emanated reincarnation of Tri Songdetsen.[135] *Sprul pa'i sku* thus signifies a finite embodied lifetime for a highly developed but still reincarnating being, whereas *sprul pa* are ephemeral and perhaps ethereal manifestations of enlightened beings that do not reincarnate.[136] So while the *Stainless Proclamations* also predicts Nyangrel's magical emanations from his posthumous residence in Dewachen,

133. *Gsal ba'i me long*, 367.5–6.

134. For the etymology and discussion of *sprul pa* in Tibetan, as well as its Sanskrit and Chinese equivalents, see Stein 1973, 417–22.

135. *Dri ma med pa*, 86 and 89.

136. See the *sprul pa* of Padmasambhava at *Dri ma med pa*, 94; of a ḍākinī at *Gsal ba'i me long*, 331. Magical emanations are initially taken to be tangible, perhaps ordinary beings, but the Dharmic context of their appearance and/or the fantastic nature of their departure convinces Nyangrel that they were magical emanations the whole time. Within the biographies, it is not clear, therefore, whether *sprul pa* are real people with special qualities, the envoys of the buddhas, or purely immaterial manifestations of enlightened awareness.

nowhere does it suggest magically emanated reincarnations.[137] Composed and amended by lineal descendants of Guru Chöwang, the *Clear Mirror* conflates *sprul pa* and *sprul pa'i sku* throughout, and this exact same convenience is afforded in Guru Chöwang's *Eight Pronouncements*, where it is stated that Nyangrel will "emit countless magical emanations (*sprul pa*)," one of which is Guru Chöwang.[138] Magical emanations and magically emanated reincarnations are quite deliberately equated in this text such that, within Guru Chöwang's oeuvre, it serves as exhibit A for evidence that Guru Chöwang is Nyangrel's reincarnation. Even Nyangrel's explicit assertion of his final rebirth is not problematic for Guru Chöwang: he acknowledges it while recollecting his prior life as Nyangrel![139]

During a visionary encounter reported in the *Eight Pronouncements*, Guru Chöwang asks Padmasambhava about his status and the various emanations of the three buddha bodies (*sku gsum, trikāya*). Padmasambhava obliges with a teaching concerning their nine types (3 x 3) whereby he finally informs Guru Chöwang, "You are the magically emanated reincarnation (*sprul sku*) of the magically emanated reincarnation (*sprul sku*)."[140] Padmasambhava further elaborates on the additional divisions and definitions of this particular category, but a key shift has been made: *sprul pa* and *sprul pa'i sku* are equivalent for Guru Chöwang (and/or his biographers) whereas they were not for Nyangrel (and/or his biographers). So despite Nyangrel's repeated assertion that he was the final reincarnation in the series, by conflating magical emanations with magically emanated reincarnations, Guru Chöwang not only displaces Nyangrel from the prophesied position of the seventeenth rebirth but potentially extends his reincarnation indefinitely. As we will see, later contributors to the *Clear Mirror* then identified Nyangrel's magical emanations as real historical persons at various stages of the text's transmission.

To conclude the first section of the final chapter, Nyangrel offers one last statement on his intent where he says, "I am going to the western realm of Dewachen. For as long as cyclic existence is not emptied, the benefit of beings will arise by means of the two exalted form bodies. In particular, my magical emanation, possessing outstanding qualities, [verb omitted] in the west." We might expect a verb of existence whereby Nyangrel would simply be referring,

137. *Dri ma med pa*, 113. This prophesizes Nyangrel's death twelve or thirteen years in the future, so the episode occurred circa 1179–80. Cf. Phillips 2004, 142.

138. *Gsal ba'i me long*, 324.4: *sprul pa sku'i rtags su/* 325.2: . . . *byang chub sems dpa'i sprul pa* . . . 325.6: . . . *sprul pa'i sku'aṃ ci yin* . . . *Bka' rgya brgyad ma*, 69.5: *sprul pa grangs med 'phro/*.

139. *Bka' rgya brgyad ma*, 104.1.

140. *Bka' rgya brgyad ma*, 109.4–5.

once again, to taking up residence in Dewachen. Its absence allows for a sufficient degree of ambiguity, however, for which a later commentator inscribed his resolution: "There is no doubt that this is Guru Chöwang."[141] This line, now provided its own space and preserved in small letters, is absent in the other version of the *Clear Mirror*, as are similarly reproduced notes that allege to identify Nyangrel's postincarnations. In the Padmasambhava prophecies that follow, a note, also absent in the other version of the *Clear Mirror*, states that Guru Chöwang is the speech emanation, which is reiterated in Guru Chöwang's biographical tradition.

Section 2 of the *Clear Mirror*'s eighth and final chapter stands out as an especially distinct section. Entitled "How the magical emanations arose in accordance with the prophecies of Orgyen Padma," it is the most definitive with regard to Nyangrel's reincarnations and preserves interlinear identifications by some later contributor/s, yet Nyangrel himself is never named within it.[142] This section may have been excerpted from a more generic set of reincarnation prophecies that was adapted less for Nyangrel than for Guru Chöwang's claim as his reincarnation. Indeed, section 2 separates Nyangrel's final testaments from the circumstances of his death that otherwise would be joined in a seamlessly continuous narrative. Unlike Nyangrel's other memories of the eighth century, some of which also occur in this chapter, this prophecy is not framed by Nyangrel remembering his life as Tri Songdetsen, nor is it attributed to some dream or vision that Nyangrel had at this time. In fact, the prophecies are not attributed to Nyangrel at all, thus section 2 does appear to have been excerpted from some other source and inserted here, thereby interrupting the first-person testimony of the primary biography that was recounted by his direct disciples.

In section 2 Padmasambhava identifies a series of incarnations in response to a pertinent question by Tri Songdetsen: "After I become a buddha, will my magical emanations arise to benefit transmigrators?"[143] The details of the prophecy remain somewhat cryptic, but the suggestions of later redactors are textually inserted to resolve any lingering questions concerning the identities of these emanations, which thereby become reincarnations as real historical persons. Padmasambhava predicts three magical emanations who will sequentially radiate as the seed syllables *oṃ*, *āḥ*, and *hūṃ* from the head,

141. *Gsal ba'i me long*, 372.1–3. Also discussed by Phillips 2004, 166–68.

142. *Gsal ba'i me long*, 372.3.

143. *Gsal ba'i me long*, 372.4. This prophetic dialogue between Padmasambhava and Tri Songdetsen bears the hallmarks of a treasure narrative, but the *Clear Mirror* does not display treasure marks (*gter shad*) for this section or include other markers to identify it as such.

throat, and heart of Avalokiteśvara, whose form Tri Songdetsen has assumed upon his enlightenment, and these three seed syllables become three human emanations who may or may not overlap chronologically. The first will be an unnamed Indian who teaches the Dharma through various forms of physical exercises, and an interlinear note here only states that he will be known as "the brahman with conch earrings."[144] His location outside Tibet renders it difficult for later Tibetan readers to suggest a historical person for that emanation, but no such obstacle confounds the identification of those who emanate within Tibet. Once again, the prophecy for the second emanation contains relatively general indications within the main text, but these are ascribed to a specific individual in an interlinear note:

> After him, a red letter *āḥ* will radiate from the throat of that buddha. By dissolving into a woman blessed by the ḍākinī Caṇḍālī who resides amid the snowy sky mountains to the northeast, she will give birth in a monkey year to a son endowed with great wisdom and compassion . . . *The magical emanation of exalted speech is the guru of La-yak, Chökyi Wangchuk.*[145]

Since Guru Chöwang is named within the main text of the opening chapters of the *Clear Mirror*, we identified the author as a proponent of Guru Chöwang.[146] Since he appears again within these interlinear notations that are absent from the *Clear Mirror* B, there is no doubt that some version of the *Clear Mirror* circulated among Guru Chöwang's disciples and was emended by them at various stages of the text's transmission. The final emanation in the trilogy is subsequently identified in yet another interlinear insertion as the famous bridge-building treasure revealer, Thangthong Gyalpo (1367–1485), but an additional, sixteenth-century or later contributor responded with an entirely distinct set of individuals. His note now spans an entire line:

> These are Shalu Khyenrab Chöjé, the great paṇḍita of Jampaling, and Pema Wangyal of Ngari. Since these three are considered the final births of Nyang and Chöwang, are these other three really them? Does one prophecy shut the door by means of a sin-

144. *Gsal ba'i me long*, 373.2.

145. *Gsal ba'i me long*, 373.4–6. This insertion is also noted by Phillips 2004, 166–68.

146. *Gsal ba'i me long*, 245, 271.

> gle opinion? I think it is determined by whichever prophecy is authoritative.[147]

Shalu Khyenrab Chöjé (1436–97) was a proponent of Kālacakra in the Sakya lineage; Paṇchen Jampaling Sönam Wangyal (1401–83) was the founder of the Gelugpa school's Jampaling Monastery in Chamdo, which lies to the northeast of central Tibet; and Ngaripa Pema Wangyal (1487–1542) was a treasure revealer who is also identified as a reincarnation of emperor Tri Songdetsen, so while Pema Wangyal may be cogent as a postincarnation of Nyangrel and Guru Chöwang, the affiliations of the other two make them unlikely candidates for such an association. Perhaps this is an attempt at intersectarian poaching, where a prior master from one lineage is identified and enthroned as a reincarnation within another. From one perspective, their reincarnation as Khyenrab Chöjé and Sönam Wangyal could absorb and effectively negate the lineages of Nyangrel and Guru Chöwang; from another, it insinuates the sanction of these later masters and their respective lineages since they are attested *to be* Nyangrel and Guru Chöwang. Regardless, the contention and manipulation present in the *Clear Mirror* aptly portrays an uncertainty with regard to the postincarnations of Nyangrel and Guru Chöwang that persisted for centuries.

Given that Guru Chöwang's materials are presented as autobiographical, for the most part they record neither the final stages of his life nor describe his death,[148] and I have yet to find an unambiguous statement of intent with regard to his own reincarnation in his primary biography, the *Eight Chapters*, but it does preserve a second coda—apparently a distinct text—appended to the original one where a catenate series of eight subsequent reincarnations are enumerated. Relying on cryptic symbols to distinguish the qualities and activities of each postincarnation, these stanzas eschew explicit data concerning persons and locations, thereby undermining their utility as prophesies to find and confirm actual individuals as the reincarnations of Guru Chöwang. They only specify a progressive refinement of the three buddha bodies that predicts Guru Chöwang's attainment of more profound degrees of enlightenment over the course of his rebirth process.[149] While later masters such as Jamyang Khyentsé Wangpo (1820–92)

147. *Gsal ba'i me long*, 374.4.

148. The coda of *Skabs brgyad ma*, 51.5–6, alludes to the death of Guru Chöwang: "when [he was] constructing the Temple of Great Bliss," which occurs in a sheep year, presumably 1271–72. This would be a slight miscalculation given that his most commonly proposed year of death is 1270.

149. *Skabs brgyad ma*, 52–53.

and Tulku Urgyen Rinpoché (1920–96) name Guru Chöwang among their preincarnations, it is unknown whether a reincarnation of Guru Chöwang was identified in the years shortly after his death. This coda seems to confirm that he would reincarnate and yet offers no recourse to those who would seek to identify those emanations. Sources for Nyangrel are consistent and explicit: many claims were made, some were contested, and while later Tibetans appear resolved to identify additional reincarnations, Nyangrel's first-person testimony repeatedly insists that he had no intention nor expectation of reincarnating again.

In contrast to the *Clear Mirror*, the *Stainless Proclamations* is definitive concerning Nyangrel's final lifetime. As translated in the previous chapter, his mother had a dream at the time of conception where four ethereal ladies explicitly address the preincarnate and reincarnate status of the son to be born to her, saying "This is the Dharma king, the last existence of the bodhisattva. By means of this birth he will not return."[150] Toward the conclusion of the *Stainless Proclamations*, the issue of reincarnation is directly addressed by Nyangrel himself when, after a long retreat, he reports:

> I impartially possessed the superknowledges and, through the manifold magical illusions and arrays, I arrived in all the buddha realms. I directly perceived the sole star in the sky of the sugatas, having mastered the empowerments, blessings, and transmissions. From this birth in existence I will not take birth again.[151]

As the very last of Nyangrel's last testaments, this comprises the final lines of the primary biography in the *Stainless Proclamations*. Continuing with its occasionally autobiographical form, Nyangrel's death is not described, and only this final testament remains to reiterate that no further incarnations are intended or expected. This biography excludes the possibility of Nyangrel's return and counters the *Clear Mirror*'s interlinear claims that Guru Chöwang was his reincarnation. Despite originally being formulated by persons of the same lineage who resided in close proximity during the same era, the *Stainless Proclamations* eluded the emendations of Guru Chöwang's disciples, and therefore we may conclude that Nyangrel's two biographies were transmitted down the lines of two closely related yet quite distinct communities. One accepted that Guru Chöwang was Nyangrel's reincarnation, and they sup-

150. *Dri ma med pa*, 85.6.

151. *Dri ma med pa*, 161.3–5.

ported this claim by redacting a proto-*Clear Mirror*.[152] The other consisted of the disciples of Nyangrel's patrilineal descendants, who ignored if not rejected Guru Chöwang's claim and who preserved a proto-*Stainless Proclamations*. Eventually, both of Nyangrel's biographies acquired the preincarnation narratives that textually originated in Guru Chöwang's *Eight Pronouncements*.

Having compared the three biographies, I suspect that the *Clear Mirror* may now preserve the earliest recension of Guru Chöwang's preincarnation narratives, even though the total *Clear Mirror* may very well have been compiled *after* Guru Chöwang's biographies. Since it contains numerous references to Guru Chöwang and his works, as well as excerpts from the fourteenth-century *Testament of Padmasambhava*, the total *Clear Mirror* must be fourteenth century or later. In assessing the internal evidence, however, the preincarnation narratives in the *Clear Mirror* are the shortest and least formulaic, whereas those in the *Eight Pronouncements* initiate each narrative with "É ma ho! After that birth . . ." and conclude each narrative with a four-line stanza of praise. I therefore suspect that the *Clear Mirror* gained the preincarnation narratives from an earlier, less refined version of the *Eight Pronouncements* that is no longer extant, and that there is a degree of cross-contamination in the transmission of both texts, which corroborates my hypothesis that they were transmitted within the same community.

The *Clear Mirror* preserves most of the initial preincarnation features from the *Eight Pronouncements*, such as a slightly annotated list followed by more elaborate narratives and the idiosyncratic enumeration schema where the first three preincarnations remain uncounted and only thirteen are enumerated, but the *Clear Mirror* lacks a narrative context for this awkward schema. It begins with an eighth-century episode in which Tri Songdetsen asks Padmasambhava to prophesize how they will meet in their future lives. Padmasambhava proceeds to prophesize the remaining events of the emperor's life as well as some details for the two that will follow, all of which are unique to the *Clear Mirror*. Padmasambhava then counts thirteen reincarnations with few details aside from their names, just as in the initial series of the *Eight Pronouncements*.

The *Clear Mirror*'s initial series concludes with Padmasambhava's prediction that Tri Songdetsen's fourteenth birth (seventeenth total) will be his last existence, whereby he will attain enlightenment and depart for Amitābha's

152. Phillips (2004, 169–70) argues that Guru Chöwang and/or his disciples possessed a version of *Gsal ba'i me long*, though it is difficult to distinguish textual details shared between the biographies from those that were orally transmitted in the decades after Nyangrel's death. Due to the close proximity and overlap between these communities, there can be no doubt that many details of Nyangrel's life were general knowledge in the area at this time.

buddha realm of Dewachen at death. Though this incarnation remains unnamed, it must be Nyangrel whose vita, such as his birth in a dragon year, are corroborated in the *Clear Mirror*'s primary biography. Following this prophecy, Nyangrel explicitly identifies himself and begins the series anew by offering more complete vignettes for each preincarnation, just as Guru Chöwang does in the *Eight Pronouncements*, but in the *Clear Mirror* a significant issue arises: having drawn the names and narratives from the opening section of the *Eight Pronouncements*, there are only fifteen preincarnations since Nyangrel is the sixteenth and penultimate preincarnation for Guru Chöwang. This is problematic for Nyangrel (or more specifically the redactors who inserted these narratives) since the prophecies state that the seventeenth incarnation will be the enlightened treasure revealer. In the *Eight Pronouncements*, Nyangrel occupied the place of single preincarnation for Guru Chöwang, but then one more is required for Nyangrel in the *Clear Mirror*. "Tara Tiu from Shang" is thereby inserted as the seventh incarnation, which corresponds with the initial series, but a narrative for that incarnation did not exist in its source text, the *Eight Pronouncements*. Those interpolating the preincarnation narratives admit just this in an interlinear note: "Since the original chapter in which he was born in Shang is not available, it is not here."

The rebirth in Shang is as essential to include in the *Clear Mirror* as it is to omit from the *Eight Pronouncements*. With the treasure prophecy specifying seventeen incarnations, the *Clear Mirror* must preserve this incarnation as a placeholder even without a vignette to narrate it, such that Nyangrel will remain the seventeenth and final incarnation. Its absence reflects the fact that the *Eight Pronouncements* never included it: only Nyangrel's biography needed an additional incarnation to avoid becoming the penultimate preincarnation of Guru Chöwang rather than the ultimate reincarnation of Tri Songdetsen. Despite the affinity for Guru Chöwang that punctuates the *Clear Mirror*, one of its redactors reserved the seventeenth prophesied position for Nyangrel who is, after all, the primary subject of that biography.

In the *Stainless Proclamations*, a very late appropriation of the preincarnation narratives would explain its much simpler recensional process. Following its opening stanzas of supplication and praise, the *Stainless Proclamations* begins its narrative with a scene on the tenth day of the first month of autumn in a monkey year.[153] Since Nyangrel's disciples have gathered to lament his impending departure for Dewachen, this is presumably in the final monkey year of Nyangrel's life (1188), so this episode frames the total biography by explaining how Nyangrel confided the details of his preincarnations and final

153. *Dri ma med pa*, 4.2.

lifetime very close to his death.[154] The historicity of this episode is tenuous at best, but the date provides a historical sheen to authenticate the details that follow.

To begin, Nyangrel's wife, sons, and cherished disciples approach him while presenting a bejeweled silver maṇḍala ornamented with gold and turquoise, and with this as an offering, they request him to detail the names, parents, regions, and so forth for each of his preincarnations, which they must do three times before Nyangrel concedes.[155] They already know that he is "the last of the fifteen catenate births of the Dharma king Tri Songdetsen," but now they beseech him to elucidate the details of the lives between them as well.[156] The *Stainless Proclamations* counts Nyangrel as the sixteenth incarnation throughout, because this is his enumeration in the *Eight Pronouncements*. By the time the preincarnation narratives were redacted into the *Stainless Proclamations*, Guru Chöwang's claim may no longer have been so controversial, and given his stature as the second of the great treasure revealers, his association may have served to enhance Nyangrel's legacy as well. In the emic view that accepts this claim, Guru Chöwang was merely filling in the details of a series that would necessarily have been confirmed by Nyangrel because they were, after all, individual expressions of the same continuum. Moreover, since the *Stainless Proclamations* shares formulaic text with the *Eight Pronouncements* that does not appear in the *Clear Mirror*, such as "É ma ho! After that birth . . . ," it becomes evident that a later recension of the *Eight Pronouncements* was the source of the preincarnation narratives in the *Stainless Proclamations*. The latter also gains "Kyé ma!" to transition between each preincarnation narrative, a versified summary to conclude it, and each has been significantly expanded, structured, and refined. Since I have yet to find any source that uses the *Stainless Proclamations* prior to the twentieth century, I suspect that this biography, perhaps just the primary biography of Nyangrel alone, sat on a shelf or in a box somewhere until it was rediscovered, edited, and incorporated into the thirteen-volume collection of Nyangrel's *Eight Instructions* that was xylographed at Kaḥthok Monastery in the late nineteenth or early twentieth century. The *Stainless Proclamations* may therefore have acquired the preincarnation narratives from the *Eight Pronouncements* as late as this publication.

154. This is the earth-monkey year of the third *rabjung*.

155. His concession concludes chapter 1 of the *Stainless Proclamations*, so the ordinal numbers of the chapters do not correspond to the enumeration of his preincarnations.

156. *Dri ma med pa*, 5.1–2. The enumeration of the preincarnations in the *Stainless Proclamations* follows that of its source for the narratives, the *Eight Pronouncements*.

The *Stainless Proclamations* is definitively the most recent and refined recension of Nyangrel's preincarnation narratives. While both the *Eight Pronouncements* and the *Clear Mirror* often, but not always, include the names of the parents, region, district, and so forth, the *Stainless Proclamations* formalizes this information into the first few lines of every narrative, thereby imposing structural consistency throughout the series.[157] It also bears updated orthography, such as the spelling of Tri Songdetsen (Khri srong lde'u btsan),[158] and it is simplified by omitting the initial list and launches directly into the preincarnation narratives, thereby circumventing the internal inconsistencies between the initial series and subsequent narratives of the *Clear Mirror*.[159] Perhaps the most significant improvement is its enumeration: instead of separating the first three (or four) lives from those that followed them, the *Stainless Proclamations* just counts them consecutively. It is more effective, both in terms of simplicity and legitimacy, to group all the lives together under the same heading, same enumeration, and same assumption of historicity anchored by the eminently historical Tri Songdetsen, which is precisely what is accomplished in the *Stainless Proclamations* alone. In doing so, it finally resolves the awkward enumeration of the *Eight Pronouncement* and the *Clear Mirror* and provides an uninterrupted progression of experiences and activities that foreshadow their full fruition as the life of the great treasure revealer.

Curiously absent throughout the *Stainless Proclamations*, however, is the prophecy declaring the seventeenth birth to be the great treasure revealer, thus any attempt to correspond to it is absent as well. Nyangrel is still celebrated as the final existence of the bodhisattva, but he narrates only fifteen preincarnations, which is the number he recalls within the primary biography as well.[160] He is therefore depicted as the sixteenth incarnation of Tri Songdetsen in accordance with his enumeration in Guru Chöwang's *Eight Pronouncements*, thereby indicating once again that this was the sole source of the preincarnation narratives for the *Stainless Proclamations*.

157. This format is well established in the Buddhist biographical tradition, extending back to some of the earliest Pāli biographies of the Buddha, such as the *Buddhavaṃsa*. See Walters 2000, 101.

158. Concerning the evolving orthography of Tri Songdetsen, see Doney 2011, 81.

159. I believe that this inconsistency appeared in earlier versions of the *Eight Pronouncements* as well but were subsequently normalized, and that the accounts of Nyangrel's and Guru Chöwang's preincarnations in the *Eight Pronouncements* and the *Clear Mirror* are the beneficiaries of editorial improvements that were transmitted between them at various points.

160. *Dri ma med pa*, 100.6.

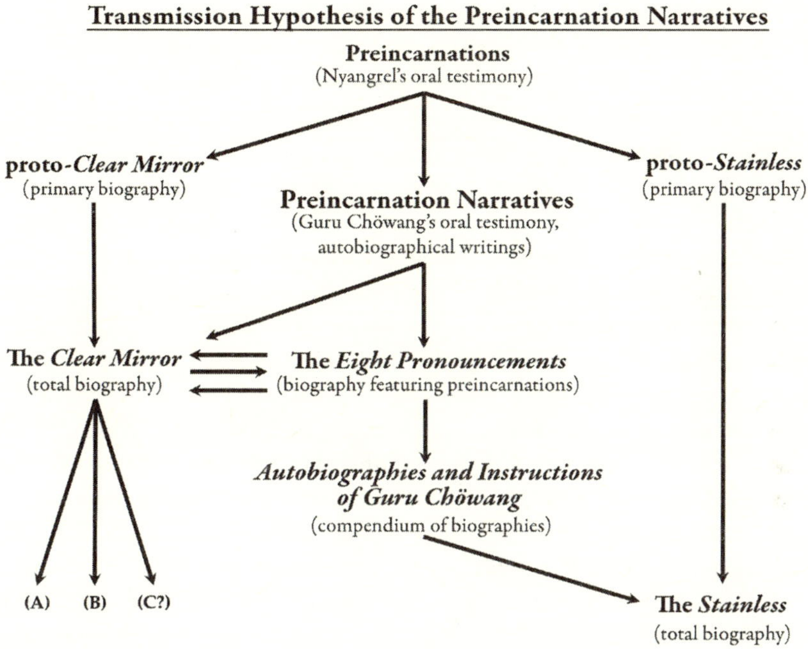

Figure 3. Each arrow signifies a single or (more likely) several cycles of copying, emendation, and redaction aligned along a general chronological descent.

To review, Nyangrel's assertion that he was the reincarnation of Tri Songdetsen and his recollection of a catenate sequence of lives between them were among his most renowned claims. Thus it circulated among his patrilineal and Dharmic descendants, including Guru Chöwang, and was recorded in his primary biographies by direct disciples. Since his two primary biographies do not share any text, I discern two distinct textual transmissions as the proto-*Clear Mirror* and the proto-*Stainless Proclamations*. Guru Chöwang then elaborated on the catenate series that Nyangrel had only generalized or enumerated, and these evolved into the preincarnation narratives that comprise Guru Chöwang's *Eight Pronouncements*. These narratives became the basis for those incorporated into the complete *Clear Mirror* and came to be featured within a compendium of Guru Chöwang's biographical materials as well. The *Stainless Proclamations* eventually obtained the preincarnation narratives from the latter collection, perhaps in a very late redaction, as evidenced by updated orthography, the various editorial improvements introduced throughout, and the total blackout of its content from other sources. Based on the very few recensions currently available to us, this appears to be the most likely transmission process for Nyangrel's preincarnations and Guru Chöwang's narration of them.

The Final Emanation

Nyangrel envisioned himself as the last in a line of catenate reincarnations who, as the fruition of Emperor Tri Songdetsen's meritorious activities, would become the enlightened treasure revealer who would ultimately depart for Dewachen at the completion of that karmic process. For Nyangrel, benefit would be effortlessly exerted through the immaterial manifestations of enlightened intent that, like the magical emanations of Padmasambhava that appeared to aid his path, would be pure and unbound by the machinations of karma. As in the biography of the Buddha, this precludes the possibility of reincarnation; enlightenment ends the cycle of rebirth by definition, which is distinct from later iterations of the Tibetan reincarnation tradition, where the higher echelons of enlightenment are attained and yet the individual returns as a magically emanated reincarnation or tulku to benefit beings as the epitome of bodhisattva activity in the Mahāyāna. Such intent has renowned Indic precedents, some of which are quite early. While its many translations guarantee variance in its exemplars, the celebrated *Instructions of Vimalakīrti* (*Vimalakīrtinirdeśa*) is estimated to have originated in the second century C.E., and both the Chinese and Tibetan versions explicitly prescribe the deliberate delay of liberation by voluntarily reincarnating into "the contaminated buddha realms in order to purify sentient beings."[161] Several centuries later the same sentiment is poetically constructed by Śāntideva (seventh century) to conclude his magnum opus, the *Way of the Bodhisattva* (*Bodhicaryāvatāra*), which was recited by the Fourteenth Dalai Lama upon his acceptance of the Nobel Peace Prize in 1989:

> For as long as space endures
> and for as long as living beings remain,
> until then may I too abide
> to dispel the sufferings of the world. (10:55)

161. Translation following Thurman 2003 [1976], 93; also see Lamotte 1976, 245. While a Sanskrit exemplar of the *Vimalakīrtinirdeśa* (維摩詰經, *Dri med grags pa bstan pa'i mdo*) was only recently recovered from the Potala Palace in Lhasa (Buswell 2014, 971), and the first Chinese translation dated to 188 C.E. is no longer extant, Lamotte (1976, xxvii) notes that this section describing voluntary reincarnation is present within the subsequent Chinese translation of 222–29 C.E., which preserves various linguistic markers of its antiquity.

And yet despite the centrality of this intention in the Mahāyāna, the possibility of its application in practice—most specifically as a set of endlessly recurring enlightened reincarnations—postdates Nyangrel; it was not among his innovations. By conflating magical emanations with magically emanated reincarnations, Guru Chöwang and his biographers not only attempted to displace Nyangrel from the prophesied position of the seventeenth rebirth but also extended his reincarnation indefinitely. For Guru Chöwang, enlightenment was not an immaterial end but an embodied continuity, spanning eternity by inhabiting multiple bodies in countless lifetimes. Nyangrel thus introduced catenate reincarnation, but Guru Chöwang extended that process beyond enlightenment, both of which were critical innovations that led to institutionalized reincarnates very soon thereafter with the final element being the promise and prophecy of future lives. With the emergence of the Karmapas in the thirteenth century, this period marks the critical nexus in the development of catenate reincarnation into one of the most definitive features of Tibetan religion.

As already discussed, the Karmapas were the first institutionalized series of magically emanated reincarnates. Aside from prophesizing the details of their next rebirth, their major contribution to catenate reincarnation is its function as an inheritance model that promotes institutional continuity.[162] This was first realized when Pomdrakpa (1170–1249?) identified the reincarnation of Düsum Khyenpa (1110–93) in 1215 or 1226.[163] The Second Karmapa Karma Pakshi (1204/6–83) was therefore born more than a decade after the death of Düsum Khyenpa and was not recognized until as many as twenty-two years after that, which is unique in the history of the line but may also reflect a more gradual process of identification that culminated in his official recognition.[164] Every Karmapa after Karma Pakshi was born within several years of his predecessor's death and recognized shortly thereafter. Although the tradition now contends that Düsum Khyenpa prophesized his return, this is very unlikely; it was Pomdrakpa who sought the reincarnation of his lineage master well after his death, thus the testaments attributed to Düsum Khyenpa are most certainly prochronisms introduced in the normalization of reincarnation and its identification strategies. Karma Pakshi is likewise said to have predicted the circumstances of his next rebirth, and his successor Rangjung Dorjé

162. Kapstein 2003, 774n78.

163. Manson 2009: 31–32.

164. Gamble (2013, 9) notes that Karma Pakshi was born into an aristocratic family and exhausted their funds in the restoration of Düsum Khyenpa's institutions, which seems to have led to his eventual recognition as his reincarnation.

(1284–1339) was the first to be deliberately sought as an infant by Urgyenpa (1229/30–1309), one of the foremost disciples of Karma Pakshi. However, it was this Third Karmapa who left the first written testament of his intention to continuously reincarnate in a catenate series: this subsequently came to define the line, normalize its prophesization and identification processes, and ensure its continuity to the present (though certainly not without controversy).

By means of the progressive innovations of Nyangrel, Guru Chöwang, and Rangjung Dorjé in particular, deliberate and nearly immediate reincarnation was soon adopted by all the sects of Tibet, both Buddhist and Bönpo. Each of these three figures claimed at least one prominent imperial-era figure among their preincarnations who, in being counted among the cabal of Padmasambhava's closest disciples, was destined to reveal the concealed texts and relics known as *treasure*.[165] As we will see, however, it was Nyangrel who popularized this karmic bond between the empire and the treasures in his seminal narrative of Tibet's conversion, the *Copper Island*.

165. The Third Karmapa Rangjung Dorjé identified himself (and his Karmapa predecessors) as reincarnations of Gyalwa Chökyang, one of the twenty-five disciples of Padmasambhava, and named quite a few additional preincarnations as well (Manson, forthcoming).

3. Treasure before Tradition

The question of authenticity has been paramount from the earliest studies of the Tibetan Buddhist treasures. Because of their allegedly ancient origins, the treasures have always been of particular interest to scholars both indigenous and not, and thus the initial question consistently asked is whether treasure texts preserved legitimate lineages of tantric praxis and, in the case of treasure narratives, historical data as well. For the most part the debate has focused on textual treasures instead of treasure relics, which would have been more difficult to repudiate in the centuries before radiocarbon dating,[166] and contemporary inquiries now draw on at least eight centuries of controversy that extends back to some of the earliest revealers. In 1264–65 Guru Chöwang composed his *Great History of the Treasures* (*Gter 'byung chen mo*), the first systematic study of the subject that represents a seismic shift in the process of defining and legitimating treasure. This is accomplished primarily in the guise of an authoritative taxonomy, and additional studies by subsequent revealers would soon follow his model.[167] Treasure thus began to be tamed into a tradition with the production and distribution of Guru

166. To date no one has attempted to radiocarbon date and thus verify the exact provenance of any text or item attested to be an original material treasure, meaning the actual item recovered by the revealer. However, were any treasures analyzed with current technologies, it is now possible to ascertain an origin within a range of three hundred years, which could be sufficient to determine whether the sample originated in the imperium. Helman-Wazny (2010, 294 fig. 9) provides a radiocarbon analysis for an example of Karma Lingpa's (1326–86) *Bar do thos grol*, a treasure renowned in the West as the *Tibetan Book of the Dead*. This particular volume is especially ornate with silver and gold ink on indigo-dyed paper, thus it appears to stem from an era when the text had already achieved sufficient renown so as to warrant such treatment in its reproduction. This indeed is corroborated by radiocarbon analysis: this volume was only produced within the last three hundred years or so, with the highest probability being 1680–1770 or even 1800–1940.

167. *Gter 'byung* rapidly became a genre unto itself once Longchen Rabjam (1308–64), Sangyé Lingpa (1340–96), and Ratna Lingpa (1403–78) produced their own histories and taxonomies of treasure. See respectively *Gter 'byung rin po che'i lo rgyus*, *Sangs rgyas gling pa'i gter 'byung chen mo*, and *Gter 'byung chen mo gsal ba'i sgron me*.

Chöwang's study; as such it presents an artificial yet nevertheless useful divide between the early treasures that preceded deliberate codification, which are the foci of the present study, from those on the long march to normalization thereafter. While certain precedents for some contents of Guru Chöwang's taxonomy can be found amid Nyangrel's materials, such explicit rubrics and definitions are mostly absent in earlier iterations of the treasure movement. One innovative feature of Guru Chöwang's efforts was his attempt to distinguish authentic treasures from those that were not, no doubt a response to a surging critique of the treasures in general and himself in particular.[168] By contrast, Nyangrel appears to have been the subject of few rhetorical assaults in his lifetime and while his biographies and narratives contain allusions to occasional skeptics, he does not appear to have composed any direct responses to them.[169] Forwarding to contemporary scholarship, the authenticity of the treasures was one of the earliest Tibetological debates and now remains among its most enduring.[170]

While the earliest Tibetologists to consider these materials typically swung from one uncritical extreme of assumed historicity to the other of total disingenuity and deceit,[171] it was A. I. Vostrikov (d. 1937) who first invoked a balancing act of academic inquiry that continues to resonate today. He argued that the treasures held a "special place in Tibetan literature" while recognizing that they had "very little value as historical sources" since, aside from some legitimately ancient fragments, the treasures appeared to be apocryphal constructions.[172] In this view the treasures are held to be important and thus

168. Gyatso 1994, 278. *Gter 'byung chen mo*, 103–4. Rok Bandé Sherab Ö (1166–1244) composed a broad defense of Nyingma doctrines and practices, including treasure recovery, in his *Grub mtha' so so'i bzhed tshul gzhung gsal bar ston pa chos 'byung grub mtha' chen po bstan pa'i sgron me*. Sakya Paṇḍita (1182–1251) was especially critical of the treasures, but Jikten Gönpo of the Drigung Kagyü was much less so. Rather than disparage the treasures, he reasserts the profundity of the transmitted texts (Martin 2001, 153–57). A broader criticism of the treasures appears to have postdated Nyangrel and stems from the time of Guru Chöwang in particular, who was the target of much vitriol. For translations of several early treasure critiques, see Doctor 2005, 32.

169. The prophecy that predicts the arrival of the great treasure revealer in the *Copper Island* cites Tri Songdetsen's expulsion of Vairocana, Nup Namkhai Nyingpo, and others as the karmic basis for skepticism toward Nyangrel's teachings. *Zangs gling ma* A, 139; H, 82b; *Me tog snying po* K, 354; M, 256.2. For a translation of A, see Kunsang 1993, 139.

170. See Gyatso 1993, 103n14; Kapstein 2000, 121–37; Gardner 2006, 61n136; Hirshberg 2012, 103–11.

171. A prominent example of the first is Csoma de Kőrös 1838, 148. For the latter, see Waddell 1939, 166.

172. Vostrikov 1970, 27–28.

authentic as cultural relics even though their origins are falsified and their content invented. With few exceptions most scholars who have explored the treasures since Vostrikov have reformulated his original premise with new levels of nuance in attempting to transcend the in/authenticity debate for more conducive lines of inquiry.[173] Janet Gyatso in particular advocates a seminal shift toward an assessment of the treasures' broader cultural function by pivoting analysis away from the question as to whether the treasures are real or fake, whether they were found as described or fabricated. In so doing, she proves that there indeed is significant value in exploring the treasures as a tradition, analyzing *how* they are presented as authentic rather than *whether* they are authentic.[174]

There is a risk latent in working within the presentation of a tradition, however, in that some aspects may remain veiled by traditional explanations; in particular, mostly absent is the diachronic process of transformation by which these strategies developed. The synchronic structures that came to define treasure did not arise spontaneously resolved even though the tradition presents them as such. Any tradition is necessarily a product of repetition, reduction, and reorganization that requires time to be tamed into accepted rubrics that approach consistency throughout a body of literature. This is not to suggest that scholars like Gyatso have ignored this process; nor have they failed to recognize significant differences between earlier and later iterations of the treasures. But so much of both the popular and scholarly literature on treasure has become so saturated by normative rubrics that they are often presented as static and singularly definitive despite the long and diverse history of treasure recovery in Tibet. While the normative treasure tradition descends from its renaissance-era antecedents, the treasures continue to be defined by the coherence of that much later tradition rather than the inspecificity and flux under which they originated. Such is the convenience of generalizations, but in focusing a case study on the biographical accounts of Nyangrel's treasure recoveries, which surely are among the richest resources for early Buddhist treasure recovery in Tibet, we see the treasures prior to their delimitation. Contemporary discussions of treasure have elucidated much about the traditions that coalesced no later than the eighteenth century through the integration and normalization of various elements, such as treasure marks (*gter shad*) and ḍākinī script. In order to understand Buddhist treasure closer to the time

173. One notable exception is Aris (1989) in which he derides all treasures as categorically false and thereby provokes many strongly worded reviews and responses. The passage on 96–97 is cited in whole or in part in Sherburne 1991, 205–6; Thurman 1991, 375–77; Kapstein 2000, 136; Gardner 2006, 66; Hirshberg 2012, 105–6.

174. Gyatso 1993, 106–7.

of its popularization, however, it is necessary to consider the treasures before they were codified into tradition, which will invite a return to the question of authenticity anew.

A few studies have focused on the early Buddhist treasures, and while some notation of important differences have been made, later iterations of the treasures and their rubrics tend to contaminate the general discussion as if "treasure" represents a resolved, synchronic continuum. As Ronald Davidson first pointed out, deceptively pervasive is the late typology that distinguishes earth treasures, exalted-mind treasures, and pure-vision literature (the last of which are not treasures *per se*) that have been "reified" both by the tradition and much of the contemporary scholarship that makes reference to it.[175] To review the main types of treasure according to normative presentations, *earth treasures* are material scrolls, texts, and relics excavated from equally tangible places of concealment. *Exalted-mind treasures* are also said to have been concealed for the benefit of future generations but within the enlightened minds of Padmasambhava's closest disciples, and thus they remain immaterial prior to their transcription during the revelatory process. The fidelity of their delivery is ensured via the immaculate expanse of enlightened awareness. Transmitted orally in the eighth century and stored within exalted mind, these texts are downloaded centuries later and committed to the page, sometimes through a meditative state where the treasure revealer dictates the text to a trusted scribe.[176] Whereas earth and exalted-mind treasures are said to have been concealed by Padmasambhava or another imperial-era personage such as his consort and aide-de-camp, Yeshé Tsogyal, *pure-vision teachings* are instructions received from buddhas in visionary journeys to their pure realms and can occur to otherwise ordinary individuals, though accomplished meditators are considered more prone to them. Conversely, treasure revealers are presented as a very special set of adepts who possess the karma and fortune to recover their quarry, which is founded on their reincarnate descent as the personal disciples of Padmasambhava himself. In sum, the terminology that distinguishes earth treasures, exalted-mind treasures, and pure visions primarily refers to their place of concealment and recovery: earth treasures are drawn from the physical ground, exalted-mind treasures from the expanse of enlightened awareness, and pure visions from the buddha realms.[177]

175. Davidson 2005, 213, and Davidson 2006, 125.

176. Chokgyur Lingpa (1829–70) would often reveal treasures in this way with Jamgön Kongtrul (1813–99) acting as his scribe and aide. As such their names are often attested together in the colophons to these texts.

177. For contemporary definitions of treasure, their revelations, and functions, see Germano 1998, passim.

The near ubiquity of this tripartite rubric is owed to the fact that the later treasures have too often come to dominate the discussion in both popular and academic forums, and its defined terms and convenient rubrics have often been adopted without regard to the long process of their refinement. By undermining the essentialization of the treasures into a synchronic, monolithic tradition through a perusal of some of the earliest extant Buddhist sources depicting them, we may rediscover the early treasures in contradistinction to the treasure tradition that would later define them.

Originating the Treasures

The etymology of the Tibetan term for treasure (*gter ma*) may be revisited, as its later significance has come to color its semantic values. Prior to the development of a tradition and distinct category of treasure, Tibetans used the term *gter* rather than *gter ma*; it seems that the nominalizer was added in recognition of its special status and likely emerged when treasure was juxtaposed as a distinct and distinctly legitimate category of Nyingma doctrinal literature beside the "oral transmissions" or *Kama* (*Bka' ma*). Looking at early precedents for this distinction, early Tibetan *gter* share many facets with the Indic tradition of *nidhi*. References are found in texts pertaining to kriyātantra that describe fierce entities standing guard over valuable items where *nidhi* may signify the container and/or its contents, just as *cache* in English refers both to the place of storage and the stuff stowed there. While designated to translate *nidhi* specifically, *gter* in its most fundamental sense relates to treasuries and mines, both of which hold items of value.[178] In presenting some of the earliest accounts of Bönpo treasure activity, Dan Martin highlights prenormative usages of *gter* where it signifies treasure, "but not primarily in the sense of luxury objects kept in a storehouse (for these there are several other terms), but in the sense of treasure troves or precious substances that might be brought up to the surface."[179] The primary implication is that *gter* are objects that may be extracted from the earth and, in possessing some kind of inherent value, are thus worthy of extraction. *Gter* originally specified things that could be mined, like gems, but the category was expanded to include manufactured products such as texts and relics that held a consecrated rather than solely monetary value.

Proscription and persecution often compel people to stow their valuables underground for safekeeping, and such contexts likely contributed to the

178. Mayer 1996, 82–90.

179. Martin 2001, 19n9.

practice of treasure concealment in Tibet as well. Tibet's earliest revealers were proponents of the indigenous religion that would come to be known as Bön. They may have been active as early as the tenth century, and some such as Khutsa Daö (1087?–1146) found both Bönpo and Buddhist materials by Nyangrel's time, thus Tibetan Buddhists adopted the practice of treasure recovery from Bönpo and dually affiliated Bönpo-Buddhist exemplars.[180] Bön lore states that the old texts and relics they recovered had survived from the time of Tibet's conversion to Buddhism by Tri Songdetsen, though some of their sources attest an even earlier period of persecution and concealment under the reign of the first "historical" king, Drigum Tsenpo.[181] According to later Bön accounts of Tri Songdetsen's reign, as Bönpo priests and ministers found themselves increasingly marginalized and replaced by Buddhist counterparts at court, and as the massive effort to translate the Sanskrit Buddhist canon into Tibetan consumed the attention and resources of the empire, adherents of the indigenous traditions found their traditions under threat and so took to burying their sacred texts and relics for posterity.

The tables would turn not long thereafter, however, and many Buddhist histories describe the reign of Udumten, better known as Langdarma (r. 838–42), as a similar time of crisis for the Buddhists. Historians contend that his reign was less anti-Buddhist/pro-Bön than simple *real economik*: state financing for monastic institutions was bankrupting the empire and required an intervention—regicide according to some accounts—to salvage its solvency. Regardless of how Langdarma's pious brother, the emperor Ralpachen, or Tri Tsukdetsen, died in 838, Langdarma's subsequent ascension of the throne and swift reduction of monastic support was unpopular among the clergy, some of whom authored this era's history, so they may have portrayed this emperor and his reign critically to the point of hyperbole.[182]

Regardless of historicity, this period of alleged persecution is when the Buddhist treasures went underground according to some early sources, but not those of the later treasure narratives that would become normative. One of the former, far less common accounts is preserved in the history attributed to Nyangrel, the *Essence of Flowers*, which depicts the flight of Langdarma's eldest brother, the ordained Prince Tsangma, when Buddhism and its proponents allegedly were under threat. Because such accounts of Buddhist treasure concealment are rare compared to the story of Padmasambhava's concealments during the golden age, it is worth reproducing in full:

180. Since this chapter focuses on Buddhist treasure, henceforth "treasure" refers to Buddhist examples unless specified otherwise. For Khu tsha zla 'od see Mayer 2012.

181. Mayer 2012, 11.

182. Yamaguchi 1996.

At the time when King Langdarma was causing the teachings to wane, his brother, the divine prince Tsangma, was exiled. Having seized the anthologies of the forefathers' words, the instructions of the profound Buddhist doctrine, the wrathful mantras, and lord Guru Padma's instructions, Tsangma absconded. After staying at Ötrana for one year, when the black [i.e., Bönpo] ministers threatened to assassinate the prince and forbade him to remain there, Nyang Tingezin Sangpo, Nup Namkhai Nyingpo, Nyak Jñānakumāra, and so forth, the great translators, gathered together and held a council.

They decided to hide all the Buddhist doctrines as treasure. [Since all the folios] were shuffled and mixed together, they turned and straightened the scriptures. They entrusted to Nyak Jñānakumāra the quintessential writings that conceal and make secret the key instructions. After he heard them and committed them to memory, he promised not to lose the writings and sealed them, appointing Ekajaṭī and the glorious protectress sisters as guardians.

They hid them as treasures of exalted mind (*thugs gter*). Additionally, 108 treasures were hidden as books at Drangsang Sinpo Mountain and several at Pal Chuwo Mountain, Sekyi Duradong, and so forth. Another 108 treasures were hidden at Kharak. The sacred Buddhist temples of Tö and Mé were reconstructed with bricks. They hid many statues and many divine daggers of Shang as treasure. They concealed twenty-eight minor treasures in the border-taming practice places of the four districts of Tibet. Padmasambhava's three doctrines in twenty-three abridged manuals together with the extensive versions were hidden at the precious dwelling of Bumthang.

Nyang Tingezin concealed Vimalamitra's Great Perfection together with their treasure seals in the households of Shaikyé in Üru. Namkhai Nyingpo concealed treasures at Khomting in Lhodrak Kharchu. After the instructions of all the paṇḍitas had been transmitted to Nyak Jñānakumāra, he instructed nine great glorious students. Once the essence of those with all the pith instructions of Namkhai Nyingpo and the rest were gathered for Nup Sangyé Yeshé, they stayed at Dregiyang fortress.

Then the divine prince Tsangma arrived at Khomting temple in Lhodrak, renovated all that had been ruined, and concealed a set of treasures. Then, having arrived at Padro, he renovated the ancient temple of Kyerchu, built it anew, and the soul documents of the forefathers, legal papers, and a vast quantity of texts were hidden

> there. He concealed others in many treasure caches such as Tiger's Lair and Lion Cave. He hid 108 treasures at Chekla. He concealed many minor treasures.[183]

This narrative portrays a time of upheaval when ancient Buddhist sites had been ransacked and the most prominent Buddhists scattered. The eldest prince, Tsangma, along with his cadre of supporters, could have been seen as a legitimate threat to the throne, but political intrigue is not intimated as the cause of their exile here. Instead the setting is one of overt religious persecution as found in many later Buddhist accounts of this period. The focus is the preservation of Buddhist scriptures through their concealment as "treasures of exalted mind" (*thugs gter*), which is the etymological antecedent of the exalted-mind treasures (*dgongs gter*) that became so prevalent in the later tradition, but this episode leaves no doubt that the term here signifies exclusively material representations of enlightened awareness, most of which were texts opportunistically concealed in physical locations. Having called together the greatest Buddhist adepts of the day, a council was held in order to determine how to preserve these treasures from the new administration that was hostile to them. After a sober assessment of their present context, its participants collectively decided that the best option was to conceal them in hidden caches. It would seem that many were inserted into natural locations such as caves and crevices in the mountains, but the episode also insinuates that some may have been sealed within masonry and statuary as the refugees renovated the Buddhist temples that had been looted and destroyed. All of these become focal points for treasure recoveries in later centuries.

Although some of Padmasambhava's writings are included among the caches in the above episode, the great tantrika himself is long gone: he is in no way involved in these acts of preservation. His own concealments would have occurred only decades prior, and many in this council are counted among his closest disciples who would certainly have been aware of—if not witness to—those activities, but Padmasambhava is not even mentioned as an exemplar to be followed. He is not forwarded as the treasure concealer *par excellence*, and it is as if Padmasambhava's treasure activity never occurred in Tibet—nor even in the *Essence of Flowers*, despite the fact that the first narrative to detail his treasure activity appears just before it in the very same document!

This textual mystery will be explored more fully in the next chapter especially, but for now it is important to introduce the existence of alternative Buddhist origin narratives concerning the treasures, those that did not feature Padmasambhava as an agent nor inspiration despite his nearly singular

183. *Me tog snying po* B, 513.3–515.1; K, 435.21–437.7; M, 315.2.4–316.3.4.

prominence in later treasure histories. While the degree of proscription and persecution during Langdarma's reign may be more hyperbole than history, the above episode succeeds in presenting what would be a cogent historical context for the concealment of Buddhist valuables under duress as the empire waned, especially in contrast to the far more renowned stories of mystical treasure concealments that occurred not in a time of crisis but at the very apogee of the empire.

Beginning with Nyangrel's *Copper Island*, the nucleus of later Padmasambhava narratives depicts his cooperation with Tri Songdetsen in converting the Tibetan plateau and all of its inhabitants, whether chthonic, terrestrial, or divine, to Buddhism. As he tamed the vast taxonomy of Tibet's domestic populace by all means necessary from Nepal to the Tibetan court, Padmasambhava's campaign is often regarded as the primary act of conversion, but the interment of Buddhist treasures throughout the natural landscape was an equally integral component of this process. Without the simultaneous subjugation and enrichment that occurred by means of their burial, say these narratives, Tibet could not have been converted to Buddhism nor would it have remained Buddhist throughout its history.

While Nyangrel's depiction of Padmasambhava's treasure concealments in the *Copper Island* and *Essence of Flowers* inspired the normative treasure histories that followed them, many of the defining features of the latter histories were inchoate if not altogether absent in Nyangrel's narratives. To summarize the plot of the normative account, Padmasambhava is said to have concealed countless treasures throughout the Tibetan landscape for the benefit of future generations. In representing his great kindness toward the Tibetan people in particular, these treasures were meant to be revealed at karmically appropriate moments when the doctrines that emerged would be of greatest relevance and benefit for the people of that time and place. Therefore Padmasambhava became not just the guru of his time but of all times, quite literally to the end of time, and this would be continuously effected by the reincarnations of his disciples acting on his behalf by endlessly revealing his instructions. Very little of this projected future is embedded within Nyangrel's Padmasambhava narrative, however. While the interment of treasure was critical to the stabilization of Tibetan Buddhism in general, the broader objectives, scope, and magnanimity of treasure concealment in the *Copper Island* is far more limited when compared to the grandiose universality proclaimed in later treasure literature. In some respects, Nyangrel's narrative is more directed toward the benefit of Nyangrel himself.[184]

184. Another difference between Nyangrel's conception of treasure and later iterations is that treasures should be continuously interred: their concealment was not meant to be limited to

Since the *Copper Island* presents a context of peace and prosperity for the time of treasure interment rather than violence and persecution, another plausible reason is needed to explain their concealment, but Nyangrel does not seize this opportunity to forward a broader vision of inestimable benefit for others. Instead the karmic legacy introduced here is Tri Songdetsen's inevitable reincarnation as the great treasure revealer, who is none other than Nyangrel. The impetus toward treasure concealment begins with the translation of scriptures considered too dangerous for public consumption but that could be used for protection, so the *Copper Island* states that "in order to safeguard the King Tri Songdetsen's royal law, Padmasambhava, Vairocana, and Namkhai Nyingpo translated the wicked mantras,"[185] which is ironic since there is much evidence that such scriptures would be proscribed by Tri Songdetsen and the Buddhist emperors who succeeded him. As in India there was a fear among the ruling elite that these magical incantations could be used against them and that literal interpretations of tantra's sexual and violent rhetoric could lead to social instability, the inversion of a ruler's objectives in translating Buddhism and distributing it throughout the populace. Moreover, as Davidson has argued, the egalitarian nature of tantric empowerment ceremonies and the enthronement of each individual as a deity within their own maṇḍala might signify the overthrow of centralized authority and thus subvert singular rule,[186] and it is clear that some of the Buddhist kings of Tibet retained a certain ambivalence toward the tantras, as evidenced by the proscription of their translation.

Later in the *Copper Island* there is another statement that references the purpose of the treasures as related to the rule of Tri Songdetsen specifically. Padmasambhava confides:

Padmasambhava or the imperium but is necessitated in response to evolving conditions. Among Nyangrel's final directives to his disciples before his death in the *Clear Mirror*, he states: "In accordance with my intent, you all must construct representations of exalted body, speech, and mind at [Mawochok] for posterity. In order to repel foreign invasions, the violent cycles that destroy, kill, repel, and suppress together with their ritual implements and supplementary items must be concealed as treasures" (*Gsal ba'i me long*, 369.5–370.1). Treasure concealment therefore consists of the rather ordinary burial of empowered objects as talismans and perhaps as offerings to enhance the strength of local protectors, which can be accomplished whenever the need arises. Additionally, given this fear of foreign invasions, the *Clear Mirror* may allude to the Mongols who established suzerainty over central Tibet in the thirteenth century, which appears to be its initial time of writing.

185. *Zangs gling ma* H, 79a3–4.

186. Davidson 2003, 131–32.

> Because the royal law is strong right now, the instructions on the life-wheel, hail, and incantations are not necessary, but they will be needed when bad times arise, so I have concealed them as treasure.[187]

Once again the focal point is the rule of the king in stabilizing the golden age of Tibetan Buddhism rather than a grandiose vision of Padmasambhava's dedication to the Tibetan people as a whole. Given Nyangrel's visionary encounters with Padmasambhava in his life and the interactions he recalled from his former one, he undoubtedly was devoted to Padmasambhava, but Nyangrel's objectives in originating the treasures in the *Copper Island* had more to do with his own life and legacy than with the vast cultural and territorial benefit with which the treasures would come to be associated. Given that treasure recoverers like Nyangrel operated on the fringes of society in the twelfth century, perhaps such broad influence seemed well beyond the range of possibility. Yet it was through the work of Nyangrel and countless others inspired by him that the treasures came to occupy such a central place in Tibetans' conceptions of their past. With the treasures' interment in that past and continual revelation over time, they came to identify Tibet as a cohesive cultural area, a sacred ground of Buddhism that reciprocally defined Tibetans as well.

While there are a number of Buddhist treasures and treasure revealers that are said to precede Nyangrel and his contemporaries, comparatively little evidence of them remains. Some of the earliest extant examples of Buddhist treasure such as the *Pillar Testament* (*Bka' 'chems ka khol ma*) and the *Heart-Essence of Vimalamitra* (*Bi ma snying thig*) are more likely to be twelfth-century products despite their claims to imperial-era concealments and eleventh-century revelations, and there is little evidence that links these texts to their credited compilers, Emperor Songtsen Gampo (d. 649) and Vimalamitra (ninth century), nor their alleged revealers, Atiśa and Dangma Lhungyal (eleventh century).[188] With so few legitimately early descriptions of treasure and treasure recovery, the primary biographies of Nyangrel within the *Stainless Proclamations* and the *Clear Mirror* are among the earliest and most extensive narratives for insights into Buddhist treasure during the later dissemination of the teachings. At that time Nyangrel was the most prominent and prolific treasure recoverer, as this mode of scriptural production spread among the Buddhists, and he subsequently became renowned as the first of five "treasure-revealing

187. *Zangs gling ma* H, 80a1–2.

188. Davidson 2005, 225–31. Cf. Martin 2001, 85–88, which notes that Atiśa is reported to have bestowed a blessing to the Bönpo treasure revealer, Shenchen Luga.

kings," an epithet that vaunts his pioneering claim as the reincarnation of Emperor Tri Songdetsen.[189]

Nyangrel and the Early Treasures

In distinct contrast to normative presentations of the treasures, an analysis of the treasure recovery narratives in Nyangrel's biographies indicates that treasures in the twelfth century were uniformly material texts and relics. While special certificates discovered in advance may offer some details, from clues hinting at the location of a cache to an inventory of its contents, for Nyangrel treasure recovery is full of surprises. Just as each recovery progresses idiosyncratically, so too do the contents emerge as a range of precious items. Treasure texts that are soteriological in nature would be expected when inventoried in a certificate, which thereby ascribes a special primacy to those types of documents, but other treasures are as often not listed, such as the array of relics, consecrated substances, and various tools of the yogin's thaumaturgical trade. By inventorying the sum total of Nyangrel's treasures from his biographies, the limited number of texts and relics suggests a range of treasure types that were being recovered in the twelfth century.

In most cases small caskets (*sgrom bu*) or boxes (*sgam*) are used as containers for these precious items, a practice attested in imperial-era inscriptions and early sources such as the *Testimony of Ba*,[190] where their construction sometimes implies a hierarchy in which containers made of rarer and more precious materials signify contents of higher esteem. In the *Clear Mirror*, doctrinal "cycles" (*skor*) of related texts emerge from caskets fashioned of tiger skins and special leathers as well as from reliquaries made of precious metals, whereas a simple clay pot or vase suffices as a vessel for propitiatory rites and consecrated substances. The *Stainless Proclamations* is more equitable, however: caskets are often defined by the contents they hold rather than the substances they are made of, thereby extending veneration more equitably toward all treasure materials. Soteriological liturgies thus emerge from "a treasure casket of the sacred doctrine" while leaving the material of its construction unspecified. In other instances, color may suffice to distinguish the contents of a container in

189. There are two enumerations of renowned treasure revealers: "the five treasure-revealing kings" (*gter ston rgyal po lnga*), all of whom claim to be reincarnations of Tri Songdetsen, and "the three supreme magical emanations" (*mchog gyi sprul sku gsum*). Nyangrel is first on both lists. See Dorje and Kapstein 1991, 145 and 121, respectively.

190. Richardson 1985, 69 and 105; Wangdu and Diemberger 2000, 24–25, 27, 30–31, 77, 104–5.

the *Stainless Proclamations*, where a black leather casket holds "countless tools that benefit or harm," and "Buddhist doctrines of ḍākinī transmission cycles" are contained within a red leather casket, corresponding to their passionate nature.[191]

Nyangrel's primary biographies attempt to itemize his recoveries exhaustively, yet certain titles and items listed in one primary biography are not always found in the other. His major doctrinal cycles are consistently corroborated, whereas the array of relics and individual texts are often not. Furthermore, Nyangrel's biographies present no categories for the different types of his treasures. As for the methods employed in retrieving the treasures, we can discern a number of strategies outlined, but these are in response to spontaneous, situational necessity rather than normative obligation. That is, it is clear from Nyangrel's primary biographies that the process of each treasure recovery is unique, and the distinct karmic context of every situation required that each recovery progress in its own way. Without a predetermined sequence of steps to follow, there are few insights into how to prepare for a recovery as well as few expectations as to how it would proceed.

Despite deviations in many details, the *Clear Mirror* and the *Stainless Proclamations* share a similar progression of events that initiates Nyangrel's career as a treasure revealer. To begin, Nyangrel receives treasure guides and texts from other treasure revealers, who provide the impetus to set out in search of his own. Then, while secluded in solitary retreat, he encounters a mysterious yogin who offers somewhat cryptic directions. These are clarified through a series of additional acquaintances, some of whom are human and quite ordinary while others are magically emanated and thus special. Following their bestowal of additional materials, especially certificates that contain information in varying degrees of detail, Nyangrel proceeds to the locations they describe, most of which are associated with the imperium. While the actual process of recovery sometimes begins with propitiatory rites, it consistently evolves into a physical process of manual labor to uncover the array of exclusively material textual and ritual items deemed treasure.

Mentors

In both biographies, Nyangrel encounters two prominent Buddhist treasure revealers who frequent the imperial sites of central Tibet. Later sources assert that some "ultra pith" (*yang ti*) instructions of the Great Perfection were

191. *Dri ma med pa*, 100.1–2.

co-revealed with a Bönpo contemporary, Nyemo Shuné,[192] but he is absent from Nyangrel's biographies, as are any other references to Bönpo influences. According to the *Stainless Proclamations*, Nyangrel met Lama Rashak and the siddha Ngödrup around the inception of his career, such that both function as exemplars and mentors, but in the *Clear Mirror* they arrive at distinct junctures in Nyangrel's life. Lama Rashak directs Nyangrel toward his first recoveries, whereas Ngödrup, who is encountered after Nyangrel has gained some renown, bestows empowerments for the treasures he had found already and thereby provides further reinforcement and legitimacy. Critical to the development of Nyangrel's treasure recoveries, these contemporaries are equally important for the Buddhist treasure tradition as a whole, and so portraits of these two twelfth-century revealers will be presented individually below.

After the death of his father, Nyangrel receives initiations and teachings from a number of other teachers, one of whom is Rashak Tertön.[193] There is little additional detail for this early treasure revealer in the historical record, but two late histories mention Rashak. Jamgön Kongtrul's (1813–99) history of the treasure revealers lists Khomting temple as the source of one of Rashak's treasure caches, which is significant since Khomting becomes a key recovery

192. Achard 1999, 54–55n4; *Rin chen baiḍūrya'i phreng ba*, 370–71. While Kongtrul's nineteenth-century account of Tibet's treasure revealers is an important source, and he likely had access to texts that are no longer extant, the historicity of such late details that are uncorroborated by earlier sources is questionable, and I reserve primacy for content from Nyangrel's biographies. Perhaps the absence of Bön influence within these early sources is intended, a deliberate omission of figures and sources that might invite criticism of Nyangrel's doctrines as non-Buddhist, but Achard notes that the categories of *ultra pith* and *crown pith* (*spyi ti*) are absent in Bönpo doxographies, thereby casting further doubt on the historicity of this exchange with a Bönpo revealer. Perhaps Kongtrul's penchant for ecumenicism informed the inclusion of certain details even when uncorroborated by other sources. For a translation of Kongtrul's account, see Gyamtso 2011, 93–98.

193. According to the *Stainless Proclamations*, Lopön Chökyi Drakpa and Chökyi Dorjé, presumably his first teachers outside the family, transmit the three core doctrines that would become the foundation of Nyingma tantric praxis: the *Net of Magical Display* (*Sgyu 'phrul* [*drwa ba'i rgyud*], *Māyājālatantra*, a root mahāyoga tantra); *Sūtra Gathering the Intent* ([*Dgongs pa 'dus pa'i*] *mdo*, a root text of anuyoga); and the mental class (*sems phyogs*) of the Great Perfection (*Dri ma med pa*, 90.4–5). The identity of Chökyi Dorjé may be lost to time, but there is at least one candidate who may be the Lopön Chökyi Drakpa listed here. The *Blue Annals* describes several Chökyi Drakpas and Chödraks. One of them was born in 1094 in Tsang province (Roerich 1949, 1008–9), so he was a contemporary of Nyangrel from the same region. He would have been in his fifties or sixties when he met Nyangrel and thus well into his teaching career. Moreover, he is listed in the section recounting the transmission of the Great Compassionate One (*Thugs rje chen po*), an epithet of Avalokiteśvara and one of Nyangrel's most important cycles, which became renowned as the *Maṇi Kambum* in the centuries after Nyangrel. The *Blue Annals* (Roerich 1949, 1010) also mentions that this individual "did not study the texts of the Nyingma school," but Nyangrel appears to have received various teachings from various specialists. These

site for Nyangrel as well.[194] Also, Dudjom Rinpoche includes an aside in Guru Chöwang's biographical sketch where his father directs him to reveal doctrines in their "pure form," which seems to specify soteriological doctrines as

---

are not presented as reciprocal exchanges where Nyangrel bestowed empowerments and such for the tantric lineages transmitted through his family. While in his early twenties, he was not yet a guru and remained only a disciple.

Another elusive teacher listed in the *Stainless Proclamations* is "the lama Dzongpa of Tsang" (*Dri ma med pa*, 90.5). Nyangrel requests the Nepali Doha tradition (*Bal po'i do ha*) and a lineage of Chö (*Gcod yul*) or "cutting" practice from this particular thaumaturge. While there is no mention of him in the *Blue Annals* section concerning Chö, this lineage, like Shijé (*zhi byad*, "pacification"), was brought to Tibet by Phadampa Sangyé (d. 1117). Robert Mayer (personal communication, April, 12, 2012) notes that one of Nyangrel's treasures specifically related to this lineage remains popular today (*Nyang ral khros ma*), though it remains unclear whether it can really be traced to Nyangrel. In the Shijé section of the *Blue Annals*, Dampa mentions that a special disciple was the worthy recipient of the mahāmudrā teachings: "The bla-ma rDzong-pa belongs to the type of individuals of spontaneous development" (Roerich 1949, 914). Perhaps this exorcist, who could have been alive when Nyangrel reached his twenties, bestowed instructions on Chö to Nyangrel, since these too were among Phadampa Sangyé's transmissions. Despite this ambiguity, what becomes clear is that many of the first teachers approached or encountered by Nyangrel were proponents of Phadmapa Sangyé's lineages, which were popular in southern Tibet at that time. This is confirmed by a trio of masters from whom he received three lineages of Shijé in the *Stainless Proclamations* and whose lives are recounted in some detail in the *Blue Annals*.

Nyangrel garners barely any mention at all in the *Blue Annals*: he only appears in the lineage of the Great Compassionate One, where he is referred to by his father's title: "Myang-tön obtained [them] from the siddha Ngödrup" (Roerich 1949, 1006). While Nyangrel himself is not listed among their disciples in the *Blue Annals*, these three masters of Shijé are positively identified as his contemporaries. The identity of the first, "Lama Lama," is obscured by a "scripto" in the *Stainless Proclamations*: this is Mal Kawachenpa (Mal ka ba can pa, 1126–1211). According to both the *Stainless Proclamations* and the *Blue Annals*, Mal was prominent in the *So* Shijé lineage (*Dri ma med pa*, 90.6; Roerich 1949, 888–90, 896). Another teacher, Lama Dartönpa (Bla ma dar ston pa) or Chüpa Dartönpa ('Chus pa dar ston pa, 1117–92), is listed in both the *So* and *Kam* (*Kaṃ*, *Skam*) Shijé lineages, the latter of which is corroborated in the *Stainless Proclamations* (in *Dri ma med pa* it is spelled *Kaṃ*, 90.6; in the *Blue Annals* it is *Skam*, Roerich 1949, 881–83, 905). The third Shijé master is the only one mentioned in both of Nyangrel's biographies. In the *Stainless Proclamations*, Nyangrel approaches Nyönpa Dönden (Smyon pa don ldan) for the *Ma* (*Rma*) Shijé lineage, and the *Blue Annals* describe Nyönpa Dönden as an important adept in this particular lineage as well (*Dri ma med pa*, 91.2; Roerich 1949, 876). He appears to be quite special for Nyangrel in the *Clear Mirror* as well, though not until later in his life.

The *Blue Annals* indicates that these three Shijé masters were very closely related: Mal Kawachenpa and Chüpa Dartönpa are listed side by side as prominent students of Shami (Sha mi, 1085–1171) (Roerich 1949, 879–81), a third-generation disciple of Phadmapa Sangyé himself (881), and Chüpa Dartönpa is listed as a direct lineage holder of Nyönpa Dönden's *Ma* transmission (876). Thus according to the *Stainless Proclamations*, Nyangrel first seeks teachings on Shijé from three of its most renowned masters of the era.

194. *Rin chen baiḍūrya'i phreng ba*, 382.6.

opposed to magical rites with more mundane objectives. The father then lists Rashak among the examples of treasure revealers whose example should not be followed: "By practicing rites of thread-cross exorcism, the Rashak treasure-finder later became merely an exorcist."[195] Yet we find Nyangrel performing the same rites as an impoverished tantrika-for-hire in his young adulthood as well, so the two professions of exorcistic rites and treasure hunting need not be mutually exclusive.

Although their initial meeting is not narrated in the *Clear Mirror*, it mentions that Rashak had previously delivered cache certificates (*kha byang*) when Nyangrel prepares to make his first recovery. In the *Stainless Proclamations*, Nyangrel has a fortuitious encounter with Rashak that occurs not long after he met Nyönpa Dönden at the age of twenty-one. Even though the simplicity of this ordinary transaction lacks so much of what defines treasure in later centuries, this may be considered Nyangrel's first treasure recovery in the *Stainless Proclamations*:

> While in the presence of the treasure revealer Lama Rashak, the sacred doctrine of the *Gathering of the Ones Gone to Bliss* emerged from four small sacks as twenty tantric scriptures together with their brief *sādhana* liturgies. Since Nyangrel requested the seven small volumes, Rashak gave him those together with the copies.[196]

Nyangrel's first treasure recovery thus occurs simply by Rashak transferring several sacks of texts into his hands, and the language is indeed consistent with subsequent recoveries where the treasures themselves are the subject of an intransitive sentence: they "emerge" on their own rather than as the object of an agent who "reveals" something. Like the cache certificates retrospectively glossed in the *Clear Mirror*, these treasures were already in Rashak's possession, but they "emerge" to Nyangrel and so are bestowed to him upon his request. Significantly, these are the tantras and liturgies of the *Eight Instructions: Gathering of the Ones Gone to Bliss*, a diverse collection of meditations and rituals focused on eight fierce deities that would become one of Nyangrel's most renowned cycles.[197] We might expect a more dramatic sequence of events for

195. Dudjom 1991, 765.

196. *Dri ma med pa*, 92.4–5.

197. This is the only description of Nyangrel's recovery of the *Eight Instructions* in the *Stainless Proclamations*, and the more elaborate narrative describing its recovery from the back of the Vairocana statue at Khomting is drawn from the *Clear Mirror* alone. This latter episode is popularly accepted as definitive; I have never found the alternate origin account featuring

the recovery of such an important treasure cycle—and we find precisely this in the *Clear Mirror*'s account of its discovery—but the *Stainless Proclamations* presents a rather mundane transaction where, based on Nyangrel's karmic connection to the cycle, Rashak simply delivers these materials into his care. How they came into Rashak's possession remains unknown, but the cycle emerged to Nyangrel regardless of whether these volumes were treasure to Rashak or not, thereby indicating that it indeed was treasure to him.

Another significant detail is that Nyangrel is recorded as having only received seven small volumes in this initial treasure recovery, yet the *Eight Instructions* has expanded into a sizeable collection in as many as thirteen large volumes today. As is common but rarely addressed explicitly, treasure cycles typically acquire many supplementary texts over the course of their transmission and so expand considerably beyond the original compendiums.[198] In many respects this is of necessity, as the pithy foundations of a cycle may lack much of the ritual and commentarial architecture to support and transmit it: mythologies of the cycle's origins, rites for the initiation of devotees, elaborate deity yoga sādhanas for intensive solitary retreat and regular group practice, rituals to effect mundane objectives and enhance soteriological accomplishment, as well as commentarial advice for any of these—all can become integrated and transmitted within a single treasure cycle. In some instances later revealers introduce such supplements from their own finds; others are simply authored but often acquire treasure status through their transmission with and function within the larger cycle.

Even though many of these latter additions may not have originally had the status of treasures, through the addition of treasure marks and the manipulation of colophons, many of these texts come to be considered integral if not

---

Rashak from the *Stainless Proclamations* described outside that text, which reinforces the thesis that the *Clear Mirror* had broader circulation whereas the *Stainless Proclamations* was unknown until recently. See note 64 above.

Nyangrel's treasure cycles of deity yoga consist of a cooperative collection of texts in which the root tantras implicitly advance the requisite claim to legitimacy. These scriptures are presented as Tibetan translations of Sanskrit originals and so allege to certify the Indic pedigree of the entire cycle, thus all of Nyangrel's deity cycles are founded on root tantras. On the basis of these, empowerment liturgies enable authorized lineage holders to transmit the cycle to disciples, thereby reviving it as a living tradition of tantric praxis. Meditation liturgies (*sgrub thabs*, Skt. *sādhana*) are the main texts distributed to disciples and thus receive the most extensive use in regular recitation, but that practice is supported by a range of texts that significantly expands the original contents of such collections.

198. Cantwell and Mayer (2010) address this issue of the augmentation and supplementation of treasure cycles as they move toward publication, taking a twentieth-century treasure text as their case study.

original components of the cycle. Since Nyangrel's biographers describe the original recovery of the *Eight Instructions* as a rather small collection, we see just how much it has accumulated over time and thus how much is the work of others as well. Moreover, since these tantric cycles are inherently dependent on ritual texts for their propagation, we can be certain that the "twenty tantric scriptures together with their brief sādhana liturgies" of the original recovery were amended with empowerment rites at the very least, and the *Clear Mirror* addresses this need explicitly when Ngödrup offers Nyangrel a range of supplementary material for the cycle that he himself had found as treasure. More controversial is the suggestion that Nyangrel himself composed original writings to meet these needs, but I suspect that post-recovery creative emendation was part and parcel of treasure recovery for Nyangrel rather than some disingenuous process of fabrication that was considered entirely distinct from it. Even in the normative tradition of recent centuries, core treasure liturgies are enhanced by ritual texts composed by means of ordinary, non-treasure authorship and yet these become regarded as treasure as well.[199]

Since Rashak had found the *Eight Instructions* earlier and gave all of them to Nyangrel in recognizing him as their rightful owner, the *Stainless Proclamations* initiates a sequence where Nyangrel receives a new treasure cycle in which he has not been empowered, thus necessitating a search for another revealer who can authorize him to practice and propagate those instructions.

> Since Nyangrel repeatedly beseeched the lord of all oral transmissions and treasures (*bka' gter*), the Lama Siddha Ngödrup, for the empowerments for the *Eight Sādhana Instructions* of secret mantra together with their oral instructions; for the sādhanas of *Complete Pacification*; and for Songtsen Gampo's tradition of the *Great Compassionate One*, Ngödrup bestowed all of them in the manner of filling a vase to the brim and also delivered many treasure site certificates to him.[200]

Nyangrel is thus empowered into the cycle of his initial recovery and then receives instructions for two others for which he has a special affinity, the Shijé

199. A perusal of Chokgyur Lingpa's treasure cycles uncovers that many supplementary works, according to the colophons, were composed by Jamgön Kongtrul well after the recovery event. These will often display treasure marks on every line. Treasure marks following lines quoted from the root sādhana, as in a feast liturgy (*tshogs 'khor*), would be prerequisite, but they commonly follow Kongtrul's original work as well. Perhaps this is the work of copyists rather than Kongtrul, but one point is that all of these contributions came to be integral components of the treasure cycle and thus regarded as treasure texts as well.

200. *Dri ma med pa*, 92.5–93.2.

Figure 4. Main statue in the temple of the Great Compassionate One, the northern temple on the first floor of the Jokhang in Lhasa. Having been destroyed in the Cultural Revolution, neither the statues nor their encasements are original, but this is the space from which Ngödrup is said to have recovered the *Great Compassionate One* in the twelfth century. Photo by the author, 2011.

teachings attributed to Phadampa Sangyé and the diverse cycle concerning Emperor Songtsen Gampo as the bodhisattva Avalokiteśvara, which would become the foundation of Tibet's national mythology as formulated in the *Pillar Testament* and the *Maṇi Kambum.* For the most part, the siddha Ngödrup remains as historically sketchy as Rashak, but the *Blue Annals* corroborates Ngödrup in the transmission line of Avalokiteśvara; he is largely known for this detail alone.[201]

Since Nyangrel receives the *Eight Instructions* from Lama Rashak in the *Stainless Proclamations* and then proceeds directly to Ngödrup for its empowerments, the two revealers serve identical functions as mentors that support Nyangrel in his initial recoveries. In the *Stainless Proclamations* Ngödrup authenticates Nyangrel's original recovery and authorizes those to come, but in the *Clear Mirror* Ngödrup plays a distinct role since he appears when Nyangrel's treasure career is well underway. Nyangrel has already established himself

201. Roerich 1949, 941; *Rin chen baiḍūrya'i 'phreng ba*, 371.3–372.6. Blondeau (1984, 77–123) traces a debate as to whether Drupthop Ngödrup was conflated with a Bönpo revealer who shares a similar name, Shötön Ngödrup (Bzhod ston dngos grub). She concludes that they were not the same individual.

as a prominent treasure revealer who has recovered a number of cycles related to Ngödrup:

> When I, Nyangrel, was staying in the upper valley [in Central Tibet], the one called Siddha Ngödrup Gön had come to Samyé. While I was working at Samyé, he was invited by a patron to the upper part of Yarlung. Uncontrived devotion welled up in me, so I went to meet Siddha Ngödrup, which delighted him as well. He exclaimed, "This guy is the genuine emanation of Tri Songdetsen!" Then the guru siddha showed me five scrolls and the profound doctrines of *King* [*Songtsen Gampo's*] *Great Compassionate One* cycle, both of which he had extracted from that deity's temple in Lhasa. He said, "Although I extracted them, you are the capable one in whom its empowerments exist." Giving them to me he said, "These wondrous treasures are yours."
>
> When I confided that I had the secret mantra *Gathering of the Ones Gone to Bliss*, Guru Siddha Ngödrup replied, "I have the introductions, empowerments, and oral precepts for that! I will bestow in their entirety the introductions, empowerments, and blessings for that which is called the *Cycle of Wrathful Mastery*. Now the oral transmissions from Guru Padmasambhava to myself will remain unbroken." For several days after this, I felt as though drunk from beer. He also taught me many of the collected tantras of secret mantra, the cycle of the [*Gathering of the*] *Ones Gone to Bliss*, Shijé, and so forth.[202]

Quite similar to Rashak's bestowal of the *Eight Instructions* in the *Stainless Proclamations*, the *Clear Mirror* has Ngödrup present Nyangrel with an array of already extracted treasure materials, but grammatically Ngödrup is a clearly demarcated agent who hands them to Nyangrel. With respect to these treasures, it seems that their process of emergence is already complete and Ngödrup now bequeaths them to Nyangrel, their rightful owner, who at this point in his life has become an accomplished revealer of treasures himself.

In sum, Nyangrel's biographies tone down any sense of innovation in the time leading up to his first recoveries. Instead he is presented as the karmically destined recipient of established traditions: neither the texts he finds nor the methods he employs are original. Rather than come forward independently with wholly new cycles, Nyangrel's first treasures are those that had

202. *Gsal ba'i me long*, 349.3–350.3. For another translation, see Phillips 2004, 137.

already been recovered by other contemporaries and delivered into his hands. As Nyangrel proceeded with his treasure career, he would continue to rely on the guidance and materials offered by treasure revealers, but others would soon come to his aid as well.

Yogin Envisioned as Instigator

Although Nyangrel received directions, certificates, and even whole treasures from other revealers, an encounter with a mysterious yogin accelerates the approach to his first independent recoveries in both biographies. Though he is prone to pure visions (*dag snang*) and dreams (*rmi lam*), these do not accurately describe the context of this encounter.[203] Nyangrel is present and awake in ordinary space and time, and there is no indication that the yogin is anything other than material until he departs. The yogin appears to be a physical being with special qualities and abilities rather than an ethereal or oneiric vision, which could be induced by and thus reduced to an internal experience.

Serving the same function as the empowerments of his youth, auspicious encounters are both catalysts and results, causes and effects that precipitate esoteric activity by demonstrating that Nyangrel is ripe for it. Such teleology is not problematic: it is necessary and legitimating by demonstrating the economy and definite efficacy of karma. In these episodes just prior to his independent treasure recoveries, the appearances of these emanations are causal in that they propel Nyangrel, both personally and materially, toward the location of these treasures. The yogin instills confidence by prophesizing that Nyangrel is destined to recover the treasures and then provides a variety of textual materials to aid his search for them. These manifestations are also resultant because they appear as the fruition of the lifetimes of meritorious activity and tantric practice initiated by Tri Songdetsen according to Nyangrel. Karma thus remains the primary undercurrent of the narratives, driving the story in stages as auspicious causes from previous lives produce their necessarily auspicious results in his present one.

The karmic seeds sown in his former life as Tri Songdetsen remained potent but latent, requiring the full complement of proper conditions to ripen as the fruit of treasure recovery. While the very existence of other revealers such as

203. The last third of the *Stainless Proclamations* mostly details Nyangrel's experiences in retreat, which are defined by visits to other realms in pure visions (see *Dri ma med pa*, from 129). In the *Clear Mirror*, a series of three special dreams occur during childhood (*Gsal ba'i me long*, 326–28).

Rashak and Ngödrup portend that the time for Nyangrel to recover the treasures has arrived, Nyangrel's encounter with the young yogin provides the final condition for their more extensive emergence. It was this catalyst that caused his karma for treasure recovery to manifest. The accounts in each biography concur with each other, despite diverging on the details, indicating that this encounter was one of the main narratives passed down and thus could have originated in some form from Nyangrel himself.

In the *Clear Mirror*, this encounter provides the basis for Nyangrel's impending treasure recoveries not just karmically but materially as well, and it may include a hint to a source of the latter. Aside from the confirmation gained through the emanation's directives, Nyangrel obtains a series of material certificates that will lead him to his first caches. They meet while Nyangrel is engaged in a one-year retreat at Mawochok:

> One evening intrinsic awareness glowed as manifest luminosity. I recalled the series of my past and future lives, and the next day as the sun rose at dawn, I heard a boy outside my door earnestly call out "Look! Look!" When I went to look, I saw a yogin dressed in white, dreadlocks piled atop his head and adorned with the six bone ornaments. Although I did not recognize him, I welcomed him inside and arranged a cushion, whereby he caused warmth to spread throughout the hermitage.[204]

Initiating the encounter, Nyangrel experiences the luminosity of ultimate reality directly that enables him to know his "past and future births." Following the re-cognition of his past lives and foreknowledge of his future one, none of which are described, Nyangrel beholds a young yogin at his front entrance. As the boy appears when the sun breaches the horizon, it seems as if the young yogin emerges out of the sunbeams themselves. Rather than finding him in a dream or a disassociated vision, this boy enters the hermitage and rests on the cushion set out by Nyangrel. Upon entering the yogin declares,

> "I am the space yogin, Wangchuk Dorjé.
> Son/Boy! You are endowed with karma and fortune.
> Padmasambhava protects you with the transmissions and
> empowerments.
> All the profound doctrines of secret mantra
> are now in the hands of the ḍākinīs:
> supplicate them immediately!

204. *Gsal ba'i me long*, 335.5–336.2.

Is Khomting temple around here?
Is Drak Sinmo Barjé around here?"
I replied that they were and took refuge.[205]

The magical emanation appears to be the perfected reflection of Nyangrel himself: both are young yogins bearing a yogin's signature accoutrements, such as dreadlocks and bone ornaments, but Nyangrel does not recognize him as an acquaintance or familiar entity, enlightened or otherwise, which is a curious detail to include. Dudjom Rinpoché identifies this yogin as an emanation of Padmasambhava, since he is explicitly identified as such in the *Stainless Proclamations*, but this is an example where the two biographies have been tacitly conflated.[206] Here the space yogin is explicitly not recognized as Padmasambhava or anyone else known to Nyangrel, and the yogin speaks of Padmasambhava in the third person. Since he is not Padmasambhava, "the space yogin Wangchuk Dorjé" may be an alias for another guru who was the source of Nyangrel's early treasure directives: his father, Nyangtön Chökyi Khorlo.

We saw that earlier in the *Clear Mirror*, the text confides that Nyangtön Chökyi Khorlo's secret name is Dorjé Wangchuk Tsal. The yogin's name, Wangchuk Dorjé, is a simple inversion of his father's secret name with Tsal appended as a final syllable signifying "the dynamic expression of." Is this yogin the dynamic expression of Nyangrel's own father? As a descendent of one of the great imperial clans, Nyangtön Chökyi Khorlo may have passed knowledge, if not guiding materials, relating to the whereabouts of old treasure caches to his son. While there is nothing to confirm that the father and yogin are one and the same, the name of this yogin in the *Clear Mirror* may imply that Nyangrel gained access to some of his first treasures via his father. The episode continues:

Having said that, I joined my hands and the yogin exclaimed,
"É ma! How completely wondrous!
There really are profound doctrines, treasures of exalted mind,
pure cycles
that were concealed by Master Padmasambhava in those two places.
Son/Boy! You must open the treasure doors to the sacred Dharma.
Care for the karmically endowed, the people, the disciples!
Diligently enhance the benefit of beings!
I will tame the transmigrators of all directions."

205. *Gsal ba'i me long*, 336.2–4.

206. Dudjom 1991, 755.

> He delivered three scrolls to me and said, "One is a cache certificate, one is a site manual, and one is a supplemental certificate."[207]

This is the critical moment because the three scrolls are finally bestowed to Nyangrel, thereby enabling future recoveries. After entrusting the certificates, it is time for the yogin to depart.

> Having said that, he got up. He was about to go out the door when I thought to ask for the details. I went to accompany him, but he passed, dissolving into the center of the closed door like a rainbow in the sky.[208]

Just as he arrived with the first rays of dawn, the yogin dissolves into light as he departs. Although he is clearly special, this is the first specific indication that the yogin possesses special abilities, or *siddhi*, at the very least, if he is not indeed a magical emanation of Padmasambhava, as Nyangrel deduces at the conclusion of their encounter in the *Stainless Proclamations*. There the yogin bears additional marks to indicate that he is more than ordinary, but overall the episode is remarkably similar:

> At the age of twenty-five I was setting the retreat boundary, and just when I offered a maṇḍala and made guru supplications, a red yogin with dreadlocks down his back appeared in the doorway. Holding a barley bowl bearing the letter *ka*, he wore a white blanket and conch-shell earrings.
>
> After giving a river-silk[209] scroll to me the yogin confided, "This region of yours, Drak Marpo, it is like a lion leaping into the sky. This lion and the four great ministers in the four directions capture the rays of the rising sun within them, and the sunset's beams are gathered as one. Since the treasure doctrines of secret mantra are at Drak Marpo with their protectors, I, the yogin beggar, need not remain. As you are the king of the region, the lord of mantra hold-

207. *Gsal ba'i me long*, 336.4–337.1.

208. *Gsal ba'i me long*, 337.4–5.

209. *Chu dar gyi shog dril.* Davidson 2005, 415–16n35: River silk is "a board-like or felt-like material made from pounding water weeds . . . It is placed first on the list of materials on which *gter ma* may legitimately be copied (*bris gzhi*) in Guru Chos-dbang's *gTer 'byung chen mo*, p. 102.4."

> ers, I offer these treasures to you. Uncover them by relying on this cache certificate."[210]

The *Stainless Proclamations* and the *Clear Mirror* display an uncommon measure of correlation here. The location is Nyangrel's retreat; the time frame is his young adulthood; the one encountered is a yogin with dreadlocks and other key accoutrements; the yogin delivers treasure certificate/s and then departs mysteriously. The *ka* on the barley bowl is an interesting inclusion in the *Stainless Proclamations*: as the first consonant in the Tibetan alphabet, *ka* seems to reference Great Perfection rhetoric concerning *ka dag* or "alpha purity," which is a quality of the intrinsic awareness (*rig pa*) that instigated this episode in the *Clear Mirror*. The protectors of the treasures are again noted, though they were identified as ḍākinīs in the *Clear Mirror*, and the yogin enables Nyangrel's first recovery by bestowing a cache certificate. Here it appears to be a single document of the more general variety, but the impact is the same: it confers authority upon Nyangrel to proceed with the recovery of treasures concealed at Drak Marpo, the central peak within a natural maṇḍala defined by a prominent "minister" or mountain in each of the four cardinal directions. Once again, this is the primary objective of the yogin's visit, and upon delivering the certificate he prepares to depart:

> The yogin turned around and passed by Nyangrel. Nyangrel immediately beseeched him to stay, but the yogin would not listen and departed across the valley behind [his retreat]. After that the lama himself got up and right away went to query the people of the valley, but they said that a yogin like that had neither come around nor been seen. Though they searched as far as a day's journey, no one had seen him. Since Nyangrel saw the yogin who had now disappeared, he deduced that the yogin was a magical emanation of Guru Padmasambhava.[211]

Though not quite as miraculous as the dissolution into the door in the *Clear Mirror*, the yogin here also departs under mysterious circumstances, and the nature of his disappearance is such that Nyangrel takes him to have been a magical emanation that arrived to aid his path.

210. *Dri ma med pa*, 93.5–94.4. For another translation, see Gyatso 1986, 25.

211. *Dri ma med pa*, 94.4–6. Note that even within this single, critical episode, there is a shift in voice: it begins in the first person where the narrator specifies that the scroll was given "to me," but it concludes in the honorific third person when "the lama" got up in search of the yogin.

Treasure Certificates

In both biographies the primary objective of the mysterious yogin is to deliver one or more scrolls to Nyangrel. These material documents are of as many as three types in Nyangrel's biographies and hierarchical in the sense that they preserve information with increasing degrees of specificity for treasure recoveries. While the *Clear Mirror* describes all three types, the yogin in the *Stainless Proclamations* only bestows a single cache certificate that is augmented by his oral testimony. *Khajang* (*kha byang*) is often translated as "guide," but this is an interpretive rendering; "cache certificate" is more literal.

In Nyangrel's biographies the reception of a cache certificate initiates the recovery process. Its contents vary depending on whether it is relied on alone or with the aid of other certificates, but its most important function is to confer authority to the treasure revealer who possesses it and thus is destined to reveal the cache/s it describes. *Kha* specifically designates the "mouth," or aperture, of the treasure cache itself, whether that space is concealed or open. *Jang* alone can signify a quality of expansiveness, while its diminutive *jangbu* (*byang bu*) denotes a "piece."[212] Both meanings seem to be at work here: *khajang* signifies a brief note on a scrap of paper or small scroll that belies the vast significance of its contents. For the one who comes into its possession, it is far more than a guide: the certificate confirms a karma-based authority of eminent domain over the site it identifies as well as its contents.

In all of Nyangrel's major recoveries, he first comes into the possession of a cache certificate before proceeding with the recovery, but the certificate bestowed in the *Stainless Proclamations* is particularly detailed. It contains information sufficient to identify the site and locate its caches, and it provides an inventory of the treasures concealed therein. In the *Clear Mirror*, however, the cache certificate only directs Nyangrel to a general location, thereby requiring him to endure further trials to learn the precise locations and contents of the caches. These are most often provided by two other types of written materials. "Site manuals" (*gnas yig*) identify the site and locate the caches, and "supplemental certificates" (*yang byang*) hold the most precise information. As would be expected, a site manual contains more explicit descriptions of the site and may contain clues that help pinpoint the cache's location, which becomes especially critical when the site named in the cache certificate is in fact a small mountain. The third and most specific scroll in the *Clear Mirror* is a supplemental certificate that bears the most specific details concern-

212. Gyatso explores the etymology of *byang* and its diminutive *byang bu* in "The Relic Text as Prophecy" (Unpublished, 2).

ing the location of a cache, its contents, and how to extract them. In at least one instance, a supplemental certificate is found midway through a recovery that leads Nyangrel to another cache close by. Both cache certificates and supplemental certificates are described in Nyangrel's *Copper Island Biography of Padmasambhava*, and these along with site manuals later become normative in the treasure tradition.[213]

After the delivery of the scrolls and the analysis of their contents, Nyangrel's two biographies diverge once again. They preserve two distinct accounts of Nyangrel's treasure career, and while they agree on some important details, such as the site of his first recovery, they conflict on many others, such as the site of his second. Likewise, the processes described in each biography differ, so each narrative must be considered separately before evaluating the range of examples collectively.

Treasure Recovery Narratives in the Stainless Proclamations

According to the *Stainless Proclamations*, after reading the cache certificate, Nyangrel sets out with an entourage of disciples for the rock mountain of Drak Sinmo Barjé Chen (Brag srin mo sbar rjes can). Now lying outside Neshi town in Tsomé county, it still bears the striations after which it was named "Rock Bearing the Claw-Marks of the *Sinmo*," a reference to the monstrous progenitor of the Tibetan people who is believed to have strafed these hills.[214] The presence of Nyangrel's disciples here should not be confused with the public treasure recoveries (*khrom gter*) of later revealers. In the *Stainless Proclamations* these are laborers and aides involved in the physically demanding process of treasure recovery, whereas in public treasures a dichotomy is preserved between the revealer and his audience, whose foremost function is to passively bear witness. In both cases, however, the presence of others provides

213. *Zangs gling ma* A, 145.3–4; *Me tog snying po* K, 358.3. The process of defining and redefining these terms is evident in the progressive series of treasure histories, which are also studies in the typology of treasure by revealers from Guru Chöwang on. See Guru Chöwang's *Gter 'byung chen mo*, 151.3–7, 159.5–6, as well as sections from Ratna Lingpa and Pema Lingpa translated in Thondup 1986, 72–76.

214. Nebesky-Wojkowitz 1956, 280: The *srin po* and *srin mo* were indigenous Tibetan deities prior to the introduction of Buddhism that were subsequently equated with the *rākṣasa* and *rākṣasī* of India. Due to the extensive taxonomy of semi-divine, nonhuman entities indigenous to Tibet, trying to render the various classes in English or using biblical categories only conflates their various identities, temperaments, and interests. As Nebesky-Wojkowitz writes, even relegating them to their accepted Sanskrit equivalents erodes their indigenous identities.

verification. Whereas the solitary revelations of the Ten Commandments by Moses and the Book of Mormon by Joseph Smith require others to suspend disbelief and accept that these scriptures are in fact the Word of God and not their own, Nyangrel's discoveries in the *Stainless Proclamations* always occur in the presence of others, who can testify to their authenticity.

Arriving at the site with his cabal of disciples, Nyangrel confronts a series of obstacles that impede his progress, the first of which is that he cannot even decipher the certificate. As a result, his first recovery begins haltingly and with much confusion:

> Having kept [the contents of the cache certificate] secret, the master and his six students dug around in a cave resembling an ogress' ear at the base of Sinmo Barjéchen. After nothing emerged they made prayers of supplication. A ḍākinī prophecy came forth directing them to pitch a tent at the base of a huge rock. Though they looked in every direction, they did not understand [where the prophecy directed them] so, after performing a gaṇacakra feast one evening, they made more supplications.[215]

Upon their first round of supplication for additional instructions, a ḍākinī prophecy "comes forth" to aid their quest, but even this results in only further confusion to the extent that they cannot even follow its most explicit instructions to erect a shelter. Instead, they perform a feast offering in an attempt to gain further guidance, but they would soon come to wish that they had heeded the ḍākinī's prophetic advice:

215. *Dri ma med pa*, 95.3–5. Even in the *Stainless Proclamations*, focused as it is upon a single treasure revealer it presents as legitimate, the treasures seem to be protected by several layers of security. A consequence of this is that Nyangrel, the very individual who is destined to recover the treasures, must succeed in additional trials to prove it. In the event that his certificate fell into the hands of someone who did not retain the proper karmic connection, its directives are so generic that the cache would remain undiscovered.

This conflicts, however, with the infallibility of karmic process such that the certificate and the authority it confers can only fall into the hands of the destined individual. Since all appearances are karmically determined, it would seem that anyone who possesses a certificate is karmically destined to possess it by definition. Likewise, anyone who discovers a treasure cache should be its destined revealer, yet these layers of security prove that this is not the case. Clearly, neither those bandits who plundered the imperial tombs after the collapse of the empire in ancient times nor the red cadres of the Cultural Revolution who pillaged Tibet's sacred sites in the twentieth century are taken to be "the karmically destined fortunate ones" described in treasure prophecies, and yet the caches were emptied all the same. Therefore, there is a rather striking and unresolved paradox that emerges when the idealistic constructs concerning how the treasures are meant to be revealed confronts the harsh political realities of Tibet's history.

Figure 5. Drak Sinmo Barjé with striations said to have been made by the claws of the ogress visible at right. "Drak Sinmo rock near Neshi," photograph by Hugh E. Richardson, 1950 (detail). Copyright Pitt Rivers Museum, University of Oxford, 2001.59.4.22.1.

> At dusk countless mundane treasure-guarding *drekpa* gathered. Displaying terrifying forms, they proclaimed fearsome sounds. When it thundered and hail fell, Lama Nyang's gaze subjugated them, overpowering them through his meditation. His actions neutralized the *drekpa*, and they stood down on their own accord. Obsequiously offering the very essence of their life force, they promised to be subjects and servants.[216]

The feast provokes the treasure guardians, a cohort of haughty entities who attempt to disperse Nyangrel and his retinue with their monstrous appearance and with an intense hailstorm, which signifies that they have finally arrived in the right place. Earlier and later treasure revealers alike often describe their confrontations with monstrous treasure protectors who stand guard over the

216. *Dri ma med pa*, 95.5–96.2.

caches, only relenting once the revealer proves their claim by overwhelming them in thaumaturgical combat, just as Padmasambhava is said to have done during his original conversion and appointment of Tibet's semi-divinities. While his entourage might perceive only the weapons of the assault (hail) and not those who wield them, Nyangrel proves his degree of attainment and status as the destined treasure revealer by directly perceiving and overwhelming their attackers. Having arrived at the correct location of the treasures and proven himself sufficiently realized, the weather subsides, the guardians subdued.[217]

With the unruly locals thus quelled, Nyangrel finally progresses toward the recovery of the treasures unimpeded. He is now met by a host of ḍākinīs who aid his search and who herald the arrival of Padmasambhava himself:

> Infinite karmic and gnostic ḍākinīs gathered at midnight and bestowed a variety of empowerments, prophecies, and siddhis. In the early morning, Nyangrel came face to face with Guru Padmasambhava, who, after conferring empowerments, prophecies, and blessings, said,
>
> > Karma-endowed birth, worthy vessel!
> > You will open the spontaneous treasure doors of the two benefits
> > with the key of enlightened mind.
> > You will open the lama-blessed treasure doors
> > with the key of the direct path, devotion.
> > You will open the treasure doors of meditation-deity siddhi
> > with the key of the four yogic sessions.
> > You will open the treasure doors of ḍākinī enlightened activity
> > with the keys of samaya, feast, and torma.
> > Right here is the treasure door of my oral lineage.
>
> Then moving toward a massive boulder, he dissolved into its side. Nyangrel directly witnessed the Guru's dissolution, and the next morning a masonry wall inconceivably appeared there. By building

217. See the long chapter on the classifications and forms of *drekpa* in Nebesky-Wojkowitz 1956, 253–317. A difficult question concerns just what these *drekpa* are in the emic sense: are they autonomous individuals who never roam far from the quarry they have been oath-bound to protect? Or are they indistinguishable from their natural manifestation as severely inclement and potentially lethal weather? The answer seems to be that they are both. An etic temptation might be to interpret them as precisely equivalent; the clouds and hail, thunder and lightning are indifferentiable from the voices and forms of the *drekpa*. However, adepts sometimes claim to perceive such beings via special perception gained through realization whereby their forms and accoutrements are described in great detail.

> a ladder to that spot, they dismantled the wall, revealing a cave with one pillar and two beams. The Guru's throne, maṇḍala, supreme instrument, vajra, bell, hand *kīla*-dagger, and so forth came into view.[218]

After Padmasambhava prophesizes Nyangrel's impending accomplishments, he directs him to the exact location of the treasure cache by dissolving into the middle of what must presumably be a massive boulder so tall as to require the makeshift construction of a ladder. In the morning light they look to the spot where Padmasambhava had dissolved, and instead of a nondescript rockface, they see that the masonry of some structure has been uncovered, thus signifying the presence of a cavity within the boulder. Using the ladder to reach the wall now apparent on the boulder's face, they break through the stones to reveal a large space inside, which is Padmasambhava's feast hall exactly as described in the original cache certificate. Given the description of the masonry as well as its two beams and a pillar, the cavity appears to have been excavated and then reinforced with architectural supports during its imperial-era construction, and Padmasambhava's personal ritual implements remain preserved and intact, just as he had left them.

Having fully proven himself, Nyangrel confronts no further obstacles at Drak Sinmo Barjé and excavates container after container of imperial-era texts and relics by digging, though there are additional steps required to find each additional cache. To begin they dig to the right of that maṇḍala (the center of which is Padmasambhava's throne) as precisely directed in the original site certificate. They uncover the first treasures it promised, which are sādhana liturgies presumably relating to each set of treasure protectors who had been mustered to this particular site by Padmasambhava. These texts will prove essential when preparing to depart Drak Sinmo Barjé.

The emergence of the supplemental certificate is especially valuable since Nyangrel has thus far relied on the original site certificate alone. This supplemental certificate, discovered only upon the successful recovery of the first cache of texts, provides further instructions for finding additional treasures concealed at the site. It also is coded and requires a "key" (*lde'u mig*) to decipher it, providing a degree of precedent perhaps for the encryption and compression technologies in the ḍākinī scripts that would become so prevalent for later revealers. While the *Copper Island* notes that Padmasambhava conceals some treasures that had been composed in "the symbolic language of the ḍākinīs," which is listed with the "demonic languages of yakṣa and rākṣasa" in addition to the human dialects of India, Nepal, and so forth, there is no

218. *Dri ma med pa*, 96.2–97.3.

reference to special treasure scripts in Nyangrel's biographies.[219] While the initial cache certificate led him to Drak Sinmo Barjé and instructed him to dig to the right of the maṇḍala, this supplemental certificate confides that there is another cache an arrow's length from the throne to the left.

His karmic authority fully confirmed by these recoveries, Nyangrel then engages in further ritual practice to accelerate and intensify the process. As a result the ground to the left of the throne collapses and reveals a series of treasure caskets bearing several of what would become Nyangrel's most renowned cycles:

> After offering a feast they made supplications. Within an aperture in the rock that had opened up was a treasure casket of sacred doctrine from which emerged doctrinal cycles of the Great Compassionate One, of the Secret Ḍākinī (Mkha' 'gro gsang), and of the Guru Vidyādhara (Bla ma rig 'dzin), together with the auxiliary instructions for each individual cycle.[220]

The first of these later became renowned as the *Maṇi Kambum* that cemented Avalokiteśvara as the patron deity of Tibet, and the latter two may be ancestors of the *Fierce Black Lady* (*Khro ma nag mo*) and *Fierce Guru* (*Gu ru drag po*), which have been transmitted within the lineages of Mindröling Monastery especially and continue to be attributed to Nyangrel. While such doctrinal cycles focusing on soteriological praxis would remain among the most prevalent genres of treasure texts, they are by no means the only type of trea-

219. *Zangs gling ma* A, 133.6; H, 99b.1. Ḍākinī scripts are said to mystically compress and encrypt entire cycles onto a single or several small scrolls, which the revealer then expands into a complete, ordinarily legible Tibetan text. The cooperation of the destined revealer's karma with their enlightened awareness functions as a cipher to decrypt the code, thus enabling him or her to download the text from the expanse of enlightened awareness and transcribe it to the page in Tibetan. A few lines of code may then expand into several volumes of text written in standard Tibetan script (see Gyatso 1998, 172–74).

There have yet to be any systematic studies of ḍākinī scripts, but this would prove quite difficult because, for one, the scripts defy systematization. They are irregular across the spectrum of treasure revealers and their recovered materials. According to tradition this is precisely the point: they must be legible only to their destined revealer, so scripts that can be read by anyone must be excluded as examples of ḍākinī script. Indic ornamental scripts such as Ranjana, Vartu, and Lañdza appear on the title pages or to visually mark sections in many Tibetan texts, treasures included, but these should not be mistaken for ḍākinī scripts. Similarly, another common error is to mistake the *visarga* following Tibetan reproductions of some Sanskritic syllables, as after the invocation É ma hoḥ, for treasure marks.

220. *Dri ma med pa*, 97.6–98.2.

sures recovered by Nyangrel, who finds an array of texts and relics in subsequent caskets.

Liturgies relating to the local protectors emerge first, which are followed by cycles of the greatest soteriological value to mark the climax of the recovery. As the extensive recovery at Drak Sinmo Barjé begins to wind down, Nyangrel discovers diverse items with a variety of powers, purposes, and functions:

> From within a siddhi treasure casket emerged the bone ornaments of Guru Padmasambhava and his consort; the top part of a Namshel Karmo statue; a *sen* statue of a red-faced *rākṣasa*; *gandharva* pills and seven-births pills; the five transgressive substances (*pañca*[*makāra*]); red arsenic powder (*sindūra*); pills made from the soil of twenty-four sacred places; a hand-scoop *kapāla*, and so forth. Furthermore, a gold empowerment vase with undried water, a *ḍamaru* drum, trumpets of men's and women's thigh bones, a *kīla* dagger, vajra, bell, and so forth arrived.
>
> From within a multicolored leather casket, general doctrines, longer and shorter histories of the doctrine, inconceivable doctrinal cycles of questions and answers, and countless site certificates for treasures that existed elsewhere arrived. From within a black leather casket emerged life-saving medicines, evil mantras that kill, mechanized slingshots, long-range arrows—countless tools that benefit or harm.[221]

This is the most detailed inventory of Nyangrel's nontextual thaumaturgical treasures provided in either of his biographies. They are categorized as "beneficial" or "harmful" according more to their active use rather than their passive substance, as the category to which each treasure belongs is ultimately determined by their application, just as medicine can heal when administered correctly and kill when not. Many of the beneficial treasures are consecrated substances imbued with blessings, some of which are for consumption. In this instance Nyangrel uncovers a veritable pharmacopeia stocked with various pills (*ril bu*) of special provenance, with many items pertaining to the healing arts as well. Other treasures might be distributed in rituals to consecrate, empower, protect, and/or provoke realization, or they might be kept as potent talismans to magnetize positive circumstances and/or to ward off danger. In contrast, "harmful" treasures comprise an arsenal of weapons that may inflict harm through being wielded directly in combat, more subtly as through

221. *Dri ma med pa*, 98.2–99.2.

poisoning, or symbolically by means of ritually effected transference. Rituals for manipulating the relative world remain among the professional repertoires of tantric adepts today, and many tools of this trade are found among the contents of Nyangrel's caches. Thaumaturgy is his bread and butter before treasure recovery proves to be a more sustainable and lucrative profession, and he may have continued performing such rites throughout his life.[222] These items recovered as treasure would be considered especially potent, as they would increase the efficacy of any activity that relied on them and thus the prestige of anyone who wielded them as well.[223]

Finally, it is important to note that historical materials are found amid the caches at Drak Sinmo Barjé, which are also considered treasure despite their lack of any explicit thaumaturgical or soteriological purpose. Since these "histories of Buddhism" (*chos 'byung*) are drawn from the penultimate casket of multicolored leather, they are considered less valuable according to both the chronological and material hierarchies of this treasure recovery process. The *Stainless Proclamations* gives no indication of their extent nor content and makes no reference to the two elaborate narratives attributed to Nyangrel, the *Copper Island* and the *Essence of Flowers*, though we shall see in the next chapter that a section unique to the *Essence of Flowers* refers to Nyangrel's *Copper Island* as a history of Buddhism. Furthermore, the *Essence of Flowers* has never been considered a treasure even if it reproduces much treasure material. Since the *Copper Island* is as definitively a treasure text as much as the *Essence of Flowers* is not, only the former is a candidate for inclusion among these histories of Buddhism found as treasure.

Despite being so vague as to deny identification, these histories would be the only possible candidates for the *Copper Island* within Nyangrel's biographies; no mention of that text or anything that could resemble it is made else-

222. Prior to Nyangrel's treasure recoveries in the *Clear Mirror*, he completes two thread-cross rites (*mdos*) at the request of a patron (*Gsal ba'i me long*, 331). Thread crosses, consisting of sticks or dowels woven with geometric patterns of string or yarn, ensnare malevolent beings who have been fomenting difficulties at a specific location. The thread cross is then discarded with its captives at a crossroads so that those beings cannot find their way back. Such ritual detritus can still be found occasionally at the intersections of Tibetan areas, such as those around the Boudhanath stūpa in Kathmandu. See Blondeau 1990b, passim, and Nebesky-Wojkowitz 1956, 369–97.

223. There are also a number of statues described, though none of the representative images (*sku tshab*) of Padmasambhava. A few that remain extant today are attributed to Nyangrel, but none are listed among his recoveries in either of his primary biographies, and once again it is Guru Chöwang who provides one of the earliest references to this particular type of treasure (*Skabs brgyad ma*, 26.2). For a photo of one such statue attributed to Nyangrel, see Thondup 1986, figure 1 (opposite 144).

where. However, a late contaminant in the preincarnation narratives in the *Stainless Proclamations* presents Nyangrel as referring readers to a *Great History of Buddhism* for details of Tri Songdetsen's reign, which would presumably be the *Copper Island* or the *Essence of Flowers*. This reference is absent from the correlate narratives within both the *Clear Mirror* and Guru Chöwang's *Eight Pronouncements*, thereby proving that it is among the latest contaminants to the preincarnation narratives and reflects a time when Nyangrel's Padmasambhava narrative was already well known. Since these historical treasures in the episode above include the same (albeit prominent) historical genre as the contaminant, this invites scrutiny as to whether the discovery of historical treasures is merely a contaminant as well.[224] In sum, both the redactional provenance of these historical treasures within Nyangrel's biographies as well as their content remains unknown, but the documentation of their discovery may suggest that some of the old texts Nyangrel sourced for his narratives were considered treasure and thus retained a special valuation as well.

Having recovered all the treasures listed in the cache certificate bestowed by the yogin, all those listed in the supplemental certificate that was found onsite, and even treasures in addition to those, Nyangrel is satisfied that all of the treasures have been found at Drak Sinmo Barjé and prepares to properly conclude the process of his first recovery. Although the *Stainless Proclamations* claims to reproduce the text of the initial cache certificate "in detail," the biography now divulges instructions that had not been disclosed previously:

> Then, just as prescribed in the cache certificate, he excellently made

224. Cf. Doney 2014, 14 and n68. Doney takes these general references to histories among Nyangrel's treasure recoveries to be supporting evidence that the *Essence of Flowers*, if not the *Copper Island* itself, is cited in the *Stainless Proclamations*. His argument hinges on this biography's mention of a *Great History of Buddhism* (*Chos 'byung chen mo* at *Dri ma med pa*, 10.2) because this historical genre, *chos 'byung*, is a component of the title for the *Essence of Flowers* and for later, more elaborate titles of the *Copper Island* as well. While summarizing his past life as Emperor Tri Songdetsen in the *Stainless Proclamations*, "Nyangrel" directs his audience to his own work if they desire to know more about the period.

It is telling, however, that this reference does not appear in the equivalent preincarnation narrative in *Gsal ba'i me long*, 282.4–283.2, which is much shorter and less elaborate, and this reference is indeed absent in Guru Chöwang's repeated narration of his and Nyangrel's shared preincarnations throughout the *Eight Pronouncements* as well. Rather than demonstrating an early reference to either of Nyangrel's narratives, Doney provides further evidence for my argument (Hirshberg 2012, 27–30 and 51–54; reiterated above on pages 80–81) that the *Stainless Proclamations* is only the latest recension of these narratives, which did not originate with Nyangrel but with Guru Chöwang. This reference to *Chos 'byung chen mo* in the *Stainless Proclamations* is clearly one of the most recent manipulations of the preincarnation narratives and therefore is the most distanced from whatever comprised the original.

Figure 6. This contemporary statue of Padmasambhava is the central figure on the second floor of Samyé Monastery. According to the head khenpo at Samyé, a *kutsap* statue of Padmasambhava recovered by Nyangrel is installed at its heart center. Photo by the author, 2011.

> a treasure substitute. After opening the treasure aperture, he first made a vast thanksgiving to the treasure-protecting ḍākinīs and *drekpa*, and then after opening the maṇḍala of the Great Compassionate One, Nyangrel practiced and beheld the divine assembly of Avalokiteśvara that pacifies transmigrators. After opening the maṇḍala of the [Secret] Ḍākinī and practicing it, he beheld the divine assembly of subjugating ḍākinīs. And finally, by practicing the Guru himself, he beheld his form together with his ornaments.[225]

Having taken so much from the site, the cache certificate recommends that Nyangrel leave a substitute in place of the treasures he removed, which becomes a "postrequisite" for later treasure revealers. Not a novel idea even in Nyangrel's time, substitutes or replacements are described in the biography of the great Bönpo treasure revealer Shenchen Luga (tenth century).[226] Given Tibetan religion's proclivity for animism and its concerns about upsetting any of the malignant entities roaming the landscape, an idea integral to indigenous beliefs is that an item of value must be left in exchange when something is extracted from the natural environment.

In order to ritually conclude the recovery and depart the site, Nyangrel must practice each liturgy in the order that it was found. He begins by arranging an extensive offering for the treasure protectors by relying on the propitiatory rites discovered to the right of the maṇḍala within his first cache of texts. He then proceeds through each of the major soteriological cycles, not just reciting them but showing signs of attainment specifically related to each and thus demonstrating once again that he possesses a profound connection to these teachings cultivated over several lifetimes. He masters them and so becomes master of them, the adept who is destined to retrieve and reintroduce these doctrines to the world. As he begins to do so, the *Stainless Proclamations* relates that he quickly attracts disciples while withholding the most secret instructions in accord with tantric protocol concerning the circulation of esoteric doctrines.

Nyangrel's second treasure recovery occurs in Pearl Crystal Cave at Juniper Ridge (Mu tig shel gyi spa ma gong). The exact location is somewhat obscure, but the *Blue Annals* record that Mutik was among the sites in Lhodrak where a Drigung Kagyü center was established, and it is also listed alongside the Kharchu hermitage, probably the renowned imperial-era Chakpurchen, which lies

225. *Dri ma med pa*, 99.2–5.

226. Martin 2001, 84.

in the mountains near Khomting temple.[227] If this is correct, then Mutik is also very much within Nyangrel's home region, and a pattern clearly emerges in which Nyangrel relied on the area that was most familiar to him for his treasure recoveries.

Upon arriving at Mutik no further tests, trials, or complications induced by local protectors challenge his authority, therefore it seems that his first recovery at Drak Sinmo Barjé was sufficient to prove that Nyangrel was the destined treasure revealer for all of his caches. Moreover, he no longer relies on aides, human or otherwise, or even on additional certificates for clues to the locations of treasure caches, since all he could need were found at Drak Sinmo Barjé. In the *Stainless Proclamations*, the first major recovery really is the watershed moment in Nyangrel's karmic evolution from Tri Songdetsen to enlightened treasure revealer. The ḍākinīs and protectors now welcome his arrival at each site, and the treasures emerge without hindrance or delay:

> While practicing at Mutik Shelgyi Pamagong at dawn on the eighth day of the first month of autumn, the ḍākinīs of the four lineages arrived in vivid splendor and circumambulated Lady Tsogyal.[228] They placed doctrines of ḍākinī transmission cycles in a red leather casket and doctrines of the seven secrets, the heart scrolls of the ḍākinīs, in a copper locket. After bending a rod of gold into a swastika, they placed it at Nyangrel's heart. Having entrusted a book-box of 108 questions and answers to Nyangrel, he prostrated and the ḍākinīs bestowed the four vase empowerments.[229] Having inserted their tongues into his mouth, they bestowed the four secret empowerments. Having inserted his secret vajra into their most intimate spaces, they conferred the four insight-gnosis empowerments. Having directed the threatening gesture toward his heart and thereby introduced the instructions of the precious Word

227. Roerich 1949, 695 and 953.

228. Nor brang o rgyan 2008, 520: the ḍākinīs of the four lineages are: white ḍākinīs of great bliss (*bde chen dkar mo*), golden ḍākinīs accomplishing benefit (*ser mo don grub*), various red ḍākinīs (*dmar mo sna tshogs*), and variegated perfected ḍākinīs (*sna tshogs mthar phyin ma*).

229. A recension of a treasure attributed to Nyangrel and bearing a similar title to this text remains extant. Kunsang 2008, 157–66, translates an excerpt from the *Questions and Answers of the Lady* [*Tsogyal*] (*Jo mo zhus lan*). Kunsang 1990, 1994, and 2008 translate several other treasure excerpts attributed to Nyangrel, several of which are drawn from Jamgön Kongtrul's nineteenth-century *Rin chen gter mdzod*. Their transmission is unknown.

> empowerment, they initiated him. After bestowing prophecies, the ḍākinīs departed into the sky.[230]

The mere presence of Nyangrel in meditation at Mutik magnetizes the ḍākinīs and inspires them to relinquish their quarry. Compared with the initial episode, treasure recovery is now effortless and automatic: Nyangrel is neither an agent nor even a "revealer" but one to whom the treasures are revealed. Once bestowed, the ḍākinīs proceed with an escalating regimen of empowerments that become explicitly sexual in nature. Nyangrel first shows deference to Lady Tsogyal and her retinue of ḍākinīs who reply by bestowing the vase empowerments. Having met in the consecration of this coronation rite symbolizing the elevation of Nyangrel as their equal, the ḍākinīs osculate (make out with him) as a means of transmitting the secret empowerments. This foreplay progresses into the third empowerment, which typically authorizes the manipulation of the channels, winds, and drops (*rtsa lung thig le*) in the practice of sexual yoga, so the ḍākinīs confer that authority with direct experience by engaging him in intercourse. The climax of the ceremony occurs when the ḍākinīs direct the threatening *mudrā* at him in their delivery of the fourth empowerment, the introduction to reality itself. Nyangrel thereby becomes empowered as an experienced lineage holder such that the transmission of these cycles remains unbroken and legitimate.

Though the eroticism of this second recovery is striking, the description of Nyangrel's third recovery at Samyé Monastery is spectacular in its own way. There is a slight delay to recovering the cache concealed there, but it is so effortlessly and definitively overcome that it may not be regarded as an obstacle at all. As in his first treasure recovery at Drak Sinmo Barjé, obstacles tend to be personified by entities with a propensity for violence, but the only hindrance in this episode is a basic human reluctance to relinquish something precious:

> After arriving at Samyé Nyangrel went to the plain of the main temple and instantaneously recollected fifteen prior births like a reflection dawning in a mirror. Having made the offering that completely purifies all appearance and existence to Samyé's religious representations, rainbow tents gathered and a great rain of flowers fell. Nyangrel declared to the sacristan, "Open the door! I wish to prostrate to the representations!" But the ruler of the region, the Samyé Tsepo, said, "Since this person is a treasure revealer and wants to remove the treasures, don't open the gates! If he takes out the treasures, the

230. *Dri ma med pa*, 99.5–100.6.

> vitality of the place will be lost, and it will be inauspicious."[231] The gatekeepers securely guarded them, so the lama Nyangrel said, "Well then, since I am the real lord of glorious Samyé, if the gates will not open, they indeed must be securely guarded!" After producing four physical manifestations of himself, one sat on the Dharma throne [made from] the roots of medicinal *yobok* trees and preached publicly while the other three manifestations walked on the three circumambulation routes of the triple-storied temple. No one could believe it! Wherever they looked, outside or in, they saw manifestations of Nyangrel. Once faith arose in the Tsepo and all the subjects, they handed over all the keys to the treasuries.[232]

Nyangrel's arrival at Samyé functions as a mnemonic that induces the recollection of his past lives, since this was the temple commissioned by his primary preincarnation, Emperor Tri Songdetsen, and thus is quite literally the foundation of Nyangrel's life. It is to this life that he refers when identifying himself as the "real lord of Samyé," and it was here that his karmic connection to the treasures was forged in the presence of Padmasambhava himself. Specifically due to that very karma, latent yet potent for four centuries, Nyangrel has returned to these gates again. This is the culmination of the karmic teleology that drove the process of reincarnation over sixteen catenate lifetimes; his recollection of them upon arrival confirms the magnitude of the moment. Tri Songdetsen and Nyangrel are distanced by time but neither continuum nor title: this is the sovereign's return to glorious Samyé. Foremost among the treasures discovered here are seven additional sādhanas related to the *Eight Instructions* and cycles concerning the Great Perfection.

This is the final recovery narrated in the *Stainless Proclamations*; following it is a summary of sites and an inventory of the treasures recovered by Nyangrel throughout his career, including those detailed in the narratives that precede this section. Drak Sinmo Barjé is again highlighted as an especially important cache, but "the temples of Kharchu, Bumthang, Khawo Gangsang, Samyé, Chimphu, and so forth" are explicitly mentioned as well. Khawo Gangsang is obscure, but all the other cache locations are a short journey from Nyangrel's home.[233] Of interest for the following chapters is a concluding reiteration that

231. For a lineal history of the *Bsam yas btsad po*, see the autobiography of their descendant, Khro phu Lo tsā ba Byams pa dpal (1173–1225): *Byams pa dpal gyi rnam thar 'khri shing ma*, TBRC W1CZ1880.

232. *Dri ma med pa*, 100.6–101.6.

233. *Dri ma med pa*, 102.2–4. Only adding to the mystery of Kha bo gang bzang's location,

Figure 7. Some of the contents of Samyé's relic cabinet. Many were discovered as treasures but others are said to have been directly bequeathed. At top left is Padmasambhava's seal; left of center is the skull relic of Śāntarakṣita. Photo by the author, 2011.

Nyangrel found historical treasures; two genres are specified, histories of Buddhism (*chos 'byung*) and chronicles (*lo rgyus*), again suggesting the possibility that the historical narratives attributed to him, or at least elements of them, were recovered as treasure, or perhaps he used some of the "outlines" (*khog dbub* [*'bubs*]) of these treasures to structure them.[234]

In reviewing Nyangrel's treasure career in the *Stainless Proclamations*, there is a linear progression: beginning as a karmically destined but untested adept, he matures into a treasure revealer replete with signs of attainment. The transition is quite steep in this account, since as soon as he succeeds in the trials at Drak Sinmo Barjé, his recovery of the treasures continues virtually unobstructed from site to site. This is quite distinct from the narrative within the *Clear Mirror*, which describes an alternating process of challenges and successes, obstacles and breakthroughs, that define his emergence as the great treasure revealer.

Karmay 1972, 110, cites an unidentified prophecy text that predicts the arrival of a blessed emanation in "Khar bo gang bzang shar mgul."

234. *Dri ma med pa*, 103.6.

Treasure Recovery Narratives in the Clear Mirror

Unlike the *Stainless Proclamations*, the *Clear Mirror* describes Nyangrel as recovering his treasures independently, and no retinue of disciples or anyone else accompanies him. As the reincarnation of Tri Songdetsen, Nyangrel is the only one who possesses the karma to recover the treasures, and all others are excluded from the process. The *Clear Mirror* often presents these narratives explicitly in the first person and thereby accentuates his singular responsibility, but his solitary pursuit still relies on a series of fortuitous meetings with special individuals who aid the approach to his quarry.

His aforementioned encounter with the yogin—a magical emanation of Padmasambhava who bestows certificates—initiates the process, but Nyangrel will need more help to succeed in his first recovery at Drak Sinmo Barjé. He follows the directions provided by the yogin and, perhaps with the aid of other certificates previously received, locates the rock described by him. Like the *Stainless Proclamations* this initial information is not sufficient to recover the treasures:

> After arriving at the base of Drak Sinmo Barjechen, I looked around and found a rock resembling a lion leaping into the sky, but the treasure did not appear by rapping on it with a chisel. According to the site certificate, a sound like the call of a cuckoo should have been emitted, but this did not occur.[235]

As in the former account, Nyangrel's first major recovery is stymied by his inability to locate the precise boulder described in the cache certificate. He finds one that seems to resemble it, but Nyangrel does not hear "a sound like the call of a cuckoo" when tapping the stone with his chisel, perhaps the telltale sign of its concealing a hollow space within. Having failed to find the correct rock, Nyangrel beds down for the night, resolving to wait for daylight to resume his search anew.

Later that night Nyangrel has another encounter that is symbolically weighty even if its exact significance is unclear. The vivid entities and their appearance are given no further commentary or context, and yet their dramatic arrival and the instructions they bestow result in Nyangrel's first major treasure recovery in the *Clear Mirror*.

235. *Gsal ba'i me long*, 338.1–2.

> That evening at dusk, I was staying at the mouth [of a cave] shaped like a bell near a pool shaped like a fish when five threatening (*dmar po*) horsemen intermingled with four friendly (*zla'o*) horsemen materialized. The one deftly leading a vicious dog said, "Through good fortune a white horse has come to possess a tiger-pelt box and a leopard-pelt box. If, having taken off your hat and placed it atop the boulder, you prostrate and wish for the siddhis of the profound doctrine, you will find them within these [boxes]. Then an apparition who is said to be the magical emanation of the treasure protector will appear offering two leather boxes."[236]

The dog-handling horseman directs Nyangrel to a boulder and suggests that he perform a sequence of idiosyncratic actions that, once followed, will result in the emergence of his initial treasure containers. As it is inconceivable that someone would otherwise know to perform this precise series of actions at this random place, these movements function like a kinetic code that adds an additional layer of security for the cache. Nyangrel presumably completes the sequence as instructed before leaving Drak Sinmo Barjé. Then:

> When daybreak arose I departed. On the roadside I encountered a woman loading a white jenny with two huge sacks. The woman asked, "Venerable one, what doctrine do you know? Should I give you one or something else?" In reply I requested a doctrine, and that woman revealed a small tiger-pelt casket from within one huge sack and announced, "Inside this are the profound instructions" and dropped it into my lap. "Upon reaching the new year I will return again." Then she snuck up from behind and clocked me with a garland of skulls such that I was knocked unconscious for a while. As soon as I came to I looked around, but that woman was gone, and though I searched later I did not find her. I inquired in other areas, but there was no one who had seen her. It is said she was actually Lady Tsogyal.[237]

In the previous evening's encounter, the rider confided that a "white horse" would be bearing treasure caskets, and Nyangrel meets a woman loading a

236. *Gsal ba'i me long*, 338.2–5. B 121.5 reads *bse* (leather/hide/pelt) instead of *gser sgam* (golden box) to describe the treasure boxes, which syncs with the pelts predicted by the rider above as well as that which will soon be received below.

237. *Gsal ba'i me long*, 338.5–339.4.

white female donkey that seems to fit the description. Taking a brusque tone from the start, the woman peppers Nyangrel with a couple questions before bestowing a single casket in answer to his request, then she coldcocks him as a farewell. Just as the initial yogin he meets is identified as Padmasambhava in person, this woman is said to be Lady Tsogyal; thus there is a degree of correlation between the preliminary encounter and the first actual treasure recovery here. The *Clear Mirror* proceeds with a strong sense of continuity, both karmically and thematically, and yet it will become evident that he is missing half of his quarry: the woman makes no mention of the leopard-skin casket, and despite her promise to return in a year, both her and the latter treasure casket soon drop from the narrative. Nyangrel then returns to "the hatted boulder" at Drak Sinmo Barjé, locates the cache within it, and inventories his first major treasure recovery, including the contents of the tiger-pelt casket handed to him by the woman. As in his first major recovery in the *Stainless Proclamations*, this cache contains several of what would become his most renowned cycles, such as those of the Great Compassionate One, Secret Ḍākinī, and Fierce Guru, as well as an array of thaumaturgical and ritual items. He then returns to Mawochok to perform a three-year retreat on the Great Compassionate One.

Some time after the conclusion of this meditative sojourn, Nyangrel's next recovery begins with an obstacle and once again progresses through a chance encounter that may be the most mundane of all those described in either of his biographies. This occurs at Khomting, one of the original border-taming temples commissioned by Emperor Songtsen Gampo that was established on the southern limits of Tibet near Bhutan. Directed to Khomting in the initial certificates, Nyangrel now ventures farther south from Mawochok, past Drak Sinmo Barjé, to Khomting, where he confronts the same problem as before: he cannot locate the cache described in the certificate.

> Upon arriving at Khomting temple, among the twenty-one treasure cavities on the back of the Vairocana statue that were attested in the site manual, the center one did not appear. While returning up the road from Khomting, I was stuck behind several merchants when one of them addressed me, saying, "Last night I was circumambulating the temple and happened to find a finger from a statue, so I kept it. Yogin, are you going up or down?" I replied, "I can go wherever." The merchant said, "If you go back down, please take this to the temple," and the statue's forefinger was proffered.[238]
>
> At those words, I stowed it away carefully and went back down

238. *Gsal ba'i me long*, 340.6–341.3.

> toward Khomting. When I reached the area of Khotöser Lake, a dog ambushed me, and I fell into an irrigation channel. I stripped my sash into bandages and discovered that the statue's finger had crumbled. In finding a scroll among the fragments, the site manual emerged. With that in hand I returned to Khomting, but the sacristan would not open the door. I gave him a bribe of one gold coin, [entered, and] welcomed a great treasure cache from the back of the Vairocana statue. In the treasure repository were two caskets, one dark burgundy and the other grey. From within the burgundy casket emerged six small volumes containing 130 distinct works of doctrine: the mother and child tantric scriptures of the *Eight Instructions: Gathering of the Ones Gone to Bliss* and many abridged liturgies condensed into scrolls.[239]

This is the more famous account concerning Nyangrel's recovery of the *Eight Instructions*, which contradicts the account in the *Stainless Proclamations* of its bestowal from Lama Rashak. A correlation, however, is the small size of the original compendium as contrasted by the thirteen-volume editions of Nyangrel's *Eight Instructions* that exist today.[240] Also of interest here is the cache's location within a massive imperial-era statue, since Tibetans, whether Buddhist or Bönpo, have inserted religious texts, relics, and assorted offerings within stūpas, statues, and other representations as part of consecration rites for centuries. These treasures at Khomting are described as old manuscripts taken from an object in which such items were customarily placed.[241]

In the *Clear Mirror* this recovery at Khomting is the final episode that fully narrates Nyangrel's treasure recoveries; only succinct summaries are provided thereafter. The latter discoveries include his third major recovery at Samyé that primarily consists of Great Perfection scriptures, thereby corroborating some details of this cache and its contents as described in the *Stainless Proclamations*. The *Clear Mirror* is more specific, however, in that it distinguishes these Great Perfection treasures with a doxographical rubric that was

239. *Gsal ba'i me long*, 341.3–342.1.

240. One of Nyangrel's original *Eight Instructions* volumes was allegedly preserved at Mawochok, which may have been the one attested by Ngari Paṇchen Pema Wangyal (1487–1582), but it was destroyed in the Cultural Revolution (Gyatso 1986, 33n44). More recently Dudjom Rinpoche (1907–84) claimed to retain one of the original volumes with other Nyangrel treasures in his private collection (Tulku Thondup, personal communication, 2010). One such kīla-dagger, or *phur pa*, is pictured in Thondup 1986, plate 8.

241. Martin 2001, 19n9.

Figure 8 (left). "Temple of Khoting at Lhakhang Dzong," photograph by Hugh E. Richardson, 1950 (detail). Copyright Pitt Rivers Museum, University of Oxford, 2001.59.4.37.1.

Figure 9 (right). "Image of Vairocana at Khoting temple at Lhakhang," photograph by Hugh E. Richardson, 1950. Copyright Pitt Rivers Museum, University of Oxford, 2001.59.4.36.1.

touted by Nyangrel but failed to gain traction more broadly (though in some transmissions, such as *Black Ultra Pith*, it persists to the present). While the Atiyogayāna of the Great Perfection had already come to be regarded as the apex of esoteric Buddhist theory and praxis among twelfth-century proponents of Nyingma, Nyangrel promoted a hierarchy that placed Ati or Transcendent Pith beneath Crown Pith (*spyi ti*), Ultra Pith (*yang ti*), and Direct Transcendence (*thod rgal*); Nyangrel seems to have held the Crown Pith in especially high esteem.[242] As in India, newer traditions relied on supersessionary rhetoric to degrade those that preceded them as less powerful, less expedient, less profound, and so forth, and Nyangrel adopted the same strategy to promote these new classifications of the Great Perfection.

Collection and Compilation, Augmentation and Fabrication

Having thoroughly reviewed all of Nyangrel's treasure recoveries in his primary biographies, which are among the earliest and most elaborate sources detailing Buddhist treasure recovery, it is clear that every single treasure

242. *Gsal ba'i me long*, 342.5 and 356.6–357.1. Also see Germano 2005, 22.

described therein is material and withdrawn from a physical place of concealment.[243] Categories such as earth treasure (*sa gter*) are not used because such a designation is redundant and unnecessary. Additionally, the association of material treasures with the ground that bore them would soon carry a pejorative sense that would be employed in the critiques of opponents who derided the treasures as "earth Dharmas" (*sa chos*), thereby acknowledging their content as Buddhist in nature but inferior.[244] This attitude may reflect Indic if not indigenous notions of immaculacy and contamination, where vaunted items such as scriptures should be distanced from the ground and things associated with it, which are considered impure.

At this stage of treasure recovery, whether Bönpo or Buddhist, there were few precedents for the immaterial treasures that became so prevalent and definitive of treasure in later centuries.[245] The terminological antecedent for "treasures of exalted mind," *thukter* (*thugs gter*), appears in some concluding summaries in the final chapter of the *Clear Mirror*,[246] and it is also used within the main narrative of the primary biography when the mysterious yogin, the catalyst for Nyangrel's treasure career, bestows several certificates to Nyangrel and directs him toward two sites. The correlate recovery narrative describes exclusively material items drawn from real places of concealment, so when the yogin exclaims, "É ma! How totally amazing! In those two places there really are profound doctrines, treasures of exalted mind (*thugs gter*), pure cycles, that were concealed by Master Padmasambhava," this appositive list indicates actual material texts alone.[247] This "exalted mind" refers to the enlightened

243. Early in the *Clear Mirror* a "sky treasure" is described as the source of the *Four Great Origins of Mañjuśrī* (*Gsal ba'i me long*, 237.5–6), but this appears in the opening chapters of the text that are among the later additions to his primary biography. Furthermore, this instance of sky treasure is not even found by Nyangrel but another revealer. The coda to his treasure career also mentions a sky treasure, but its materiality or lack thereof is not clearly defined. The term corresponds to some later and more elaborate rubrics where treasures are categorized by their place of concealment among the five elements, the fifth being sky or space (*nam mkha'*). None appear within the narratives of Nyangrel's recoveries themselves; all are material and are drawn from terrestrial caches.

244. See the translation of Jikten Gönpo's critique in Martin 2001, 157.

245. Martin's 2001 analysis of the Bön treasure tradition also limits their recoveries to the material. In general there are far more correlates between Nyangrel's methods and the Bönpo practice of treasure recovery than between Nyangrel and the later Buddhist treasure tradition that counts him as one of its earliest and most important proponents.

246. Nyangrel "entrusts his instructions of the great exalted-mind treasures" to his disciples at the end of his life (*Gsal ba'i me long*, 356.2), and "the teachings of the great treasures of exalted mind spread like the sun dawning in the sky" after his death (361.5).

247. *Gsal ba'i me long*, 336.5.

awareness of Padmasambhava himself, the original source of those instructions; it does not refer to a recovery method that relies on immaterial compression and direct download; there is no evidence that such had been conceived in Nyangrel's time. Padmasambhava's concealments in the *Copper Island* do not insinuate anything but material treasures, actual physical objects, and no prediction is made for their discovery anywhere but from their terrestrial caches. In short, treasure for Nyangrel was uniformly analog; "security measures" such as mantric cryptography had been prevalent for centuries in India,[248] and some indigenous antecedents may have already been in development in Tibet, but there is no question that the advanced technologies utilizing the compression, encryption, storage, downloading, and decoding of Dharma data, which together would enable the revelation of immaterial treasures of exalted mind (*dgongs gter*), had yet to be designed. Whereas Nyangrel's biographies and narratives present all treasures under the single category of analog materiality, Guru Chöwang defines several subtypes in his *Great History of the Treasures* that introduce a new degree of diversity and categorization, inviting a shift toward immaterial treasures and thereby taking a momentous step forward in the methodology of treasure recovery.[249]

The most prominent verb associated with the discovery of Tibetan Buddhist

248. White 2003, 243.

249. Foremost among Guru Chöwang's distinctions are treasures of exalted body, speech, and mind (*sku gsung thugs kyi gter*) (*Gter 'byung chen mo*, 87.5). Some of their subcategories, however, as well as a fourth and final type of treasure especially, begin to introduce the possibility of the immaterial. Guru Chöwang primarily defines treasures of exalted body as physical representations of a buddha's form, such as statues, but he also describes one that "arises as a pure appearance from the compassionate mind of the disciple" (87.7). Akin to a visionary or oneiric encounter where a subject perceives the form of a deity, this "treasure" constitutes an experience and a revelation, and yet nothing but the memory of the event is retained. By contrast, Nyangrel's treasures always signify a material quarry to be carried offsite. Guru Chöwang therefore introduces a classification for an immaterial type of treasure, but since this pure appearance does not result in an actual object of any kind, it remains quite distinct from the exalted-mind treasures of the later tradition, where legible texts are ultimately produced. Guru Chöwang groups scriptures under the category of exalted speech treasures, whereas exalted-mind treasures are physical objects, such as stūpas, that symbolize enlightened awareness.

Following these treasures of exalted body, speech, and mind, Guru Chöwang introduces a fourth and final type of treasure that he defines as "treasures that ascertain the true essence, the nature of reality," which functions as a final catch-all category that provides the broadest possible definition of the term *treasure* (96.6). He writes: "Since the root of all treasures is suchness . . . treasures are the exalted mind of the victors of the three times" (97.2–3), which seems to quite closely mirror the significance of *thugs gter* in Nyangrel's works. For Guru Chöwang this links all treasures to their ultimately immaterial original source while legitimating anything that is claimed to be treasure, thereby allowing for significant creativity both in the recovery of treasure texts and their contents. Perhaps in response to the scathing critiques levied against

Plate 1. Circa thirteenth-century thangka depicting Nyangrel's lineage of the Fierce Black Ḍākinī (*khros ma nag mo*) from the Chö (*gcod*) tradition, with Padmasambhava at top center and presumably Nyangrel at lower left. This is one of the oldest *thangka* paintings of Padmasambhava. Courtesy of the Shelley & Donald Rubin Collection: http://www.himalayanart.org/items/188.

Plate 2. Nyangrel's area of activity. Topographic image (maps.google.com; locations approximated based on Dorje 2009 and satellite imagery from Google Earth) of Lhodrak in south-central Tibet and northern Bhutan. Keeping to a relatively small and familiar area, most of Nyangrel's treasure sites were easily accessible by following the Tamshöl River, which is visible as a deep gorge running southwest from just below Mawochok, past Drak Sinmo Barjé, and all the way to Khomting temple near the border with Bhutan. Samyé was a longer trek to the north but also within a few days' journey.

Plate 3. (opposite) The Samyé valley from Hepo Hill, with the Copper Island of the Three Realms at far left and Samyé Monastery at right. Photo by the author, 2011.

Plate 4. The main temple at Lhodrak Kharchu, one of Nyangrel's treasure recovery sites. Photo by Gyurme Dorje, 1994.

Plate 5. The revered stūpas of Tukten Chorten and Tashi Öbar at Nyangrel's hermitage and residence, Mawachok, which contain the relics of Nyangrel and his son, Namkhapel. Photo by Gyurme Dorje, 1994.

treasures is "to reveal" (*ston*), but this is largely because it defines those who find them, the "treasure revealers" (*gter ston*). This compound appears in Nyangrel's biographies as well, yet the transitive use of the verb alone occurs only once within all of his recovery narratives.[250] An exhaustive analysis of the verbs used to describe treasure recovery in both biographies reveals that Nyangrel rarely "does" anything; the consistent use of intransitive sentence constructions mitigates his agency. He is literally omitted from the action and is merely the one present to directly receive the treasures when the time has come for them to emerge on their own. His agency is mostly limited to searching and digging, and yet even then it is the treasures that "emerge" from their cache rather than Nyangrel who actively removes them. The treasures may reveal themselves to Nyangrel, but only once does he actually "reveal" the treasures.[251]

Rather than a causal process of active revelation or production, these narratives underscore the fruitional karmic process of passive manifestation where the treasures simply appear to Nyangrel. The erosion of agency underscores the karmic context by which the treasures emerge, which is the fruition of Nyangrel's past life as Tri Songdetsen that is the driving force of

---

him, Guru Chöwang took it upon himself to devise a typology that would legitimate his textual production.

Doctor (2005, 23) has found some early occurrences of the term *dgongs gter* in the *Heart Essence of the Ḍākinīs*, which is attributed to Shangtön Tashi Dorjé (1097?–1167). This is preserved with Longchen Rabjampa's fourteenth-century *Four Parts of the Heart-Essence*, however, and the nature of its transmission is unclear.

250. *Gsal ba'i me long*, 342.5.

251. Between Nyangrel's two primary biographies, there are thirty-nine verbs that result in treasure recoveries. This tally only counts instances where the verb appears explicitly: preceding phrases to which a final verb distributes but remains merely implied are not included (though the ratio of intransitive to transitive verbs would be even greater in favor of the intransitive if they were). In total, only eleven distinct verb instances are transitive where Nyangrel (and/or his cabal in the *Stainless Proclamations*) function as agents. Four of these eleven constructions describe the manual labor of treasure recovery, which is digging or chiseling (*brus pa* at *Dri ma med pa*, 95.1, 97.3; *brkos pa* at 95.4; *bcod* at 99.2). The remainder are verbs that describe the transitive action of retrieval, such as "extracted" (*'don pa / bton pa* at *Dri ma med pa*, 95.3, 102.2; *Gsal ba'i me long*, 338.1); "unveiled" (*zhal phyes pa* at *Dri ma med pa*, 102.5) and "taken out" (*phung* at *Gsal ba'i me long*, 340.6); or "welcomed" (*gdan drangs* at *Gsal ba'i me long*, 341.6, 351.2), which is weak compared to the others.

In contrast, twenty-eight distinct verb instances rely on intransitive sentence constructions and therefore lack an agent even though their "revealer" is present. The treasures "emerge," (*byung* at *Dri ma med pa*, 96.3, 97.4, 99.2; *Gsal ba'i me long*, 338.2, 340.1, 340.2, 340.2, 340.3, 340.4, 340.5, 340.5, 341.1, 341.5, 342.1, 342.2, 342.3, 342.4); "arrive" (*byon* at *Dri ma med pa*, 98.2, 98.4, 98.5, 99.1, 103.3, 103.6, 103.6, 104.3) and "come forth" (*thon* at *Dri ma med pa*, 92.5, 94.3, 95.3) as the subjects of their own intransitive sentence constructions. (Note that duplicate page references here are distinct instances of the same verb on a single line.)

the narratives. While this form of causality is somewhat generic, meaning that it does not incorporate the more elaborate karmic theories and rubrics of the Abhidharma literature, it does promote the more fundamental Buddhist perspective that all appearances of the world are karmically produced, thus all experiences of the individual are direct manifestations of their own karma. In Buddhism the law of karmic cause and effect is natural law, a universal principle as fundamental as gravity, if not more so. As the reincarnation of Padmasambhava's patron, host, and heart disciple, Nyangrel lives as the product of very special conditions that effectuate very specific results. His recovery of the treasures has literally been lifetimes in the making, and as the inevitable fruition of that karmic process, their emergence to Nyangrel is not so supernatural as quintessentially natural.

Given all of his textual production, it is striking that neither of Nyangrel's biographies record him as ever committing a single letter to the page. Every piece of literature associated with him is found as treasure or at least defined as such; creative authorial agency is categorically denied, ignored, or expunged from his biographies. Nevertheless, given some of their innovative contents, it is difficult to deflect the critical suspicion that at least some of his treasures, or some components of his treasures, were authored by his own hand. Discussion of what this fabrication might constitute, however, has remained mostly accusatory: if any content is new rather than drawn from old material, the creative process of textual invention is portrayed as the fraudulent composition of apocrypha. While it is often true that "what is new legitimates itself as the old that has been forgotten,"[252] this dichotomy between the old and the new may be as simplistic and problematic as in/authenticity when applied to the Tibetan treasures.

When Western scholars began to consider a millennium of Tibetan treasure recovery, often with an emphasis on the exalted-mind treasures of more recent centuries, a widespread skepticism developed in response to the purported origins of the treasures as relics of the imperium, found as described. No matter how we dance around the issue rhetorically or methodologically in an attempt to circumvent a more direct and disrespectful repudiation of the tradition, it seems to be the case that many Western scholars believe that the treasures are false precisely in the way that many Tibetans believe them to be true. Their concealment by Padmasambhava and his contemporaries never occurred; their imperial-era origins are unfounded; and their contents are predominantly if not uniformly the fabrications of their revealers. Ignoring for a moment the Orientalist assumption of hermeneutical superiority embedded

252. Assmann 2006, 100.

in such views, textual analysis does tend to reveal that treasure texts very often bear the scripts, orthography, terminology, doctrinal trends, and "prophecies" of events from the era of their revelation rather then the time of their alleged concealment. Contemporary apologists emphasize that the ultimate nature of the treasures transcends the comprehension of ordinary minds, including those of Tibetologists, but even in light of such unchallengeable contentions, critical analysis does tend to undermine the origins of the treasures as traditionally attested. Nevertheless, it is as problematic to stigmatize the entire treasure tradition as "false" as it is to assume that all treasures deemed authentic by the tradition are "true" in every respect. Scholars like Janet Gyatso, Matthew Kapstein, and Ronald Davidson have succeeded in progressing the conversation beyond that simplistic dichotomy, but an assessment of Nyangrel's treasures invites the reconsideration of emic positions and the interjection of greater nuance into the in/authenticity debate.

By identifying several imperial and post-imperial fragments within Nyangrel's treasures, Cathy Cantwell and Robert Mayer have begun to prove that some early treasures were not just "what they pretend to be" but what they claim to be: texts compiled from the rediscovered folios of old manuscripts, some contents of which may have originated in the time of Padmasambhava or shortly thereafter.[253] Cantwell and Mayer focus on a Dunhuang manuscript titled *Supreme Pacification: The Concise Enlightened Activity of Transference* that precisely corresponds to a text preserved in each of Nyangrel's largest collections of the *Eight Instructions*, though under different titles.[254] Cantwell and Mayer conclude that "despite the slightly variant titles, there is no doubt that the text, from start to finish, is the same" and that "the only possibility is that Nyangrel found the text intact."[255] Elsewhere they discover that Nyangrel's

253. Kapstein 2000, 136, concludes with his commentary on the in/authenticity debate: "the treasures are not exactly what they pretend to be, and yet they flow inexorably from the depths of the Tibetan cultural and religious system. Every discovery is also a memory. The treasures are exactly what they pretend to be."

254. IOL Tib J 331 (III): *Zhi ba'i mchog 'pho ba'i 'phrin las bsdus pa*. In the Mtshams brag *Bka' brgyad*, its title is *Byin rlabs phun sum tshogs pa phur pa'i sgrub pa bi ma las mdzad pa zhi ba yon tan spo ba'i cho ga* (9.5: 351–65). In the Gangtok *Bka' brgyad*, the corresponding text, *Zhi ba'i mchog brtan g.yo ba'i cho ga* (9.3: 62.4–77.5), is contained within a compendium of related documents under a single title, *Byin rlabs phur pa'i sgrub pa*, all of which correspond to the practice of the meditation deity Vajrakīla. These same texts appear in sequence in the ninth volume of the Mtshams brag edition but are helpfully separated by title pages.

255. Mayer 2011a and 2011b. In comparing Nyangrel's treasure text to canonical Nyingma tantras that may have been available to him, Cantwell and Mayer note a correspondence between some of his Vajrakīla treasures and the *Perfection of Activities Tantra* (*'Phrin las phun sum tshogs pa'i rgyud*), but their analysis reveals that the shared material is presented in a different order

Copper Island reproduces a stanza of praise for Padmasambhava culled from another Dunhuang manuscript. Given the emendations evident within it, Cantwell and Mayer theorize that their tenth-century manuscript underwent at least two rounds of prior editing and copying, thus this stanza could have originated not long after Padmasambhava's visit to Tibet.[256]

While these are the first philological confirmations that some treasure elements were definitively drawn from old manuscripts, these surely are not the only examples of such correspondence. Is it so untenable to allow that some of his sources may have been drawn from hidden caches under special circumstances that, in the eyes of Nyangrel's biographers if not Nyangrel himself, relied on the unexpected intervention of mysterious personages and the direction of cryptic certificates, all of which would have been interpreted as the fruition of uniquely fortunate karma in a Tibetan Buddhist context? It is reasonable to conclude that some elements of Nyangrel's treasures were found as described in his biographies. At the very least, these correspondences prove that Nyangrel was not exclusively a fabricator of apocryphal scriptures and an artisan of fake relics but an excavator and editor of old manuscripts who incorporated excerpts if not whole texts into new collections such as the *Eight Instructions* and new narratives such as the *Copper Island*. Within the latter, Padmasambhava explicitly advises Tri Songdetsen to occupy himself with this very endeavor once he awakens in his future birth as the great treasure revealer:

> As the essence of wealth, copy the texts of the gurus, peruse and review them . . .
> As the essence of activity, copy the texts and give them to whoever wants them.[257]

Copying, perusal, and review are part and parcel of the methods of textual production that became known as treasure recovery. The intertextuality inherent in such methods reflects the standards of Tibetan tradency, where passages understood to be authoritative are copied from earlier exemplars into

---

and that Nyangrel's treasure is more faithful to the Dunhuang text than to any of these tantras that postdate it. They conclude that "we can safely dismiss the suggestion that Nyangrel might have taken out exactly the same sections and reordered them in exactly the same way as the Dunhuang text." Thus it appears that he found this old manuscript and directly incorporated it into the *Eight Instructions* as a treasure text.

256. Cantwell and Mayer 2012, 93.

257. *Zangs gling ma* H, 84a1 and 84b2.

new documents, a practice prevalent throughout Tibetan commentarial literature, historical narratives, and Nyangrel's treasures as well.

The full process of treasure recovery must have extended well beyond the excavations that initiated it, but this is rarely if ever implied, admitted, or described in the biographies of treasure revealers. Nyangrel's accounts of textual treasure recovery uniformly present their documents as whole, intact, ready to be read and practiced: in the Drak Sinmo Barjé recovery in the *Stainless Proclamations*, Nyangrel prepares to leave by practicing and displaying signs of accomplishment in each of the cycles he recovered, thereby strongly insinuating that the core sādhanas of these cycles were complete as recovered and so unmanipulated—at least when first practiced. Yet elsewhere the biography is careful to mention that supplemental yet indispensable rituals like empowerment rites were obtained from other sources, such as his mentor Ngödrup. Presumably these were previously recovered as treasures as well, or the language at least suggests that these ritual texts are considered treasures upon their transfer to Nyangrel, regardless of how they were originally constructed. Always sensitive to a critique of fabrication, treasure revealers consistently describe their quarry as found whole, but I suspect that while the early treasures signify material items extracted from hidden caches as a basis, this never precluded significant editorial work and compilation on the part of the revealer. A process of redaction and reformulation was a necessary step not in the initial excavation of a treasure but in its full revelation, which culminated in its reintroduction to the general populace. Some "fabrication" was an essential part of the treasure recovery process, even if its practice remained controversial. At least some early treasures do not warrant the general accusation of falsification leveled by many indigenous and academic critics.

Henk Blezer has demonstrated that Karma Lingpa (fourteenth century) excerpted available documents to construct parts of the *Liberation through Seeing in the Liminal State* (*Bar do thos 'grol*), a treasure text that helped carry Tibetan Buddhism into the Western mainstream with its translation as the *Tibetan Book of the Dead*.[258] This leads him to conclude that Karma Lingpa "should be regarded as a creative editor rather than as a visionary revealer of Padmasambhava's hidden teachings,"[259] but I would counter that these two designations are by no means mutually exclusive. In collaboration, these two operations adequately describe how early treasures were found and processed. The compilation and emendation of rediscovered sources, some of which were attributed to Padmasambhava, into new compendiums was by no means the

258. For biographies of this text and its translation, see Cuevas 2003 and Lopez 2011.

259. Blezer 2001, 302.

smoking gun of inauthenticity but was part and parcel of the process through which these texts were re/introduced. Likewise, Cathy Cantwell and Robert Mayer have demonstrated how Dudjom Rinpoché Jikdral Yeshé Dorjé (1904–87) synthesized an array of old materials with original writing to restore and complete a treasure cycle and document how he was compelled to do so by one of his own treasure-revealing teachers.[260] Clearly this method of textual recovery has both ancient precedent and recent practice and has been considered both legitimate and standard in many Buddhist communities for much of that span. And yet the collapse of this dexterous and elaborate process into a single moment of treasure "revelation" has invited suspicion and critique, which is ironic since such marvelous revelatory accounts are designed to dispel them.

As Ronald Davidson writes, "Their new rituals, doctrines, and narratives were not composed of whole cloth, but parts worked into new clothes, clothing that simultaneously revealed and concealed reality."[261] The treasures contain the potential to reveal the reality of their provenance because they preserve textual correspondences (and/or the lack thereof) that may be uncovered through textual analysis, but the treasures conceal reality in that the rather mundane elements of their fabrication are often obscured by fantastic origin narratives and selective if not falsified accounts of their recovery. Davidson appreciates that the treasures provided the opportunity for Tibetans to develop indigenous traditions, most especially the Great Perfection, but like Kapstein he expresses the assessment prevalent throughout much of the field of Tibetan Buddhist studies: the treasures are cultural relics and authentic as such, but most are apocryphal fabrications legitimated by historical fictions. This does not exclude the possibility that some treasures were found as described, but to date that evidence had been lacking. In a tradition steeped in skillful means, where activities that would be considered negative under most circumstances can be considered positive when intended for the benefit of others, anything is possible.

While many are apocrypha by definition, all of these treasure texts are Buddhist products and so retain a degree of authenticity as such. Those that are the most compelling philosophically or poetically, and those that best represent the tradition even as they transform it, tend to become vaunted as authentic scriptures regardless of how they originated. Documents that read as inspired by enlightened awareness and so inspire faith are reflexively legitimating, which seems to be as good a model for authentication as any. Indeed, there is strong precedent for this in India where among the valid sources of *buddhavacana*

260. Cantwell and Mayer 2010, 70–73.

261. Davidson 2005, 243.

according to the *Samādhi of Direct Encounter with the Buddhas of the Present*, a Mahāyāna sūtra dated to the second century, is the illumination of "inspired eloquence" (Skt. *pratibhāna*, Tib: *spobs pa*). Paul Harrison glosses this as "the ability to give voice to the truth on the spur of moment, often in public," but this certainly applies to the process of authorial composition in private as well. Despite being newly enunciated or written, these inspired products too are authentic *buddhavacana*.[262] With this the definition of a "treasure" becomes quite fluid, and that which separates a treasure text from other religious documents foremost depends on more specific claims concerning its manner of revelation.

Treasure revelation was one method for slipping the yoke of the Tibetan obsession with Indic pedigree and orthodoxy such that a genuinely Tibetan Buddhism, one adapted to the cultural constructs and needs of the Tibetan people, could evolve. As evidenced by the diverse cultural forms and philosophies of Buddhism prevalent in the world today, this indigenization, assimilation, and innovation of Buddhism over the long course of its history is definitive of Buddhism itself. As the first of the great Buddhist treasure revealers, Nyangrel employed his talents as an archaeologist, researcher, tradent, author, and tantric adept in his quest to reconstruct the shattered relics of his patrilineal and reincarnate inheritance, not only into cohesive collections of tantric praxis but into new perspectives on Tibet's collective past as well.

262. Harrison 2003, 124.

4. Drawing Honey from Historiography

HAVING THOROUGHLY PERUSED the methodologies and inventories of Nyangrel's treasure recoveries, the mode of textual production for which he is most renowned, the uniqueness of another text attributed to him can be appreciated: *Honey Nectar, the Essence of Flowers: A History of Buddhism* (*Chos 'byung me tog snying po'i sbrang rtsi'i bcud*). This would be the one text Nyangrel did *not* reveal as treasure. Instead its four codas repeatedly claim that Nyangrel relied upon a more conventional process of historiographical research and recomposition to write the *Essence of Flowers*, even when treasure texts are explicitly cited among its sources.

The cover page of its oldest recension is blank, and the history thus appears to have originally been title-less.[263] Its present title was extracted at some later date from a poetic stanza in the prologue that functions as a kind of "introphon." This explains the title's nine-syllable meter, relative dearth of grammatical particles to aid translation, and the unresolved variance of translations in secondary sources as a result of it. What was adopted as the title of the volume is a single line of verse composed as an appositive list where its grammatical function is only elucidated by a final verb in the line below it, which is thus omitted in the title itself. The "title" is the nominative object for a rather eloquent metaphor describing Tibetan historiography. Writing in the first person, "Nyangrel" presents this metaphor for the compilation of his history, provides some insight into it by elucidating the meaning (and some indication

263. Manuscript M's cover page features only the stamp of the *Staatsbibliothek* that holds it in Berlin. Meisezahl notes that the manuscript as he first encountered it included a "handwritten inventory label" (*Hand stammende Inventarzettel*) that I take to mean a card listing the text's contents tucked into its protective cloth covering. According to Meisezahl, the card identified the text as the *Great Religious History of the Old School* (*Rnying ma'i chos 'byung chen mo*), though this may be a topical genre for cataloging as much as a title for the volume itself—it would have sufficed for either given the contents. The card also included one additional term below the main script that read only "kagyü" (*bka' rgyud*), presumably indicating the sect of that name. The card's provenance and intent thus remains unclear, and it was not photographed by Meisezahl, no longer accompanies the volume in Germany, and appears to have been lost. For a discussion of how the manuscript was found *in situ*, see Meisezahl 1985, 10.

of how to translate what became the title as well), and claims authorship of the product:

> The history of Buddhism [that is like] honey nectar, the essence of flowers,
> was gathered by a bee-like one, clear minded and intelligent.
> The exemplary ancient histories and chronicles
> transmitted by fortunate scholars, the precious vessels,
> the writings that spread in the earlier and later teachings,
> and the statements of scholars
> have marvelously been handed down from generation to generation
> in accord with the stages of the sūtras and tantras, the scriptures and testaments.
> Without error, I, Nyangrel, arranged sequentially
> in one place all the scattered texts.[264]

While I follow the Western convention and refer to our twelfth-century treasure recoverer as "Nyangrel" throughout this book, this stanza is one of very few Tibetan literary references where Nyangrel is simply named "Nyangrel." This name is rarely used by Tibetans, who tend to refer to him by his clan and personal names, Nyang Nyima Öser, or more formally as Ngadak Nyang (Sovereign Nyang), presumably in reliance upon the imperial title acquired from his preincarnation Tri Songdetsen. In describing his methodology as one that relies on the collection of authentic sources that are excerpted and aligned into a linear historical narrative, he constructs a metaphor that elucidates what became the title of the text. Nyangrel likens the historian's scholarly enterprise to honeybees that fly from flower to flower, extracting the nectar essence of each that, once gathered and processed, becomes refined into a narrative as sweet as honey. The author is therefore the intelligent honeybee who explores the meadows of libraries and presumably hidden caches, going from text to text as flower to flower, extracting excerpts like nectars to be processed and refined into the honey of a complete narrative.[265]

In the opening stanzas that precede this statement, Nyangrel twice elaborates on the significance of that nectar. First he describes the Buddhist doctrine (*chos*) as the nectar (*bdud rtsi*) that dispels the afflictions and results in liberation, thus the essence of Nyangrel's honey history is imbued with at least

264. *Me tog snying po* B, 3.3–5; K, 2.7–12; M, 1.3.2–6 and 3.3.2–6.

265. This analogy is drawn from Indian Buddhist literature, where it is reproduced in such renowned works as Śāntideva's *Bodhicaryāvatāra*. See Shantideva 2006, 111 (8.16).

half of the soteriological potential of Buddhism. It remains to be seen whether it is meant to purify the cognitive obscurations to omniscience as well.[266] The author also relates that "nondual enlightened mind is a stream of nectar," thus this historical narrative is representative of ultimate reality itself.[267] Aside from advocating for the transcendent and irrefutable authenticity of the work, the verses present a rather lucid and precise metaphor for Nyangrel's particular brand of historiography, which is founded on intertextuality and tradency, the transmission of previously held knowledge through the replication and reorganization of what are taken to be authoritative excerpts into new compendiums.

The *Essence of Flowers* has been celebrated by contemporary scholars as one of the foremost sources for Tibetan history through its alleged time of composition in the twelfth century, yet this belies the text's obscurity throughout its eight centuries of transmission. It survives in only three manuscripts of a single recensional line, a modern edition based on two of those manuscripts, and a digitally input version of that publication in Tibetan Unicode. Unlike the *Copper Island*, the *Essence of Flowers* was never xylographed nor widely distributed, and it has yet to be found explicitly cited or quoted in any subsequent source. This latter fact may stem in part from its transmission for some time without a single explicit title that could be cited. Adding both to the value and intrigue of the *Essence of Flowers*, contemporaneous histories of Buddhism are excerpted by later historians and yet, unlike the *Essence of Flowers*, the texts themselves are no longer independent and wholly extant. However, there are certain unique shared details that suggest the *Essence of Flowers* may have been referenced by Butön (1290–1364) when he wrote his renowned *History of Buddhism* and/or Lama Dampa Sönam Gyaltsen (1312–75) when compiling his *Mirror Illuminating the Royal Genealogies*, but it is equally probable that Nyangrel, Butön, and Lama Dampa relied on some of the same early sources that are now lost.[268] In sum, while there are certain parallels between the *Essence*

266. *Me tog snying po* B, 2.2; K, 1.4–5; M, 2.1.3.

267. *Me tog snying po* B, 2.5–6; K, 1.13–14; M, 1.2.5 and 3.2.5–6.

268. The editor of the Lhasa edition, Khyenrab Ösel, relates that he found only one history that cites *Me tog snying po: Mdo smad chos 'byung* by Brag sgon pa Dkon mchog bstan pa rab rgyas (1801–70) (*Me tog snying po* K, vii). However, *Me tog snying po* does not appear to be cited within presently available versions of this text (see the bibliography to *Mdo smad chos 'byung*, 3–15).

While Lama Dampa does not cite *Me tog snying po* specifically, Sørensen (1994, 161n449) mentions that *Rgyal rabs gsal ba'i me long* shares details with it that do not appear in other sources with parallel narratives, including available recensions of those that Nyangrel relied upon, such as the *Bka' chems ka khol ma*. For example, *Me tog snying po* and *Rgyal rabs gsal*

of Flowers and a few histories that postdate it, it has yet to be found explicitly cited in any history, may simply have drawn upon corresponding sources, and ultimately appears to have had little direct influence on later Tibetan historical writing.

In terms of its provenance, all of the sources that comprise the *Essence of Flowers* seem to originate in the twelfth century or before, and its tantric genealogies conclude with contemporaries of Nyangrel as well; thus its overt internal content does not immediately betray a process of significant manipulation after his time. The exceptions, however, are the concluding sections of the *Essence of Flowers*, where analysis demonstrates that the narrative indeed underwent multiple redactions and indicates that additional sources were interpolated throughout an earlier version of the narrative. Even in concurring with the assessment of the *Essence of Flowers* as a twelfth-century history, an analysis of its composition and transmission problematizes Nyangrel's authorship while clarifying the logic behind its attribution to him.

Three Volumes, One Recension

It will become apparent that several hands contributed to the *Essence of Flowers*, but for the time being we will refer to them collectively as "Nyangrel." Only three manuscripts are known to remain extant at present, two reproductions of which served as the basis for what has become the most widely available and thus the most cited version of the text. Printed in a modern *dbu can* typeface, the Lhasa edition (*Me tog snying po* K, after its editor, Khyenrab Ösel) is in fact an amalgam of manuscripts A and B, but a manuscript found by Richard Meisezahl (manuscript M) in Berlin proves to be the earliest version of the *Essence of Flowers* and therefore the best exemplar for philological analysis.

As described by Khyenrab Ösel in the introduction to his edition, he journeyed to Bhutan in 1982 in search of two manuscripts of the *Essence of Flowers*

---

ba'i me long are the only sources to present the birth year of emperor Srong btsan sgam po, a detail of long-running controversy. See *Me tog snying po* M, 120.2.2, where the ox (*glang*) year is inscribed on the margin above the first line and compare with Sørensen 1994, 161. Van der Kuijp (2013b, 118) also notes some parallels between *Me tog snying po* and Butön but is hesitant to suggest that Butön used it: "there is no evidence that he was directly familiar" with *Me tog snying po*. For a very brief discussion that inspired van der Kuijp's far more detailed analysis, see Szerb 1990, 139–41.

Another history that focuses on the three Buddhist kings, *Byang chub sems dpa' sems dpa' chen po chos rgyal mes dpon rnam gsum gyi rnam thar*, has been attributed to Nyangrel due to its topical similarities with *Me tog snying po*, but Doney (2011, 73–89) offers a convincing refutation of this thesis.

that had been published in 1979. Designated manuscripts A and B, these were the only known versions of Nyangrel's history at the time; thus he compared the two to publish a modern publication that, while not a complete critical edition according to the standards of Western methodologies, nevertheless identified important variants between manuscripts A and B, interpolated corrections, updated some orthography, and noted lacunae throughout the edition, all of which are framed within different types of brackets to distinguish them. Manuscripts A and B are therefore the bases of the 1988 Lhasa edition; the latter is not a distinct recension with an independent philological value for determining the transmission of the *Essence of Flowers* prior to it, but it remains the only version of the history in print.[269]

In general A and B are very similar, but A is an "incomplete" copy as described by the edition notice: about twenty-five consecutive folios are missing from the middle of the text, and the manuscript abruptly ends toward the conclusion of the *Copper Island* narrative within it.[270] Rather than stop at the end of an episode or chapter, manuscript A breaks off in the middle of a sermon by Padmasambhava[271] (see figure 10). Nevertheless, what remains of A was more faithfully transmitted than B, which is maligned in the publisher's preface as "corrupted." This manuscript continues straight through the *Copper Island* narrative and ends with several codas and colophons, thereby preserving a series of distinct postscripts for the *Essence of Flowers*. Nyangrel did not contribute any of this concluding material, however, which is proven upon considering the Berlin manuscript.

While Khyenrab Ösel was compiling his edition from manuscripts A and B, Meisezahl had concurrently embarked on a similar project but with a different

269. Cf. Doney 2014, 2, where it is noted that *Me tog snying po* is reproduced alongside *Zangs gling ma* in Jamgön Kongtrul's nineteenth-century *Rin chen gter mdzod*, but this is in error: manuscripts A and B were added as two additional volumes to a 1979 extended publication (*Rin chen gter mdzod chen po'i rgyab chos*) and are not original to Jamgön Kongtrul's collection. Nyangrel's history was never xylographed, and it was not published in any form until these photolithographic reproductions in 1979.

270. The publisher indicates these missing pages in *Me tog snying po* A by inserting a single blank folio in place of them (203–4). The text is interrupted at the bottom of page 202 (=K, 116.21), which is followed by the blank folio, and resumes at the top of 205 (=K, 141.19). One page in the Lhasa edition (K) is equivalent to about one folio in A, so roughly twenty-five folios are missing. Manuscript A is thus deemed "incomplete" both for missing this internal segment as well as for the abrupt interruption of the narrative well before its conclusion.

271. This corresponds to chapter 38 in *Zangs gling ma*. The interruption in *Me tog snying po* A occurs at K, 377.10; *Zangs gling ma* A, 183.6. The text concludes with a completion particle as a natural grammatical stop, but it is an awkward one within the broader context of the narrative and well before its natural conclusion.

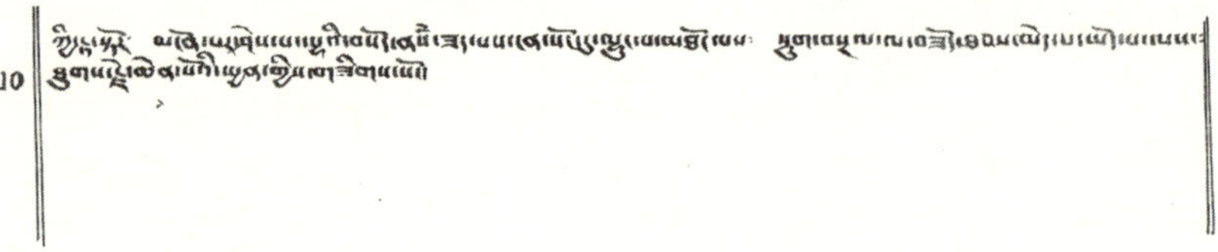

Figure 10. Last page of the *Essence of Flowers*, manuscript A.

manuscript with a distinct methodology. His work focused on a manuscript of Nepalese provenance that he uncovered in the State Library of Berlin. Meisezahl also succeeded in obtaining the two Bhutanese publications that were the focus of Khyenrab Ösel's work and thereby conducted a comparative analysis of all three manuscripts. Rather than attempt to produce a critical edition as a new recension, Meisezahl's primary objective was to publish a photo-facsimile of manuscript M introduced by a comparative analysis. As part of this project, Dagyab Rinpoché created a detailed table of contents and helped compile indices of place and personal names that, while far from registering all occurrences, remain quite useful.

Manuscripts A and B share a number of elements absent in M, such as several lines of notes in their opening pages, and as mentioned, B bears clear evidence of additional manipulations.[272] Given the paucity of exemplars, some lingering questions remain concerning the transmission of A and B, but it appears that all three manuscripts are part of the same recensional stream, with A and B being later redactions. Manuscript M is definitively the earliest extant witness and therefore is the best referent for philological analysis. The discussion below will demonstrate that M is quite far removed from whatever may have been the "original" document, but it remains the most faithful to it among the exemplars available to us. It also preserves many codicological features, effaced by the editing and copying of what became versions A, B, and K, that illuminate the transmission of what is now known as the *Essence of Flowers*.

272. Compared with manuscripts A and B, M is continuous through the prologue. Compare *Me tog snying po* M 5.1.5 with A 5.6–6.3 and B 4.3–6, where . . . *te/* and *gcig* . . . are interrupted by several lines of small writing, which are reproduced parenthetically in K. Meisezahl 1985, 14, provides several examples of extrapolations or "corruptions" that are unique to B. Additionally, B is the only version to display some treasure punctuation marks (483). This is remarkable not just because of their rare appearance here, but because this section is excerpted from *Sba bzhed* and not *Zangs gling ma*! Compare with *Sba bzhed* S, 67.9–12.

One Volume, Three Manuscripts

Manuscript M consists of at least three distinct manuscripts that were compiled into a single volume.[273] The first manuscript is represented by only the first three folios, whereas the second repeats two of those folios before proceeding to the remainder of the historical narrative that ends on folio 525, which is not the end of the total volume as it exists today.[274] With pagination restarting from 1 and scribed by a distinct hand, both of which are evident only in M, a third manuscript appends an additional twenty-one folios to the *Essence of Flowers*. Therefore, even though each of the four colophons in this addendum ascribes authorship to Nyangrel, its contents were not written by him, for even as it repeatedly claims that the *Essence of Flowers* was his product, these details were not included in the original text. If Nyangrel did not author the colophons in the addendum, it begs the question of how much he contributed to the *Essence of Flowers* that precedes it as well. More reliable evidence of his authorship must be sought elsewhere in this early *History of Buddhism*.

The first three folios of M are whiter than those that follow and cleanly calligraphed in black and red ink. Darker paper, a heavier-handed script, and duplicate pagination on the fourth folio signals the interruption of the first manuscript for another. The pagination of the second manuscript repeats folios 2 and 3 and duplicates much of its text, thereby indicating that only the very first folio of the second manuscript is missing. The overlap of folios 2 and

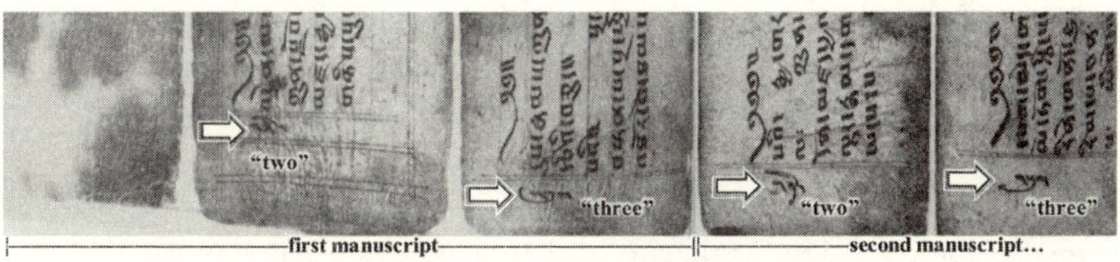

Figure 11. Pagination and script samples from rectos of folios 1–5 in manuscript M. Note the repetition of folio numbers and the handwriting variation between the three initial folios and the two that follow them. Among other distinctions, this can be recognized by comparing the *ukhyü* (*dbu mkhyud*) that "head" or begin each recto. The first manuscript displays two curls with some flourish in the tail, whereas the second displays three curls with a heavier, straighter stroke. Folios reproduced from Meisezahl 1985, 1 and 3.

273. Meisezahl 1985, 12–13, identifies two manuscripts within M and terms a third concluding section as an "addendum."

274. Meisezahl 1985, 12. For a catalog entry of this manuscript, see Everding 2014, 3–9.

3 is such that the third folio of the first manuscript is entirely redundant and could have been discarded. Comparing M with A and B, manuscript A is interrupted well before reaching the addendum material, but a copyist or editor of B left a special stroke (*shad*) before the addendum to mark a disjunction:

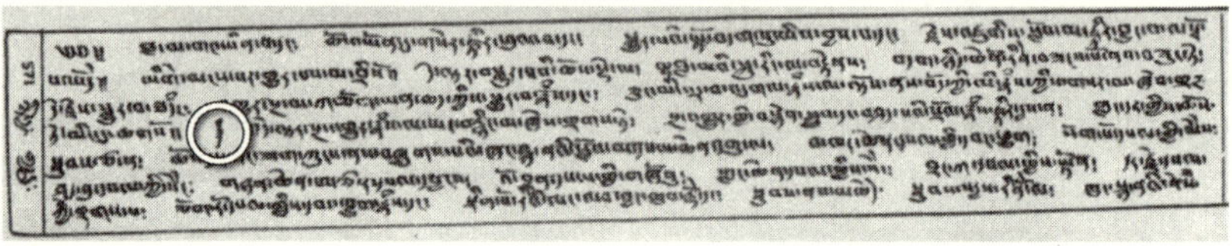

Figure 12. *Me tog snying po* B, 571, with a special *shad* (circled) signifying a break in the source text.

The copyist for this section of B thus recognized a shift but continued the pagination through to the end of the text, thereby enabling B to present the illusion that the *Essence of Flowers* was continuous from start to finish.

While Khyenrab Ösel, the editor of the modern Lhasa edition (K), compared the texts of A and B and noted his editorial decisions within special brackets, he omitted all of the internal markings unique to those manuscripts. In this way, he completed an eight hundred year process of redaction whereby the *Essence of Flowers* finally became a single text that visually appears to have been composed in its entirety by Nyangrel. Though but one piece made of many parts, the addendum to the *Essence of Flowers* itself is a distinct compilation that became seamlessly integrated into that text through repeated copying. Since K has become the most available and thus the most cited version of the text, the presence of an addendum has most often gone unnoticed and accepted as part of the original document. The text after the editorial mark in B retains some subtle stylistic and historical evidence that suggests the contrary, but only M retains clear markers that definitively distinguish an earlier iteration of the *Essence of Flowers* without the addendum.

Nectars and Flowers, Excerpts and Sources

As described by the metaphor of the prologue, the *Essence of Flowers* relies on nectar-like excerpts drawn from myriad sources to produce the honey of its narrative. Indeed, the text is largely an amalgamation of excerpts from available texts knit into a narrative. In contrast to the eloquence of the metaphor, the construction of the text itself is rather inelegant: aside from the prologue that initiates the text and the series of coda that conclude it, there are few signs of editorial effort that would seem prerequisite in the composition of such a complex history: transitions between sources, eras, episodes, and topics are thin if not altogether absent. A complete source analysis of the *Essence of Flowers* is well beyond the objectives of the present study;[275] what follows is an introduction to its historiographical selection and integration of sources, highlighting those that are relevant to Nyangrel's golden age narrative especially, that seeks to distinguish those elements of the *Essence of Flowers* that might be traceable to him from those that were introduced later in the text's transmission.

Among the most defining features of the *Essence of Flowers* is that, despite its purported intent to present a complete history of Buddhism in India and Tibet through the twelfth century, its total content is heavily weighted not just toward Tibet but to only two emperors. While there are sketches for a selection of pre-Buddhist emperors, the reigns of Songtsen Gampo and Tri Songdetsen comprise nearly half of the total volume. These emperors are the foundations for two of Nyangrel's primary projects, indisputably among his most significant contributions to Tibetan literature and culture. The first consists of his treasures concerning Emperor Songtsen Gampo as the embodiment of Avalokiteśvara, the Great Compassionate One, that soon became renowned and expanded as the *Maṇi Kambum*. This collection is among the main sources for national myths that identify Avalokiteśvara as the patron deity of Tibet. The second major project is the focus of the present discussion, where Nyangrel's *Copper Island* and the *Essence of Flowers* portray Tri Songdetsen as the patron of Padmasambhava who actualizes the establishment of Buddhism in Tibet, tames its hosts, and conceals treasures throughout the landscape. Not coincidentally, Padmasambhava is considered an emanation of Avalokiteśvara, thus Nyangrel's devotion to the deities and emanations of the padma buddha family is intricately intertwined with thematic and soteriological consistency throughout many of his major works.

Within the *Essence of Flowers*, Songtsen Gampo's reign functions as the historical precedent for and introduction to the activities of Tri Songdetsen and Padmasambhava. Songtsen Gampo's construction of the first Buddhist temples, dispatch of Thönmi Sambhota to devise a Tibetan script for the translation of Sanskrit Buddhist scriptures, and installment of buddha images at the bequest of his Nepalese and Chinese tribute brides serve as prelude to Tri

275. Sørensen 1994 traces the alignment of *Me tog snying po* and many of the sources used to construct it, such as *Bka' chems ka khol ma* and *Maṇi bka' 'bum*, with the fourteenth-century *Rgyal rabs gsal ba'i me long* by Lama Dampa Sönam Gyaltsen.

Songdetsen's construction of Samyé Monastery, massive translation project, and sponsorship of treasures buried throughout the Tibetan landscape. While the apotheosis of Songtsen Gampo as the embodiment of Avalokiteśvara had already been initiated in texts like the *Pillar Testament*, the collaboration of Tri Songdetsen and Padmasambhava was less established, and the *Essence of Flowers* can be seen as a vehicle for the glorification of this duo.

Here the story of Tri Songdetsen and Padmasambhava is drawn almost exclusively from a single source: Nyangrel's *Copper Island* provides the primary narrative. This is interspersed by a handful of scattered details and excerpts from the *Testimony of Ba* or perhaps from an extinct source that was independently excerpted for both the *Essence of Flowers* and the *Testimony of Ba*.[276] Since the Tibet section of the *Essence of Flowers* is structured by a selective but chronological succession of Tibetan emperors, we find the entirety of the forty-chapter *Copper Island* narrative in the *Essence of Flowers* with the exception of its first five chapters, which depict Padmasambhava's life prior to his arrival in Tibet. Content derived from the *Copper Island* and the *Testimony of Ba* is enhanced only by an elaborate description of Samyé Monastery and a poem that depicts Padmasambhava's transformation into a garuḍa to wrangle the nāgas there, both of which may be unique to the *Essence of Flowers*.[277] These additions strongly suggest that the *Essence of Flowers* could not have been the source for the earliest attested recensions of the *Copper Island* since all of them exclude these elaborations. Both the *Copper Island* and earlier, unextended versions of the *Testimony of Ba* conclude with the reign of Tri Songdetsen's successor, Mutik Tsenpo or Muné Tsenpo (an unresolved historical controversy),[278] thus the *Essence of Flowers* must rely on other sources to narrate the remainder of the empire. After Tri Songdetsen's death and Padmasambhava's departure from Tibet some time thereafter, the *Copper Island* narrative concludes, and the *Essence of Flowers* then narrates the history of Tibet through the inception of the later dissemination by drawing on the *Extended Testimony of Ba* (*Sba bzhed zhabs btags ma*).

The *Essence of Flowers* favors the *Copper Island* to the exclusion of the parallel account in the *Testimony of Ba*. The *Copper Island* and its reproduction in the *Essence of Flowers* revise the historical narrative concerning the estab-

276. Van der Kuijp 2013b, 162 and 167–68, suggests the common reliance of *Me tog snying po* and *Sba bzhed* on an earlier source.

277. Doney 2011, 87–88.

278. There is significant confusion concerning the succession directly after Tri Songdetsen, which is reflected by the *Copper Island*'s presenting the reign of Mutik Tsenpo whereas the *Testimony of Ba* concludes with the reign of his brother Muné Tsenpo. For a detailed discussion of this issue, see Dotson 2007.

lishment of Buddhism in Tibet under the reign of Tri Songdetsen. According to the *Testimony of Ba*, Padmasambhava was summoned to ritually beat into submission the hosts of obstructing forces such that the first Buddhist monastery could be constructed. Having been warned by anti-Buddhist ministers of a potential rivalry, Tri Songdetsen quickly grows unsettled by Padmasambhava's success in these endeavors, and the emperor deports him after as little as a few weeks, deploying a team of archers in hot pursuit. Not only did Tri Songdetsen deport Padmasambhava, he sought to assassinate him! Padmasambhava's last words on Tibetan soil were that his work there was incomplete: he did not conceal the treasures and he did not participate in the consecration of Samyé Monastery. Moreover, the emperor is depicted as a gullible ditherer who was easily manipulated by his anti-Buddhist ministers. Since Nyangrel identified himself as the treasure-revealing reincarnation of Tri Songdetsen, the *Testimony of Ba* account would have been thoroughly discomfiting: it undermined the foundation of his activities, his enlightenment, and his livelihood.

The *Copper Island* presents a competing narrative whose rosier perspective of Tri Songdetsen's reign promotes a thoroughly established karmic basis for Tibet's evolution into a land of Buddhism. The *Testimony of Ba* account threatens Nyangrel's self-conception certainly, but it also undermines the karmic foundation for Buddhism's establishment in Tibet. If the establishment of Buddhism were flawed and incomplete, how could a flawless and authentic Buddhism develop there? Since Nyangrel is the reincarnation of Tri Songdetsen, the omniscient revealer of buried treasures who remembers the details of that past life, he claims a rather unique editorial authority to revise the historical record. Nyangrel's *Copper Island* and his *Essence of Flowers* are the first sources to complete the apotheosis of the imperium into a golden age of Tibetan Buddhism. Having excluded all of the dissonant details from the *Testimony of Ba*, the *Essence of Flowers* replicates the *Copper Island* narrative verbatim and only borrows elements that support the primary drive of its account, the thoroughly successful establishment of Buddhism in Tibet, with details that were absent in the *Copper Island*.

The integration of these enhancements is not always so seamless, however, and a glaring anachronism occurs at the very end of the Padmasambhava narrative in the *Essence of Flowers*. Corresponding to the conclusion of the main narrative in the *Copper Island*, Tri Songdetsen dies, and Padmasambhava offers his parting advice to the various peoples of Tibet for nearly forty folios in manuscript M.[279] Although the most recent recension of the *Copper Island*

279. The death of Tri Songdetsen occurs at *Me tog snying po* K, 357.8; M, 257.3.6; *Zangs gling ma* A, 142.5; H, 85b.

describes the enthronement of Mutik Tsenpo immediately after the death of Tri Songdetsen, this episode is absent in early recensions, and he is not explicitly described as the king of Tibet for more than twenty folios in the *Essence of Flowers*, thereby suggesting that he has yet to ascend the throne.[280] Given this correction in later recensions, it seems that later redactors recognized this to be problematic as well. Padmasambhava finally takes leave after a series of didactic songs and instructions where the *Copper Island* concludes, and the *Essence of Flowers* must rely on other sources to structure the remainder of its narrative, yet any sense of chronological or topical continuity is lost because a review of Tri Songdetsen's reign is inserted here even though it ended forty folios prior.[281]

Rather than proceed directly into the reigns of Tri Songdetsen's sons, the *Essence of Flowers* first inserts a distinct section unattested in the earliest recensions of the *Copper Island* that summarizes Padmasambhava's time in Tibet. It states that the master remained for fifty-one years, served as the court chaplain throughout the reign of Tri Songdetsen, and departed for Ngayap temple in the southwest during the reign of Mutik (M) or Mutri (B/K) Tsenpo. After this the *Essence of Flowers* states that the *History of Buddhism*, specifically referring to Nyangrel's account of Padmasambhava, has concluded. Next is the standard colophon to the *Copper Island*, but it is interrupted before the final verb that describes its concealment as treasure, a defining feature of every recension of the *Copper Island*'s colophon. Here there is no mention of Nyangrel (or anyone else) as the revealer of this narrative, nor is it admitted to be a treasure: the *Essence of Flowers* omits all internal evidence that would betray the status of its foremost source as a revealed text. The relevant content of the *Copper Island* has now been exhausted and provides no further data for replication in the *Essence of Flowers*.

The history proceeds with a distinct list of the many scholars who participated in the great imperial translation project and some of the titles as representative products of Tri Songdetsen's reign, but the text then anachronistically reverts to recount his corralling of the various Tibetan clans that defined the beginning of his reign. The coda then features two lists that function as a bibliography for its account of Padmasambhava.[282] Given that independent recensions of the *Copper Island* do not describe any of its sources, this coda embedded within the *Essence of Flowers* is unique and postdates the

280. *Me tog snying po* K, 376.13–14; M, 272.3.2; *Zangs gling ma* H, 107a4–108a2.

281. *Me tog snying po* K, 391.16; M, 283.1.6.

282. *Me tog snying po* B, 460; K, 393; M, 283.3. Van der Kuijp 1995, 41–42, reviews this list and explores the significance of its genres.

original Padmasambhava narrative. After this bibliography, a disjunction in M betrays the insertion of additional titles by a later contributor who, as will be detailed below, may have been none other than the author of the *Essence of Flowers*’ second colophon, given the precise replication of several somewhat obscure titles.

The *Essence of Flowers* then parallels if not transcribes what appears to have been a less-redacted ancestor of the *Extended Testimony of Ba*, beginning with the appointment of Ba Yeshé Wangpo as the first abbot of Samyé Monastery (late eighth century), through the collapse of the empire (mid ninth century), to the invitation of Atiśa, the training of Rinchen Sangpo, and the inception of the New Translation period (late tenth / early eleventh centuries), which is interspersed with excerpts from additional sources. The problem, however, is that whereas a tradent of the *Essence of Flowers* succeeded in inserting relevant excerpts from the *Testimony of Ba* at appropriate moments in the *Copper Island*’s chronology, s/he failed at the conclusion of the *Essence of Flowers.*

Despite being one of the defining events of Tri Songdetsen’s reign in many histories of the period, the Great Debate between Kamalaśīla, representing the Indian advocates of a gradual path, and Hashang Mahāyāna, who defends Chinese assertions of sudden enlightenment, is absent in the *Copper Island*. As with other missing details from the reign of Tri Songdetsen, the *Testimony of Ba* is the go-to resource to fill them in, but rather than insert the Great Debate at its appropriate chronological moment, which would be in the latter years of his reign after the completion of Samyé, it appears long after the description of his death. This marks the exact place where the *Copper Island* ends and is awkwardly spliced by the *Testimony of Ba*, which then becomes the main source for the remainder of the *Essence of Flowers*.[283] Perhaps the interpolation of the

283. The replication of this episode includes several lines that are absent in *Sba bzhed* G but present in S, which again indicates that an ancestor of S was used for *Me tog snying po*. Note that Meisezahl’s 1985 photofacsimile (M) reproduces three verso on one page followed by their three recto on the next, so it appears in some citations that the text goes backward (i.e., 286–85). Compare *Me tog snying po* K, 395.19–96.6; M, 286.4–285.3.4 (main text); *Sba bzhed* G, 62.13–18 (underlined); *Sba bzhed* S, 53.9–14 (**bold**): ***de’i dus su pho brang rim dgu’i*** *sgo* ***khang du mkhan*** *po bo dhe sa ta’i* ***dbu la*** *gor bus* ***phra brgyab*** *pa ltar mdzad nas/* ***zhal chems ye shes dbang po la bzhag*** *nas* ***sku gshegs*** *so/* ***de’i spur has po ri’i rgyab tu bzhugs nas mchod rten gcig bzhengs*** *so/* ***der btsan pos ye shes dbang po*** *chos dpon du* ***ring lugs su bskos****/ mdun pa yang bla’i ’og tu bton/* ***rab tu byung pa mang pos chos gra’i dpon*** *dang/* ***nya ma’i dpon*** *kyang so sor* ***bskos/ na bza’*** *rnams dang/ rgyal blon mang pos ’phan gyis sbyor/ slob dpon* ***ring lugs*** *pa* ***la zla ba re*** *re’i phogs la nas khal bdun cu/* ***chos gra’i dpon la*** *nas khal* ***sum cu rtsa lnga chos slob pa la*** *nas khal* ***bcu gnyis*** *re* ***thang du bcad/*** *slad kyi ye shes dbang po mngon shes dang ldan* ***pas/...***

In this excerpt, *Me tog snying po* includes nearly all of the text from *Sba bzhed* G and S. The only text included in G that is absent in S is Khenpo Bodhisattva’s full name, which could have

Testimony of Ba was the work of a subsequent redactor rather than that of its purported author, Nyangrel himself? Analysis of the final sections of the text sheds much light on its compilation and transmission.

Coda to an Earlier Essence of Flowers

As we saw, Meisezahl's crucial discovery was the presence of an addendum, a distinct manuscript subsequently appended to his manuscript of the *Essence of Flowers*. This is made apparent by the paleographical and codicological analysis of manuscript M, since its concluding twenty-one folios display distinct pagination, are written in the hand of a different scribe, and display patterns of damage and degradation that differ from those that precede them. Unique to this addendum is the colophon of a previous copyist: written on both sides of a single folio, the copyist's colophon belongs at the very end of the entire volume but at some point was exchanged with the first folio of the addendum.[284]

The copyist's colophon in manuscript M appears very late in the volume yet not quite at the end of it, where it belongs. Manuscript A is interrupted well before this section, whereas B either omits this colophon or was sourced from an *Essence of Flowers* that lacked it. Unfortunately, the omission of previous copyist colophons is standard practice; their replication within a volume would provide an invaluable paper trail for tracing the transmission of a text. In recalling that only the first three folios of the volume comprise the first manuscript of M, the final folio of the second manuscript (525) displays fewer

---

been extrapolated rather than based on G. Conversely, the lines from ...***ring lugs su bskos/*** (line 4 above) to ***slad kyi ye shes dbang po***... (final line above) contain elements that are only present in *Sba bzhed* S, thus indicating that an ancestor of S was the source text instead of G. Moreover, *Me tog snying po* follows S in sequence but offers far more detail. While all of this additional text could be extrapolation, it may also be the case that an ancestor of S was significantly less redacted. Given the wholesale copying of *Zangs gling ma* just prior to this section, I suspect that the same methodology was used and thus the latter hypothesis is more likely: a less redacted ancestor of *Sba bzhed* S was copied into *Me tog snying po*.

284. When M was appraised during a recent Tibetan manuscript project in Germany, the cataloger moved this folio back into its proper place within the volume and penciled page numbers throughout the addendum, which will be obvious to anyone who now encounters M in Berlin. Meisezahl's facsimile will remain more available to scholars than the manuscript itself, however, so I have continued to discuss M *in situ* as reproduced by Meisezahl rather than as presently corrected.

than three lines of text followed by three sets of double *shad* and is concluded by the affirmation *sādhu*, or "well said." Manuscript M has definitively reached its end, or an end anyway, thus signifying that an earlier witness of the text concluded here with these lines.

Figure 13. Folio 525b, the final page of the narrative before the copyist's colophon and addendum. Meisezahl 1985, 352.2.

If we accept the addendum just as it appears in M—as a distinct manuscript appended to the text—then the final paginated folio in M preserves the coda to an earlier version of the *Essence of Flowers*. While these lines lack a formal colophon with attribution of authorship, they indeed record an intention for the composition of this history.

Though the *Essence of Flowers* begins with an overview of Buddhism in India, its focus is the transmission of Buddhism in Tibet, which accounts for nearly 80 percent of the total document. After very briefly summarizing the range of these contents, the coda of the *Essence of Flowers* reasserts the authenticity of the Nyingma scriptures by emphasizing that everything was translated and nothing was fabricated. This is a rejoinder to the critiques that had begun to assault the Nyingma transmissions and implies that his treasure activities were born of necessity: it was critical to find the tantras that legitimated these cycles. By Nyangrel's time, the early translations had come into competition with new scriptures that, being contemporary products, were more easily authenticated by establishing their Indic pedigree through the location of their Sanskrit source texts. In the last line of what appears to have been the original coda to the *Essence of Flowers*, Nyangrel upbraids the Tibetan people:

> Thanks to the reign of Lha Lama Yeshé Ö (tenth–eleventh centuries), the classification of the translated doctrines have been understood in this way since the time of Mahātma Rinchen Sangpo (958–1055). Having recognized a little dissimilarity between the translations made by the early translators before him, such as Kawa Paltsek, Chokro Lui Gyaltsen, and Shang Yeshé Dé, and those that

> came after him, the Tibetan people became infatuated with what became renowned as the New Translations.[285]

An earlier version of the *Essence of Flowers* thus concluded with this coda rather than a colophon, leaving the reader to seek authorial statements elsewhere in the text. Apparently in an attempt to assuage these concerns, the addendum includes not one but four distinct colophons, all of which attribute authorship to Nyangrel.

As was mentioned above, the first and final folios of manuscript M's addendum were exchanged. Aside from the contents, this is made evident by discerning that the colophon folio is ragged and smaller than those that it is sandwiched between, thus indicating that it once lay at the bottom of the volume. That is, since the last folio is the most exposed, functions as the bottom edges of the total volume, and bears the weight of all the others, it suffers greater friction when the volume is wrapped and unwrapped, degrading its edges more quickly. A comparison of folios 524–25 with the first folios of the addendum also distinguishes distinct patterns of water damage, thereby proving beyond any doubt that these are two distinct manuscripts that were transmitted separately for some time. Their exposure to moisture occurred on distinct occasions, and they were compiled together into a single volume some time after the damage occurred.

The question of how the copyist's colophon arrived here before the addendum is answered simply. This colophon is written on a single, stand-alone folio. Since the colophon has writing on both sides whereas the first folio includes a blank title page, this blank side was moved to the bottom of the entire volume to mitigate the risk of damaging any writing, and the colophon was moved to become the first folio of the addendum. If the original first folio is thus viewed in its proper place within the volume, the reader not only notices the previous conclusion to the *Essence of Flowers* as signified by the *sādhu* and blank lines, but also the blank page that follows it visually indicates an obvious break between an earlier version of the *Essence of Flowers* and a later addendum.

A Copyist's Colophon

The copyist's colophon, exchanged to become the first folio of the addendum in manuscript M, includes an array of valuable information, but it does not include the most crucial piece of data, the date the copy was completed. The

285. *Me tog snying po* B, 571.1–4; K, 482.11–15; M, 351.2.6–352.2.3.

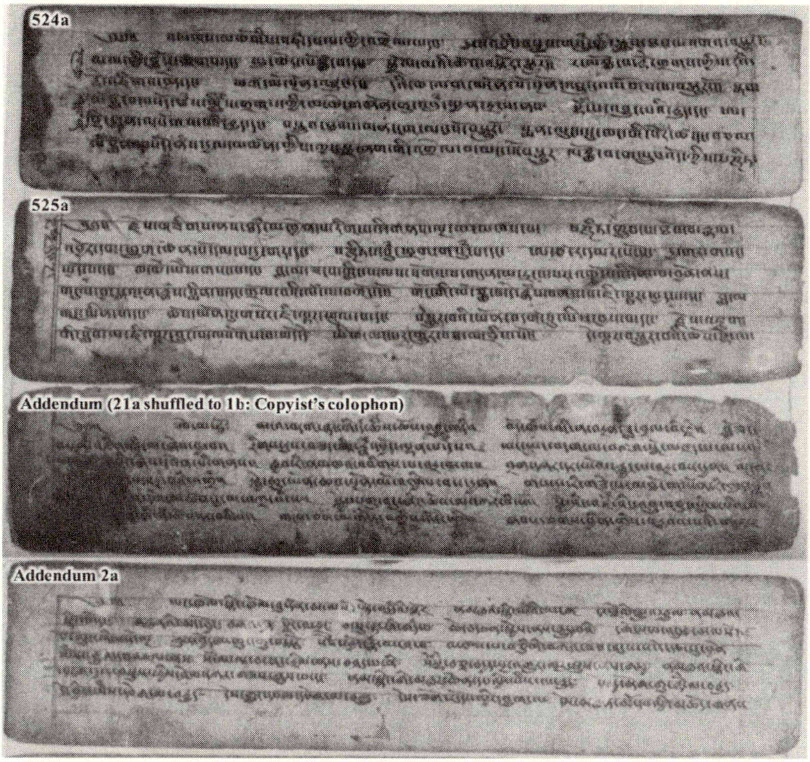

Figure 14. Rectos of folios 524–25 followed by two unpaginated folio that abut them from the addendum. Meisezahl 1985, 351–52.

copyist identifies himself as "Chöphel, the blind old monk" and proceeds to name his guru, his sponsor, how much he was paid, the place from which he worked, and for how long.

> É ma ho!
> The incomparable lord here in Tibet
> by the name of Losang Tenzin Nyima,
> he of good lineage and discernment,
> repeatedly ordered me [to copy]
> this Dharma history of the sacred doctrine by Ngadak Nyang
> at the solitary retreat known as Setrö Pemading (Se khrod padma sdings).
> The mountain behind it seems to pierce the sky,
> and it is beautified by rocks that appear to be draped in white silk.

The [course of the] riverbank by the mountain in front resembles a blind mother begging for alms,
and it is embellished by the churning blue oblation waters of the Kyichu.
The mountains at right are high and lofty; the river's distributaries from the left erode them.
The ground that is arrayed with many auspicious and virtuous signs;
the ground that gathers all beings and is well disposed toward the doctrine;
the ground that births, destroys, is tilled, moistened, and matures;
the ground that gathers many scholars and spreads the sacred doctrine
is the supreme place blessed
by the footprints of the land of snow's lord, Tashi Öser.
The blind old monk called Chöphel,
having abandoned distractions of body, speech, and mind, copied for three months
and was presented four *zho* and forty *srang* of gold as an offering.[286]
By acting in accord with the lama's command, this made a proper connection.
Through the accumulation of pure virtue in striving toward this,
I dedicate the root of virtue to fulfilling the intentions of those gone to dharmadhātu and
toward the attainment of complete enlightenment by all transmigrators.[287]

Despite all these details, it is quite difficult to triangulate the data to definitively pinpoint the era when this work was carried out, though the best hypothesis may be the mid-to-late seventeenth century, after the ascension of the Great Fifth Dalai Lama in central Tibet.

All of the people listed above bear prominent Geluk elements in their names; the copyist's retreat place is somewhere along the Kyichu River (Skyid

286. Bertsch 2001, 3–4: "Allegedly in use before the reign of Songtsen Gampo, these standards of weight measurement are ancient. One *srang*, which was equivalent to a Chinese tael (slightly more than thirty-seven grams in Tibet, but variable), comprised ten *zho*; a *zho* was 1/10th of a *srang*. By the twentieth century, these weights had been manipulated for coinage and eventually functioned only as figurative ratios once they were applied to paper currencies." The inclusion of the copyist's remuneration is an interesting detail, but as these units of measurement were used in Tibet since ancient times with significant fluctuations in value, it becomes difficult to ascertain the time period of the copyist's activities based on this evidence alone.

287. *Me tog snying po* M, 351.3–352.3.

chu) that runs through Lhasa,[288] the stronghold of the Geluk school; and the Great Fifth was the first Dalai Lama to harbor a special affinity for Nyingma doctrines and narratives. Moreover, in the coda to his edition of Urgyen Lingpa's *Testament of Padmasambhava*, the Great Fifth names "Losang Nyima, Ganden Tenzin, Kunga Namgyal" among those who were entrusted with overseeing the editing and copying of that text.[289] On the one hand this appears to name three different individuals, but when acknowledging contributors to his edition of the *Testament of Padmasambhava*, the Great Fifth often uses cardinal numbers ("the three") to indicate a set of individuals. Here there is no indicator of plurality, thus this series may state the various names of a single foreman (*dbu mdzad*) tasked with overseeing the reproduction of his *Testament of Padmasambhava*. If this is the case, then the Losang Tenzin Nyima who commanded Chöphel to copy the *Essence of Flowers* is likely the Losang Nyima Ganden Tenzin who is credited here as fulfilling the exact same role. The Great Fifth also states that he consulted various editions of Padmasambhava's life, and given its prominence within the *Essence of Flowers*, it stands to reason that he would commission the reproduction of this history. And yet while the *Copper Island* is explicitly described as an exemplar for his edition of the *Testament of Padmasambhava*, he does not cite Nyangrel's *Essence of Flowers*.[290] While none of these details alone are sufficient to definitively prove the provenance of the addendum that now accompanies manuscript M, they collectively point toward a single hypothesis: the Great Fifth Dalai Lama or someone involved in his revision of the *Testament of Padmasambhava* commissioned a copy of the *Essence of Flowers*, and one or more of the three manuscripts now comprising manuscript M are the remnants of that product. Manuscripts A and B would therefore postdate the seventeenth century, but

288. Everding (2014, 7n**) contends that Meisezahl (and myself following him) are incorrect with regard to the conflation of M's Skye chu with the Skyid chu, suggesting instead that the river identified here is the Skyer chu that flows through La yag, the birthplace of Guru Chöwang in close proximity to Nyangrel's home and areas of activity. This would indicate that the circulation of the *Essence of Flowers* was so minimal that it may never have penetrated its area of origin, and would suggest that this region's abutment against Bhutan is the only reason why two manuscript recensions were discovered there and reproduced in the twentieth century.

289. *Padma bka' thang*, 511.6.

290. Lest we mistake his reference to "the Lhodrak tulku's *History of Buddhism*" as Nyangrel's, earlier in the coda the Great Fifth specifies the Lhodrak tulku and history of his esteem: not Nyangrel but the Second Pawo, Tsuklak Trengwa (1504–66), the throneholder of Lhodrak Drowolung Monastery, who wrote the famous *Feast of Scholars* history (*Chos 'byung mkhas pa'i dga' ston*). *Padma bka' thang*, 507.6 and 511.1.

most of the other details concerning the transmission of the *Essence of Flowers* and its persistence in obscurity remain a mystery.

Returning to the paleographical and codicological evidence of the copyist's colophon rather than its content, the colophon and the entire addendum are in a single hand that is distinct from any of those that comprise the primary narrative. The copyist of M's addendum therefore did not copy any of the volume that now precedes it. Like the first three folios of the volume, perhaps the twenty-one folios that comprise the addendum were also poached from a distinct copy of the *Essence of Flowers*; however blind Chöphel may have been, he could not have spent three months copying only twenty-one folios. Thus the vast majority of his complete version of the *Essence of Flowers* history must be lost.

Alternatively, some other copyist replicated his copyist's colophon, but this would be atypical. Such colophons are usually ignored when new copies are made or blocks carved; it is somewhat rare to find layers of colophons at the end of a volume that record the exact sequence of its transmission. An exception is in some editions of the *Testament of Padmasambhava* where the Great Fifth's coda is preserved even when a new coda is appended to the volume, but he is a uniquely towering figure of Tibetan literature and history; few command such recognition and respect.

In reviewing the final folios of M, the definitive conclusion to the main narrative, the blank title page of the addendum, and the variant scripts all vividly indicate that earlier versions of the *Essence of Flowers* ended before the addendum. When working with twelfth-century Tibetan documents with so few exemplars, the range of possibilities for what occurred along such extended lines of transmission is vast, and it thus becomes difficult to definitively confirm or refute one particular hypothesis. Yet on the cumulative basis of all the evidence presented above, it seems beyond a reasonable doubt that the addendum postdates the primary narrative of the *Essence of Flowers*. It is therefore very unlikely that any of its contents can be attributed to Nyangrel.

The Chronicle of the Later Dissemination of the Teachings

Having confirmed that the copyist's colophon is out of sequence, the first section of the addendum bears several unusual features that distinguish it not only from the *Essence of Flowers* that precedes it but from the rest of the addendum as well. In all three manuscripts the first section ends with its own title, the *Chronicle of the Later Dissemination of the Teachings* (*Bstan pa phyi dar gyi lo rgyus*), but in M alone it is further isolated by a *mangalaṃ* blessing that concludes it as well as an inverted, single curl *ukhyü* and gap that initiates the next section.[291]

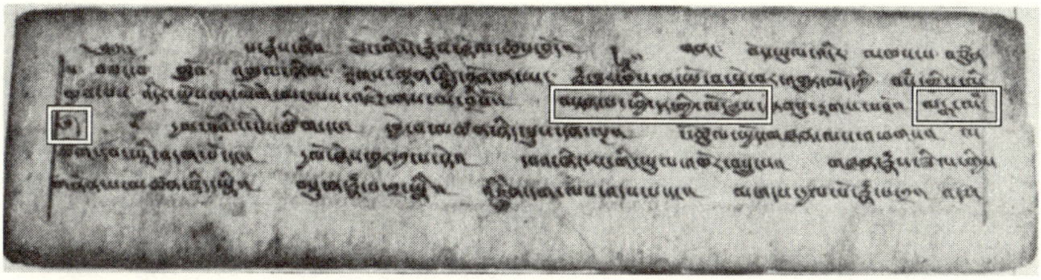

Figure 15. The conclusion of the *Chronicle of the Later Dissemination of the Teachings* in the addendum, with *ukhyü* boxed at left, title boxed off center, and *mangalaṃ* boxed at right. Meisezahl 1985, 359.2.

Ukhyü typically occur in the top left corner, preceding text only on the rectos of each folio. A copyist or tradent inscribed this inverted *ukhyü* to signify that this is where a distinct document/source concluded and another began. Within the other complete versions of the *Essence of Flowers*, neither this chronicle nor the addendum remain deliberately marked as distinct, appearing instead to be integral components of the original document.

While the "later dissemination of the teachings" most often refers to the newly translated doctrines that were being introduced from the eleventh century, the *Chronicle* in the *Essence of Flowers*' addendum primarily describes the many "early translations" from the imperial era that survived into that period as well as some that gained greater popularity thereafter. It thus serves as an inventory of the doctrines that would come to be categorized as those of the Old School, or Nyingma, and as such the *Chronicle* is aligned with the primary sectarian affiliation of the *Essence of Flowers*. Various lineages of deity-yoga praxis such as Hayagrīva and Vajrakīla are followed by several early lineages of the Great Perfection, and some of the doctrines introduced by Phadampa Sangyé in the eleventh century are featured as well. As we saw in both of Nyangrel's biographies, he received many of the latter's Shijé teachings, but so did the various branches of the Kagyü, and many renowned early exponents of that lineage are included here. Since the *Chronicle* is a doctrinal genealogy tracing the transmission of specific tantric cycles, more akin to the Bible's patrilineal sequences of "begetting" than a narrative, each lineage begins with its

291. *Bstan pa phyi dar gyi lo rgyus* runs from *Me tog snying po* B, 579.4–586.2; K, 482.16–494.19; M, 365.3.1–6 then 353.1.1–359.2.3 due to its first folio being shuffled to the end of the volume.

earliest proponents and in many cases follows the line of transmission through the late twelfth or early thirteenth century. All of the lineage holders listed therein are at least contemporary with Nyangrel, and none were born after him. The *Chronicle of the Later Dissemination of the Teachings* may indeed be drawn from this period, whereby it would remain a rare resource for the proponents of various teachings, some of them quite heterodox, that were popular in Tibet at that time.[292] Given the array of evidence that distinguishes the contents of the addendum from the narrative that precedes it, the original compiler of the *Essence of Flowers* could not have appended the *Chronicle*, yet its *terminus ad quem* in the early thirteenth century also stands as compelling evidence that the *Chronicle* and the *Essence of Flowers* that precedes it originated around Nyangrel's era. However, an assessment of the four codas and colophons that follow the *Chronicle* sows further doubt concerning Nyangrel's role in the construction of the *Essence of Flowers*, which is ironic since their objective must have been to alleviate such concerns.

Four Subsequent Codas and Colophons

After the *Chronicle of the Later Dissemination of the Teachings*, there are four distinct codas and colophons, two of which are written in the first person. As such they reiterate authorship and lend authenticity to the provenance of the total document and its contents. Yet the presence of four distinct references to Nyangrel in the addendum betrays the work of at least four redactors, and since several sources excerpted for their closing comments appear elsewhere in the history, their contributions are likely not limited to the addendum alone. This provokes the question as to how much of the *Essence of Flowers* was compiled by Nyangrel and whether he had any direct role in its formulation at all.

Following the conclusion of the *Chronicle*, the addendum shifts into verse with an homage to the kings that consists of three sections, each with a distinct meter.[293] After this homage is a dedication, summary, and colophon that together would serve as a cohesive and fitting conclusion to the total document, yet while this dedication revisits the bee, flower, and nectar metaphor

292. For an analysis of the lesser-known figures and transmissions described in the *Chronicle*, see Martin 1996a and b. Despite their extensive contributions to many of these lineages, neither Nyangrel nor his father are named and there is scant mention of Nyang, which is strange for a text that is attributed to Nyangrel.

293. Section 1 (seven syllables per line) begins at *Me tog snying po* B, 586.2; K, 494.20; M, 359.2.4; section 2 (nine syllables per line) at B, 587.4; K, 496.1; M, 359.3.5; section 3 (mostly seven syllables per line, but inconsistent) at B, 588.4; K, 496.15; M, 361.1.1.

for Tibetan historiography from the prologue, it interprets their symbolism differently. The dedication begins by relating the author's assessment of the text and its effects on him, which inspires analogies concerning the value of the *Essence of Flowers* and how it was composed. But as it progresses into high praise with honorific verbs, the dedication conveys that it was composed in response to Nyangrel's work and is not Nyangrel's praise of his own work. This person was a close reader and eloquent admirer of the text but certainly not the author of its primary narrative:

> This history is inconceivable, vast as the sky.
> Although the honeybee of my intellect cannot recognize its extent,
> through relying on the wings of the scholar's words,
> [I] discern that region of the sky: history exactly as it occurred.
>
> It is free from all fixation like the wind in the sky.
> It is complete in its luminous qualities like a full moon.
> It is the foundation for every wholesome quality like the great earth.
> While it is renowned to be as valuable as a priceless precious jewel
> to those who have faith in this biography of the ancestors who have passed,
> it is known to be as worthless as stone to the ignorant.
> Those accustomed to bad conduct and lacking in fortune
> will never come to understand this history.
>
> Gold amid earth and sandalwood among trees,
> thoroughbreds among horses and wheel-turning monarchs among men:
> just as they are supreme and rare,
> so confidence in this supreme chronicle is rare.
>
> The ocean of enlightened qualities, the precious treasury of the Buddha's teachings,
> equalizes all transmigrators in the sun of compassion.
> Those with faithful and devout minds prostrate
> to the ornament of all scholars, this precious chronicle,
> as well as to the supreme sacred beings endowed with lineage.
> All impure beings who cross over the mire [of karma and afflictions] through their conduct
> are adorned by the glorious view that delights the buddhas
> and satisfy the swarm of bees endowed with lineage.

This history is a clear mirror. [Alternate: This enlightenment is
a luminous flower.][294]
Like a lotus this "flower chronicle" gathers an ocean of enlightened
qualities.[295]
The hands of discriminative awareness
join words into a thread of memory like a garland of precious flowers
and bind my mind to the head of faith like a scarf.

This anthology is virtuous, stainless, and completely pure.
Just like this garland of precious biographies,
may a joyous feast to attract the victorious ones and their heirs
be gathered before the omniscient victors.[296]

Though it seems highly unlikely that these verses could have been written by Nyangrel, of all the text that comprises the addendum, and all of the codas in particular, these stanzas most resemble the poetic prologue to the *Essence of Flowers* that is explicitly attributed to him. To begin the dedication, its author invokes and attempts to expand upon the bee analogy from the preface but ultimately reinterprets its original significance. Duly impressed by the scope of the *Essence of Flowers*, this author admits the deficiency of his own mind that he likens to a honeybee. This admiring reader has reinterpreted the metaphor to refer to his intellect as an individual reader rather than the methodology of the one who constructed the history as in the prologue. His mind cannot conceive of the history of Buddhism on its own, so he must "rely on the wings of the scholar's words," with the scholar being Nyangrel and the words his *Essence of Flowers*.

He goes on to assert that comprehending this *Essence of Flowers* history results in spiritual attainment and perhaps even enlightenment, mirroring the

294. This line was significantly revised. The first translation is true to M, 362.3.4, which alone reads *'byung tshul 'di ni gsal ba'i me long yin/*. This is more likely to be original as it once again reiterates the subject of these verses, the history (*'byung tshul*) mentioned periodically throughout them. This again indicates that M is indeed the least manipulated version of *Me tog snying po*. The second translation reflects the revision in B, 591.1 (and K, 499.9–10, which follows it) that changes both the target and analogue of the metaphor. B and K read: *byang chub 'di ni gsal ba'i me tog yin/*, which may represent an attempt to segue into the line that follows it that, despite being present in all versions, appears to have been interjected at some later time.

295. This eleven-syllable line disrupts both the nine-syllable meter and the four-verse stanzas, thus it is exposed as an extra line inserted later, and its use of the flower metaphor again deviates from that of the prologue as well. While it appears in both M and B, this line is so poorly integrated that it stands out as an obvious contaminant.

296. *Me tog snying po* B, 591.1–592.3; K, 498.16–99.14; M, 361.3.2–363.1.1.

soteriological claims of the opening verses. Having acknowledged that "confidence in this chronicle is rare," this author then proceeds to defend the narrative and thereby implies that the *Essence of Flowers* or its more controversial contents, perhaps the narrative starring Padmasambhava, had its critics. When the bee analogy is attempted again, it has become further generalized and unfixed from its original metaphorical value as has that of the flowers. In the prologue flowers signify whole texts and their nectars are the excerpts to be processed into a complete historical narrative that is equated with honey, the processed result. Here the author deviates from the original by equating the stringing of excerpts as a "garland of flowers," which alters their function in the prologue yet provides another lucid metaphor for Tibetan historiography. Given the similarities in eloquence, style, and content, the same admiring reader may well have penned the prologue and this coda as bookends to the narrative. But if so then both attributions to Nyangrel are refutable, and this author presents distinct interpretations for a single metaphor of his own construction.

After the dedication is a summary of the *Essence of Flowers* that does not seem especially representative of its content, primarily because Padmasambhava is not mentioned despite his prominence through nearly 25 percent of the total document. The summary then concludes with prostrations to all of the kings, buddhas, and bodhisattvas before proceeding into a detailed colophon that may be more speculative than historical:

> By whom was this tale of the kings, ministers, and bodhisattvas
> compiled from base to summit?
> Responding to the sowing of repeated requests
> made by the excellent destroyer of delusion known as Dütsi Shikpo,
> Jikten Gönpo Rinpoché,[297]
> and the heir of the victorious ones, Tuo Chökyi Yeshé,
> after excellently considering however many oral transmissions and
> treasures there are,
> the one with loving-compassion that cares for all sentient beings,
> Nyangben Nyimai Öser, made [this history] by means of pellucid ideation
> alone in the glorious hermitage of Lhodrak.
> Having relinquished arbitrary embellishments and meddling (*ra chod*?),
> [he] arranged the letters.[298]

297. So as to avoid splitting the syllables of a name while preserving the nine-syllable meter, the author here follows an eleven-syllable line with one seven-syllable line.

298. *Me tog snying po* B, 593.5–7; K, 500.15–21; M, 364.1.5–363.2.2.

The first colophon to the *Essence of Flowers* is written in the third person, and it seems that this colophon with the dedication and summary that precede it are the contributions of a single enthusiastic reader who remains anonymous. He suggests that the *Essence of Flowers* was requested by three adepts, two of whom are Nyangrel's renowned contemporaries, Shikpo Dütsi (1149–99) and Jikten Gönpo Rinchen Pal (1123–1217), so their inclusion may have added clout to the *Essence of Flowers*. The third adept remains obscure.

As the primary heir of Nyangrel's *Great Compassionate One* in both the *Clear Mirror* and the *Stainless Proclamations*, Shikpo Dütsi is prominently featured as one of Nyangrel's four or five foremost disciples, yet their relationship is unattested in most other sources even when Shikpo Dütsi is listed among the lineage holders of important Nyingma cycles.[299] Active in Lhodrak as a Nyingma advocate and attested among Nyangrel's closest disciples in several sources, he seems a logical candidate to supplicate Nyangrel for a history that glorified the imperium and its products, the early translations. The second person is less expected, however, as Jikten Gönpo was the founder of the Drigung Kagyü and does not appear to have had much of a connection to Nyingma in general or Nyangrel in particular. He wrote a polemic against the treasures, though his rhetoric is mild when compared to other examples from the period.[300] Shikpo Dütsi did spend time at Drigung, however, and one of his root gurus was based in Lhakhang, named after its Khomting temple.[301] As detailed in the previous chapter, this is where Nyangrel recovered the *Eight Instructions* according to the *Clear Mirror*, and the *Blue Annals* records that proponents of Drigung maintained several active temples and retreats around Khomting and Kharchu. The most direct route between Drigung and Khomting follows the Tamshöl River right past Mawochok and was very well traveled, not just by Drigungpa

299. Shikpo Dütsi's name is inverted in all three manuscripts of *Me tog snying po* (Bdud rtsi zhig po), but it is correct in Nyangrel's biographies. *Gsal ba'i me long*, 353.4–5; *Dri ma med pa*, 110.6. Although Shikpo Dütsi is described as having spent much time in Lhodrak, his association with Nyangrel is absent throughout his biographical sections in the *Blue Annals*, and he is not mentioned among the proponents of the *Great Compassionate One*. Mikyö Dorjé is listed as Nyangrel's designated heir of Avalokiteśvara instead, but Shikpo Dütsi inherits the Ḍākinī cycle in both of Nyangrel's primary biographies. Given the paucity of data on Nyangrel in the *Blue Annals*, Gö Lotsāwa did not have access to his biographical materials, but apparently none of the sources he used for the life of Shikpo Dütsi mentioned Nyangrel among his gurus.

300. For a translation and analysis of Jikten Gönpo's *Dgongs gcig yig cha*, which is far more dismissive of Bön than anything Buddhist, including treasure, see Martin 2001, 148–82. For his polemic against the treasures in particular, see Martin 2001, 157.

301. Roerich 1949, 138.

but by Nyangrel as well.[302] This gorge was Nyangrel's primary area of activity, so it is more than likely that he and Jikten Gönpo trod the same path, but only this colophon in the *Essence of Flowers* suggests that they ever met on it. Finally, the third person said to have requested the *Essence of Flowers* from Nyangrel, Tuo Chökyi Yeshé, is unknown by that name, but perhaps an alias was Nyang Drangpa Chökyi Yeshé (*Nyang brang pa chos kyi ye shes*), evidently a member of Nyangrel's clan. Described as a disciple of Lama Shang, this Chökyi Yeshé composed a commentary on Maitreya's *Uttaratantraśāstra* in the twelfth century.[303]

It may not be coincidental that the New Translation adepts featured in the addendum's *Chronicle of the Later Dissemination* belong to the Kagyü sect. In the context of that section, this is primarily because Phadampa Sangyé's cycles were passed from Milarepa through the hierarchs of the Kagyü line, and thus Drigung is mentioned as well.[304] Additionally, the *Precious Rosary: Biographies of the Three Ancestral Buddhist Kings*, a history wrongly attributed to Nyangrel but perhaps influenced by the *Essence of Flowers*, was handled by one Shākya Rinchen at Drigung.[305] Since one of Nyangrel's foremost heirs, Shikpo Dütsi, spent time at Drigung, and since both he and Jikten Gönpo are reported to have requested the *Essence of Flowers* (and since the title card that once accompanied M was inscribed with the word Kagyü?), perhaps an early manuscript was preserved in Drigung's library. At the very least, the *Essence of Flowers* seems to have passed through the hands of those with an affiliation to Drigung, one or more of whom may have contributed to the addendum and perhaps the total document as well.

After the first colophon is a second coda that strongly resembles some versions of the *Pillar Testament* before proceeding through a very brief history of the early Buddhist treasures that culminates in Nyangrel's activities. Among the earliest sources to present Songtsen Gampo as an emanation of Avalokiteśvara, a version of the *Pillar Testament* seems to have been the source

302. Roerich 1949, 606.

303. See Burchardi 2002, 66. For Lama Shang, see Yamamoto 2009.

304. *Me tog snying po* B, 584.7; K, 493.17; M, 359.1.4.

305. *Chos rgyal mes dpon rnam gsum gyi rnam thar rin po che'i 'phreng ba*, 303.2–4. The line is obscured so the exact nature of Shākya Rinchen's activity with the text is unknown. Doney recently conducted the most thorough comparison of the *Rin po che'i phreng ba* with the *Me tog snying po* and concluded that the former was not excerpted from the latter, primarily by comparing their usage of the *Sba zhed* (Doney 2011, 73–88). These references to Drigung in the *Me tog snying po* are compelling, however: perhaps the text was held there at some time and inspired Shākya Rinchen in his [verb obscured] of the *Rin po che'i phreng ba*?

for much of the equivalent section in the *Essence of Flowers*.[306] Likewise, the lines borrowed for this coda are adapted but remain unmistakable: "This text of the king's testament is difficult to see, difficult to hear, and difficult to find . . ."[307] The *Essence of Flowers* then paraphrases the *Pillar Testament* through its vignette of Atiśa but diverges into the treasure recoveries of several figures who postdate the *Pillar Testament*'s alleged time of recovery in the early-to-mid eleventh century. The first is Drapa Ngönshé (1012–82), who is said to have recovered the *Four Medical Tantras* (*Rgyud bzhi*) as treasure, a designation that once again obscures its manner of composition, most likely by Nyangrel's contemporary, Yuthok Yönten Gönpo, who masterfully threaded old Indic and Tibetan textual fragments with new commentary.[308]

Noted after Drapa Ngönshé is Nyangrel's contemporary, mentor, and aide, the siddha Ngödrup, who is foremost recognized here for having found fragments of the Avalokiteśvara cycle known as the *Great Compassionate One*. Then, with an explicit use of the first person, "Nyang Ralpachen" once again describes his sources and approach to historiography, even though it is now the second colophon in the addendum to address the topic of methodology. While topically redundant it provides much new content:

> I, Nyang Ralpachen, gathered the treasure texts I extracted from Samyé, Tradruk, and Khomting temples; the chronicles of the later dissemination and texts well known to the ears of scholars in all the esoteric and exoteric seminaries of Tibet; unerring stories; royal chronicles; the *Secret [Imperial Succession] According to Buddhism* (*Gsang ba chos lugs*); the *Renowned [Imperial Succession] According to Bön* (*Sgrags pa bon lugs*); the *Trio of Kyangpa, Khugpa, and Bagpa* (*Rkyang pa khug pa sbags gsum*); *Gyalön Gapa* (*Rgyal blon gab pa*); *Punpo Serké Gupa* (*Spun po gser skas dgu pa*); *Singpo Natsokchen* (*Zings po sna tshogs can*); the source of the scriptures that teach the meaning of those; the oral instructions of sacred gurus; the testaments of the kings; the true speech of persons; [books on] ethics; and that which arose from flawless commentaries. Having verified all of these, I did not add or omit anything. I did not allow [the narrative] to stray into slander or [discontinuity like] a broken fence. Having excellently drawn from all the sūtras and tantras of bud-

306. For a detailed discussion of the parallels between these sources, see Sørensen 1994, 15–22.

307. *Me tog snying po* B, 594.2–3; K, 501.1–2; M, 363.2.2–3; *Bka' chems ka khol ma* A, 320.1–3; absent in B.

308. Yang Ga 2010 explores the sources and composition of the *Four Medical Tantras* in detail.

> dha speech, the treatises, and oral instructions in order, I indeed arranged them.[309]

Beginning with treasures that are attested as valid sources for historical material, this colophon again elucidates the methodology employed as well as the range of sources consulted to reconstruct the history of Tibet. In Yarlung due north of Mawochok en route to Samyé, Tradruk temple lies in close proximity to the tombs of the emperors and may have been the first Buddhist temple established in Tibet, thus it would seem a likely location for Nyangrel to recover a treasure cache. It indeed is listed as a treasure site by Padmasambhava in the *Copper Island*, but unlike Samyé and Khomting, no recoveries are described there in either of Nyangrel's biographies.[310]

The colophon then offers an abridged bibliography that lists the sources Nyangrel allegedly gathered for the *Essence of Flowers*. Among them are a succession of early historical titles, several of which comprise elements of the Five Works (*Can lnga*) that describe Tibet's imperium and the origins of the kings.[311] As introduced above, several of these titles are cited earlier in the *Essence of Flowers* in the bibliography appended to the conclusion of the *Copper Island* narrative.[312] With the anachronistic summary and insertion of the Great Debate there, this interjection of sources from the second coda suggests that the *Essence of Flowers* underwent multiple waves of redaction by several individuals, at least four of whom wrote distinct codas that implicate their editorial contribution of specific content elsewhere in the text.

Returning to the bibliography provided by the second coda, other historical genres are consulted, but special emphasis is placed on Buddhist scriptures as textual sources of history. When compared to the relatively general and inaccurate content summary provided in the coda that precedes it, this second coda is remarkably detailed and precise. This author is more familiar with the *Essence of Flowers*, the textual sources that comprise the main narrative, and even the lone historical section of the addendum that he cites explicitly as a "chronicle of the later dissemination." Oral sources are also forwarded as valid: in addition to common

309. *Me tog snying po* B, 594.5–595.3; K, 501.11–2.2; M, 363.2.6–364.2.6.

310. *Zangs gling ma* H, 81a; *Me tog snying po* K, 352.18–19; M, 255.2.5.

311. The "imperial successions" according to Buddhism and Bön are in fact two components of the first "work" of the *Can lnga*, *Yo ga [yi ge] lha gyes can*. *Zings po sna tshogs can* is the third work of that set. For a complete discussion of the *Can lnga* with translations of fragments from *Lde'u chos 'byung*, see Karmay 1998, 282–309. For a study of the *Renowned Imperial Succession According to Bön*, see Blondeau 1990a, 37–54.

312. *Me tog snying po* K, 393.13–14; M, 283.3.5–6. Also, see van der Kuijp 1995, 41–42.

authorities like scholarly monks and tantrikas, the author cites "unerring stories" and "the true speech of persons" as legitimate sources for this history. Having named his sources in detail, "Nyang Ralpachen" reaffirms that he was the author *cum* tradent of the *Essence of Flowers* in the first person. This would serve as a thorough and definitive conclusion to the text—it most likely once did—but presently it does not.

Returning to verse after this second colophon, the addendum continues with a general defense of the history and an additional first-person claim to authorship. No explicit reference is made to the *Essence of Flowers*, but some of this third coda adequately represents its content. Of relevance to the current context is a mention of "magically emanated kings," since Nyangrel helped propagate the identification of Songtsen Gampo as Avalokiteśvara. Nyangrel himself claims to be the magically emanated reincarnation of Tri Songdetsen, who in the *Essence of Flowers* is already identified as an emanation of Mañjuśrī, and the trifecta is completed in all versions of the history by identifying Ralpachen as the emanation of Vajrapāṇi. This threefold identification has since become ubiquitous in Tibet.[313] After this hail to the kings comes a one-line statement of authorship: "May this record that I, Nyang-ben, have made be worthwhile."[314] The third colophon then continues with a critique of the current age, a defense of his endeavor, and a dedication:

> When this Dharma spreads it will be beneficial to all.
> These days, when the old and ancient history is considered,
> the higher teachings on the instructions, sūtras, and tantras are denigrated;
> hypocrisy and condescension are directed against the sacred Dharma.
> Such misdeeds and misery cut the root of virtue.
> Kyé ma! What to do with those who insist on such deluded thinking?
> Nevertheless, if we give rise to confidence in the doctrine of the Great Vehicle
> through the kindness of spiritual friends,
> then may the merit gained in writing this for the benefit of beings
> swiftly lead all to become virtuous and attain buddhahood![315]

313. *Me tog snying po* B, 595.6–7; K, 502.8-10; M, 363.3.3–4. Songtsen Gampo as Avalokiteśvara at A, 247–48; B, 188–89; K, 166–67; M, 119.2. Tri Songdetsen as Mañjuśrī at A, 436; B, 313.3; K, 272.10–11; M, 199.2.3–4. Ralpachen as Vajrapāṇi at B, 302.1.2; K, 417.2; M, 363.3.3-4. A ends before the reign of Ralpachen. We also find "the three ubiquitously renowned kings" as a set in the first coda of the addendum: *Me tog snying po* K, 495.12; M, 360.2.5.

314. *Me tog snying po* B, 596.2; K, 502.13; M, 363.3.6.

315. *Me tog snying po* B, 596.2–4; K, 502.14–19; M, 363.3.6–364.3.4.

This "Nyang-ben" thus closes with a defense of the *Essence of Flowers* and the Nyingma doctrines, which are equated with the genuine teachings of the Mahāyāna.

Beginning with, "Although many dissimilar chronicles of the history of Buddhism have appeared," the fourth and final coda of the *Essence of Flowers* is in fact copied from the *Extended Testimony of Ba*.[316] Lest we be concerned that it was vice versa, the coda in the *Essence of Flowers* preserves the title of its source as the *Extended Heeding Every Letter of the Command* (*Bka' rtsi yi ge zhib par zhabs btags pa*), apparently an alias for the *Extended Testimony of Ba*, though the coda has been slightly repurposed to conclude the *Essence of Flowers* here. Text shared by the *Essence of Flowers*' fourth coda and the *Extended Testimony of Ba* is represented in bold:

> **Although many variant chronicles of the history of Buddhism have appeared, and some disparage them, some wish for them, some summarize them, some split them up, and some take them to be uncontrived, this** history is free from impurities and is genuine, **well understood** and **well written**, well studied and wisely constructed. **What has been written down by ordinary people can be mistaken.** Genuine textual traditions are exceedingly difficult to grasp. **If something is present in all the oral instructions, who among the scholars has fabricated it?** Do not give **the text** to others, **but keep it in mind. Having been written,** when held **in the vessel,** it is a jewel **treasury.** All **noble people by necessity must keep it in mind!**
>
> **The** ***Extended Heeding Every Letter of the Command***
> Make it into both abridged and extensive versions.
> Seeing them produces great wonder.
> Listen to the collections many times with friends.
> Intelligent ones distinguish correct from incorrect.
> Guarding samaya well, the view is purely realized.
> Nyangben Nyimai Öser said this.[317]

316. *Me tog snying po* B, 596.6; K, 503.1; M, 364.3.5; *Sba bzhed* S, 91.10.

317. *Me tog snying po* B, 596.5–597.3; K, 502.20-503.11; M, 364.3.4–365.1.4 (main text); *Sba bzhed* S, 91.10–92.1 (**bold**): ***chos 'byung gi lo rgyus mi 'dra ba mang*** *du* ***snang yang/ la la ngan smras/ la la zhe 'dod/ la la bsdus pa/ la la le tshe/ la la bcos ma yin te/ 'di*** [*Sba bzhed* S continues (not translated above): *sngon gyi btsan po rje blon dang/ rgya bod kyi lo paṇ chen po rnams kyi gsung dang/ dbus gtsang gi gtsug lha khang chen po rnams kyi bzhugs tshul dang/ mi 'gal bar mchis pas legs pa yin/*] *ni sel* [M: *sol*] *med rnal ma yin//* ***legs par bzung*** *la* ***legs par*** *gyis* [S: *bris*]*//* ***legs***

No, he did not. Although the colophon concludes with an ordinary verb of speech (*smra*) appropriate for a first-person subject rather than the honorific (*gsung*), Nyangrel did not "speak" the coda of another document. Instead, it is likely that the tradent who interpolated various details and episodes from the *Extended Testimony of Ba*, and who therefore can be blamed for the anachronistic splicing of the Great Debate, replicated its coda as well but attempted to refashion it to some degree for the *Essence of Flowers*. That attempt concluded with a fourth and final colophon that once again identifies Nyangrel as the author or, more literally here, the speaker of the *Essence of Flowers*.

Current scholarship on the *Testimony of Ba* locates the first extended versions to the thirteenth or fourteenth century, although it has been argued that its presence within the *Essence of Flowers* serves as proof positive of a twelfth-century origin as well.[318] Others have implicated the existence of less-redacted, perhaps twelfth-century ancestors of the *Extended Testimony of Ba* prior to the versions that remain extant today,[319] which is supported by close comparison with the *Essence of Flowers*. The various elements of the addendum must have been appended after Nyangrel, however, so it is possible that a single redactor used an *Extended Testimony of Ba* available in a subsequent century to intersperse select enhancements into the *Copper Island* narrative, interject the anachronistic summary of Tri Songdetsen's reign, and splice the *Extended Testimony of Ba*'s post-Tri Songdetsen narrative to significantly extend the *Essence of Flowers*. Upon exhausting the content of the *Extended Testimony of Ba*, he summarizes that "the people of Ü and Tsang who received their vows in Kham are present in several histories and chronicles of Buddhism." Referencing the perseverance of institutional Buddhism in northeastern Tibet after the collapse of the empire, he indicates that other sources must be sought to reproduce the remainder of the history of Buddhism in Tibet.[320]

par** slob* [S: *bshod/ 'on kyang*] *la mkhas par mdzod//* ***so so skye bos bkod** rnams* ***'khrul ba srid// *gzhung lugs rnal ma thogs pa shin tu dkon//* ***man ngag kun la yod na mkhas pa su yis byed//*** ***yi ge** gzhan la ma ster* ***blo la bzung** la* ***shod//*** ***bris nas snod du** bcangs na* ***bang** mdzod* ***nor** bu yin//* ***ya rabs** rnams la* ***dgos** kyis* ***thugs la zhog//*** ***bka' rtsis yi ge zhib** par* ***zhabs btags pa**// dpe la dog la bshad la yangs su mdzod// ngo mtshar che ba gzigs pa rnams kyis mdzod// bshes gnyen rnams la sde snod mang du thos// chos dang chos min 'byed pa'i blo gros yod// dam tshigs legs srungs lta ba dag par rtogs// nyang ban nyi ma'i 'od zer 'di skad smra//.*

318. Willis 2012, 8. Also see Sørensen in Wangdu and Diemberger 2000, xiii–iv, and Sørensen 1994, 634–35.

319. Doney 2011, 19.

320. *Me tog snying po* K, 450.3–4, M, 333.1.4–5. While the *Sba bzhed* includes additional text that is not in *Me tog snying po*, the line preceding this citation borrows from *Sba bzhed*, 87.3 (. . . *bod dad pa can* . . .) and the line following it continues from 87.4 verbatim (*mi bcu gnyis*

Like the redactors who preceded him, this fourth tradent also concludes his work by copying the coda from his foremost source text. After the fourth colophon, the *Essence of Flowers* continues with yet another summary, another first-person colophon of sorts, with "I exerted myself well in the way of Dharma," "I revealed the concealed," and a final dedication with the blessing *mangalaṃ bhavantu* invoking virtue. Only here does the *Essence of Flowers*, after so many conclusions, now finally end.[321]

Revisiting the Origins of the History of Buddhism

Without a critical assessment of the addendum, the *Essence of Flowers* has been ascribed to Nyangrel because it begins with a first-person prologue in which Nyangrel identifies himself and concludes with no less than four colophons, all of which repeatedly assert that he was its tradent. Further analysis of its construction reveals a *terminus ad quem* of figures, content, and sources in Nyangrel's time, and the vast majority of his *Copper Island* narrative is reproduced within it, so there indeed is much evidence to make its attribution to him cogent. Having identified and reviewed the addendum especially, however, doubts concerning its claims to a singular authorship spread to Nyangrel's role in its construction as well.

The splicing of the Great Debate after the death of Tri Songdetsen is a glaring exception to the *Essence of Flowers'* temporal linearity. Since Nyangrel's *Copper Island* succeeds in progressing chronologically within its own narrative, it is unlikely that he would have allowed such a glaring anachronism to mar the *Essence of Flowers*. Perhaps Nyangrel found historiography far more challenging than treasure recovery, but there are no other indications that he had difficulty integrating various sources into a single document. Based on the discussion of his treasure recoveries in the previous chapter, this appears to have been precisely his skillset! Furthermore, the *Copper Island* seems to be an unprecedented document that required not only the integration of fragments from various sources but much original writing as well, so Nyangrel must have been a rather gifted author, narrator, and historiographer. He possessed talent

lam nas log pa gcig dang bcu gsum 'ongs/), but it seems that the redactor of *Me tog snying po* was running out of real estate in his *Sba bzhed bzhags btags ma* and so acquired additional sources to complete the post-imperial narrative. Germano 2002d, 226n3, suggests that the next source replicated in the *Essence of Flowers* after the end of the *Extended Testimony of Ba* could be Rongzom's lost *History of Buddhism*.

321. *Me tog snying po* B, 597.6–7; K, 503.18–19; M, 366.1.2–3.

in each of the skills required to produce a linear history and, wherever needed, could have relied on his own authorial abilities to introduce alterations or add missing content, as would be needed to write Padmasambhava into the Great Debate. Thus in pulling at the seams of the *Essence of Flowers*, its textual patches and threadwork become evident, leading us to question whether Nyangrel had any hand in its composition at all. For this history rather artlessly integrates various sources into a single narrative, thus betraying an ineptitude with the very skills in which Nyangrel was especially proficient.

Nevertheless, the repeated attributions of his authorship would seem at least somewhat convincing. In manuscript M, the earliest extant exemplar of the *Essence of Flowers*, the first of these attributions is duplicated in the overlapping passages between M's first two manuscripts. Since this prologue and its explicit attribution to Nyangrel was included in two distinct copies now compounded together in M, it must have been an integral component of the text for some time. And despite the four attributions in the addendum being later additions to the text, the late twelfth- or early thirteenth-century *terminus ad quem* of the yogins and intellectuals listed in the addendum's *Chronicle of the Later Dissemination of the Teachings*, as well as the first colophon's identification of Nyangrel's twelfth-century contemporaries, Shikpo Dütsi and Jikten Gönpo (and perhaps Chökyi Yeshé), indicates that at least some parts of the addendum may have been appended not long after Nyangrel's time.

In sum, Nyangrel's direct compilation of the *Essence of Flowers* cannot be definitively refuted, but it seems more likely that its actual tradent was among his lineal and/or familial descendants, and that the text underwent a relatively quick succession of redactions thereafter. Meisezahl hypothesizes that one of Nyangrel's contemporaries such as Shākya Yeshé (1147–1207) wrote the addendum, whereas others suggest that some of its elements were added by his son, Namkhapel, or by another direct disciple.[322] As detailed above, while the addendum now appears as a single unit even within M, it is in fact composed of at least five parts accumulated over at least four redactions by at least four distinct redactors, which is evidenced by its four distinct colophons, each with a variant compound of Nyangrel's name.[323] Like waves lapping at the shore in a rising tide, each colophon represents a high-water mark left by a distinct wave of redaction before it receded behind another. Additional copies and redac-

322. Meisezahl 1985, 13; Germano 1994, 237n85.

323. First colophon: Nyang ban nyi ma'i 'od zer (*Me tog snying po* M, 363.2.2). Second colophon: Nyang ral pa can (M, 364.2.6). Third colophon: Nyang ban (363.3.6). Fourth colophon: Nyang ban nyi ma 'od zer (365.1.4). The prologue uses another variant: Nyang ral (1.3.6 and 3.3.6).

tions may have occurred between them, but only four contributors authored an additional colophon intended to act as a new and final conclusion to the *Essence of Flowers*. The last major redaction not only interpolated details from the *Testimony of Ba* into the Padmasambhava narrative but also significantly extended the *Essence of Flowers* well beyond the reign of Tri Songdetsen in reliance on the extended version of that source, thereby resulting in a more complete history of Tibetan Buddhism to the twelfth century and in many ways a very different document. If these manipulations indeed were late contributions to the *Essence of Flowers*, as they appear to be, then the earliest iterations of the history could have terminated at the fragmented colophon from the *Copper Island*, before the interpolations from the *Extended Testimony of Ba* and other sources carried the narrative through the end of the empire.

All evidence indicates that the *Essence of Flowers* has always been ascribed to Nyangrel, and each of these subsequent redactors named him as its source as well. Perhaps they recognized that its centerpiece, Nyangrel's biography of Padmasambhava, made it more his text than their own, even if he did not have a direct hand in compiling the *Essence of Flowers*. Such attribution need not be taken as disingenuous or even spurious: it is common for Tibetan documents to be accredited to more famous forebears, which increases the prestige of the document and often its influence as well. A more recent example is the collected writings of Ju Mipham (1846–1912), where the entire collection in as many as thirty-three volumes is ascribed to him, but an analysis of the colophons to individual texts within that collection reveals that Mipham authored a selection of these documents. Many were compiled by disciples who claim to have relied on his notes and/or oral teachings, or who excerpted sections from his commentaries for different applications under distinct titles. In this way, "authorship" in a Tibetan context can be far more inclusive than Western notions of it, which strive to definitively identify a specific individual as the originating agent of a written work. In Tibet authorial responsibility may ultimately be ascribed to the highest common denominator, the most vaunted contributor, however direct or indirect their contribution may have been. The central place of the *Copper Island* narrative within the *Essence of Flowers* may have sufficed to ascribe the entire history to Nyangrel, even if he had no direct involvement in its compilation. The history as a whole is a series of excerpts, threaded together into a single narrative, with scattered extrapolations that appear original to it. With several waves of redaction that introduced, interpolated, and appended excerpts from various sources, it is possible if not likely that the *Essence of Flowers* was constructed by others around the nucleus of Nyangrel's Padmasambhava narrative.

5. Delivering the Lotus-Born

THE REVOLUTIONARY IMPORTANCE of the *Copper Island* cannot be overstated: it is the first complete biography of Padmasambhava; it introduces a counternarrative to late imperial accounts of Tibet's conversion, most especially the one recorded in the *Testimony of Ba*; and it presents the first apotheosis of the imperium into a golden age of Tibetan Buddhism. With the identification of Songtsen Gampo as Avalokiteśvara, it is the foundation narrative of Tibetan culture. And yet despite the presence of Nyangrel's Padmasambhava narrative as the centerpiece of his *Essence of Flowers* history, and despite its renown as Nyangrel's most significant contribution to Tibetan literature, history, and culture, the *Copper Island* is not explicitly named in the extensive treasure inventories and recovery narratives of Nyangrel's primary biographies. His major doctrinal cycles are all accounted for, their concealments by Padmasambhava are recounted, and their recoveries narrated. Even countless minor treasures of mundane thaumaturgical value are carefully inventoried, yet this story of Padmasambhava and his conversion of Tibet is literally nowhere to be found.

An analysis of the origins and transmission of the *Copper Island* problematizes a range of normative assumptions concerning this preeminent work. The treasure origins of Nyangrel's Padmasambhava biography have been regarded with resolved certainty for centuries, but its absence from his biographies warrants an investigation of its source, content, and transmission. Such an investigation offers new hypotheses concerning the introduction, construction, and popularization of Nyangrel's Padmasambhava biography in Tibet.

There are many unknowns and thus many possible permutations for the three hypotheses that follow, but this is precisely the point: our understanding of the transmission of the *Copper Island* (and the *Essence of Flowers*) has become quite fixed despite the fact that, to date, we have known little more about the origins of these documents than what the tradition has dictated to us. It is practically certain that we will never know everything about Nyangrel's methods in creating these documents and their exact transmission, but by considering the full range of evidence now before us, we can relinquish an automatic preference for the normative and familiar. These theses by no means refute all that has been assumed concerning Nyangrel's delivery of Padmasambhava, the Lotus-Born, into Tibetan history, but they present viable alternatives to the received assumptions.

First Hypothesis: Source

As far as we know, it has been considered a matter of fact throughout the long transmission of Nyangrel's Padmasambhava narrative that he revealed it as a treasure text from the Copper Island of the Three Realms (*Khams gsum zangs khang gling*) near Samyé Monastery. The site that serves as the text's ornamental title was the residence of one of Tri Songdetsen's three queens in the Samyé valley. A palace for each of them once stood just beyond the immediate periphery of the monastery, but only a reconstruction of the Copper Island remains standing today.

The name of the text said to have been recovered there, *Sanglingma* (*Zangs gling ma*), has had some variance in its translation due to the ambiguity of the term *ling* (*gling*), most literally a continent or island, which the palace was no doubt designated due to its proximity to the maṇḍala of Samyé Monastery itself. The idealized universe centered upon Samyé's triple-storied temple as Mount Meru is orbited by a cosmos of freestanding temples and stūpas, some of which signify the four continents (*gling bzhi*) and eight subcontinents (*gling phran brgyad*). The queens' palaces were never integral components of this geomantic complex, however, which was made evident in more recent centuries by the construction of a circular, stūpa-capped wall that encloses the monastery and its immediate maṇḍala. Nevertheless, since the queens' palaces lie within the vicinity of Samyé Monastery, they too were designated *ling* as its satellites.

The Copper Island of the Three Realms now stands about two hundred meters south of the monastery, clearly distinct from the center and concentric circles of Samyé's grounds (see plate 3). While the three palaces of the queens at Samyé's periphery functioned as places of worship since ancient times,[324] I

324. Written at the behest of Tri Songdetsen, the *Authoritative Exposition of Samyé* (*Bsam yas bka' mchid*) explicitly refers to the Three Realm palace of another queen as a "temple" (*gtsug lag khang*, Richardson 1998, 92 and 95), and the Copper Island again functioned as such by the time of its reconstruction or renovation sponsored by the fifth Radreng (Reting) Rinpoché, Thupten Jampal Yeshé Gyaltsen (1911–47) in the 1940s. The palace was damaged during the Cultural Revolution and has continued to fall into disrepair since that time (Dorje 2009, 180–81), though paintings and capitals within the main building still vividly depict icons such

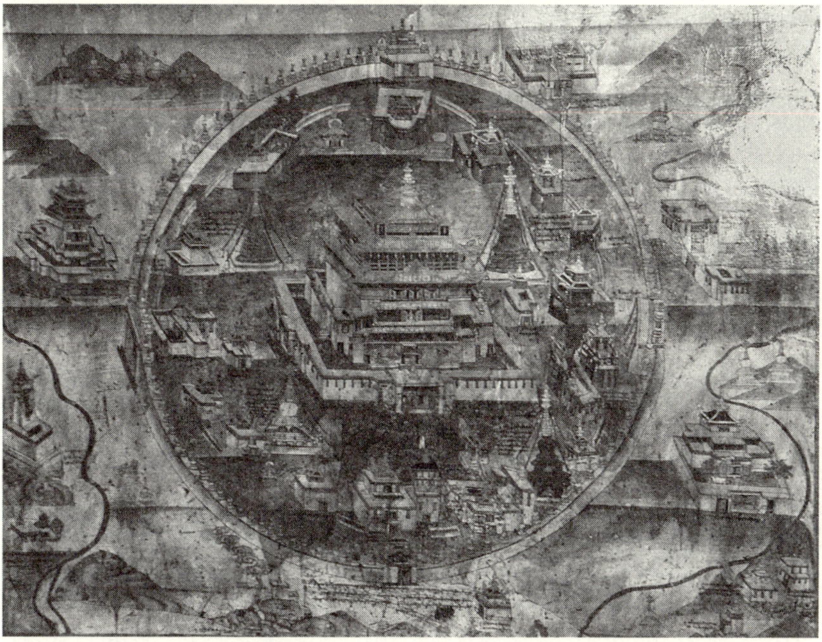

Figure 16. Mural of Samyé Monastery from the second story of its main temple, with its surrounding structures such as the queens' palaces depicted close by. The Copper Island is at middle left, correctly oriented to the south of the monastery. The tower of Yumbu Lagang in Yarlung, its location and distance approximated by its placement across a line representing the Tsangpo River, is at lower left (southeast). Photo by the author, 2011.

revert to the most literal translation of *ling* as "island" throughout rather than the more interpretive "temple" to avoid confusion with those accorded a specific geomantic function within Samyé's maṇḍala. According to later treasure lore, it was here that the biography of Padmasambhava had remained undisturbed from the time Yeshé Tsogyal concealed it around the turn of the ninth century until Nyangrel recovered it, fully complete from start to finish, more than three hundred years later.

Most versions of the *Copper Island* now contain all the hallmarks of a treasure text: treasure marks at the ends of phrases throughout the narrative, a colophon that explicitly categorizes it as a treasure concealed by Yeshé Tsogyal and revealed by Nyangrel, and an ornamental title citing its place of recovery.

as Tsongkhapa and other yellow-hatted masters. As of 2011 it was undergoing extensive renovations for use as a nunnery.

Furthermore, while some of its contents may have been drawn from popular oral narratives, it appears to have been radically unprecedented as a complete biography of Padmasambhava. Among the early sources that remain available to us, a later recension of the *Testimony of Ba* records Padmasambhava as an agent in Tibet's conversion, albeit an ephemeral one, and scattered mentions of the tantrika have been found in other written sources, but none corroborate even this minor role in the establishment of Buddhism. All available evidence indicates that prior to Nyangrel, no complete biography of Padmasambhava existed. Readers quite logically deduced that the *Copper Island* indeed was a treasure text. What other explanation could there be for its sudden introduction by the most famous treasure revealer of the age?

Yet its absence from the narrations of Nyangrel's treasure recoveries and their inventories is striking. Despite the consistency of all emic and etic assumptions concerning the provenance of this text, its origins must be reassessed: Did Nyangrel reveal his Padmasambhava biography from the Copper Island of the Three Realms? Did he even consider it to be a treasure text? If he did not compile the *Essence of Flowers*, could the *Copper Island* be the one fully original composition authored by Nyangrel's hand?

The *Copper Island* itself offers a detail that could be relevant. When Padmasambhava inventories all the treasures he interred throughout Tibet, he begins with the most precious or valuable, "the soul treasures of the king" (*rgyal po'i bla gter*) or "the soul texts of the king" (*rgyal po'i bla dpe*), in signifying that these physical documents function as external supports of the sovereign himself, preserving his vitality.[325] As the records of his speech, such treasures are the testaments (*bka' chems*) of the king, and this is exactly how the text is described within the standard colophon to the *Copper Island*: it is "the testament of the sovereign Tri Songdetsen." According to the *Copper Island* these most precious treasures are concealed on each of Samyé Monastery's three stories at the epicenter of Tibet's Buddhist universe. After these "treasuries of the doctrine" or "soul texts of the king" are secured there, Padmasambhava conceals another round of soul treasures on its most immediate periphery, within the three palaces of Tri Songdetsen's three queens that rose just beyond the maṇḍala of the monastic complex itself. Second only to those concealed within Samyé itself, these too are presumably the soul treasures of the king; the person is omit-

325. *Zangs gling ma* H, 80a6–81b4; I, 65b4–67a2; J, 104a5–6a5; K, 52a5–53a4; L, 150.2–152.5; *Me tog snying po* M, 256.1.1–256.2.4. This is an instance where *Zangs gling ma* H and *Me tog snying po* M are aligned (*rgyal po'i bla gter*) whereas *Zangs gling ma* I, despite being representative of the earliest recension as well, introduces some variants (*rgyal po'i bla dpe* instead of *bla gter*). For the benefits of *bla*-infused objects and their attendant risks in magic, see Cuevas 2010, 169–70.

ted across all recensions, thus it would seem that the prior identification distributes. If this is the case then the soul treasures of the king concealed within the Copper Island of the Three Realms are the only ones that could conceivably represent some components of Nyangrel's eponymous Padmasambhava biography.

And yet while these texts could have been sourced for the *Copper Island*, they cannot provide the entire narrative: the story continues well beyond Padmasambhava's description of his treasure concealments. The narrative does not conclude until after he leaves Tibet, therefore necessitating its concealment by another. The colophons across all recensions indeed attribute this action to Padmasambhava's consort and aide, Yeshé Tsogyal, and not to Padmasambhava himself. This being the case its exclusion from the treasure inventories within the *Copper Island* itself is acceptable, but the failure to explicitly mention such a seminal text among Nyangrel's treasure recoveries in his biographies warrants further investigation.

While Nyangrel's *Stainless Proclamations* biography generically references some treasures that are defined by historical content, his *Clear Mirror* biography fails to corroborate them: it makes no mention of any such texts among Nyangrel's finds. He does recover some treasures from Samyé Monastery in the *Clear Mirror*, yet even if the general identification of this place is meant to include the queen's palaces, the biographies concur that only a cache of treasures related to the Great Perfection are recovered in that area. Nyangrel never finds a Padmasambhava biography as a treasure text in either biography, nor does he elect to author one—or any other text for that matter—historical or otherwise. The omission of a conventionally compiled history such as the *Essence of Flowers* from both biographies is not unexpected given their focus on his treasures. Moreover, we might discern a preemptive subtext that precludes even ordinary textual production lest such authorship suggest that his treasures were fabricated as well, but the total absence of the *Copper Island* or anything resembling it from the *Clear Mirror* is problematic, since this biography alone won sufficient distribution as to be referenced for subsequent histories. The *Clear Mirror* offers no correlate for Nyangrel's biography of Padmasambhava, treasure or otherwise; according to what are presented as exhaustive inventories within it, Nyangrel never found nor authored such a text. Despite much evidence of manipulation over the course of the *Clear Mirror*'s transmission and the eventual renown of the *Copper Island*, no redactor elected to insert an episode relating its revelation into this biography. While the *Stainless Proclamations* also fails to provide readers with a definitive citation, it may obliquely provide some potential correlates for the Padmasambhava biography among Nyangrel's finds.

The closest candidates for the *Copper Island* among any of Nyangrel's treasures mentioned in the *Stainless Proclamations* would be some histories of Buddhism (*chos 'byuṇg*) found toward the end of the recovery process at Drak Sinmo Barjé, as well as some others that are generically listed with chronicles (*lo rgyus*) drawn from an unspecified location.[326] Nothing more than these two historical genres are provided, and their contents remain unknown. Emerging from a casket of less luxurious construction near the very end of Nyangrel's recovery at Drak Sinmo Barjé, these histories were not considered as important or as valuable as the treasures that precede them according to the implicit material and chronological hierarchies of the recovery process, at least not at the time when the *Stainless Proclamations* was written (or manipulated to include these genres). Nevertheless, the mention of histories of Buddhism among Nyangrel's treasures in the *Stainless Proclamations* provides the only possible correlates for his narrative focusing on the catalytic role of Padmasambhava in Tibet's golden age when Buddhism was established. While uncorroborated in the *Clear Mirror*, the Padmasambhava narrative is explicitly cited as a history of Buddhism within the *Essence of Flowers*, thus it has been understood as such for some time, but this is hardly sufficient to identify one of these minor historical treasures in the *Stainless Proclamations* as the *Copper Island*.

Despite this absence, the *Copper Island* cannot be attributed to another author, tradent, or treasure revealer. Whether popularly attested as a treasure spoken by Padmasambhava, transcribed and concealed by Yeshé Tsogyal, and revealed from beneath the foot of Hayagrīva in the Copper Island of the Three Realms, or critically theorized to be a pious fabrication only legitimated as treasure, what we now know as the *Copper Island* has always been attributed to Nyangrel. The most compelling evidence of its compiler still lies within its own narrative: in all versions of the *Copper Island*, whether as distinct volumes or embedded in the *Essence of Flowers*, Padmasambhava prophesizes the arrival of an individual who, as the seventeenth incarnation of Tri Songdetsen, will be karmically destined to recover the treasures and attain enlightenment in that lifetime. Given its details, this can be none other than Nyangrel. Padmasambhava attests:

> For the king's benefit we have translated many sacred doctrines that produce enlightenment in a single life. Since you are distracted, however, you will not apply them experientially [at this time], but you will retain a karmic connection. I have concealed them as treasure such that in the last of seventeen catenate lifetimes you will

326. *Dri ma med pa*, 98.6 and 103.6.

> meet with them again. The secret mantras, fierce mantras, and oral instructions will arise in treasure caches to a few fortunate ones.[327]

Nyangrel was the first to claim catenate reincarnation, his first attested pre-incarnation was Tri Songdetsen, and he repeatedly identifies himself as the seventeenth incarnation of the emperor. Of less relevance to Nyangrel in this particular instance but of profound importance for the later treasure tradition is Padmasambhava's allowance of "a few" fortunate ones who would also serve as treasure revealers. These few would later expand to include the reincarnations of Padmasambhava's twenty-five major and 108 minor disciples, each of whom may produce as many as five emanations with each reincarnation, thereby allowing for an ever expanding constellation of treasure revealers.[328] It is clear from this prophecy, however, that the seventeenth incarnation of Tri Songdetsen was to be the supreme treasure revealer, Nyangrel, which was first reflexively articulated within his *Copper Island.*

In the event that this prophecy was insufficient to unequivocally identify that individual, Padmasambhava provides more explicit detail concerning the exact biodata of the great treasure revealer to come:

> In the last of his seventeen catenate lifetimes, the sovereign king himself will be a person [born] in a dragon year in a place like a red horse carcass split open, which lies toward the southwest border of this place.[329]

Sources concur that Nyangrel was born in a dragon year in Lhodrak, which lies south-southwest of Samyé Monastery, the presumptive setting for this prophecy. Not for lack of trying, I have yet to visit and determine whether the region of his birth resembles the cavity of a dead horse, but the area is indeed renowned for the red-rock gorges and mountains that inspire this bloody analogy.[330] Since each of these details specifically identifies Nyangrel

327. *Me tog snying po* K, 352.1–5; M, 254.3.4–6; *Zangs gling ma* H, 79b2–4. *Zangs gling ma* A, 134, is translated in Kunsang 1993, 136.

328. This scenario bears a striking resemblance to the *Samādhi of Direct Encounter with the Buddhas of the Present Sūtra.* See Mayer 1994.

329. *Me tog snying po* K, 354.18–21; M, 256.3.2–4; *Zangs gling ma* H, 82b.4–6. For a translation of the equivalent section in *Zangs gling ma* A, 138 see Kunsang 1993, 139. However, also note that additional identifying details have been inserted, such as the actual place name, Tamshöl, and that he would be born into a "noble family" or imperial clan, neither of which are present in earlier iterations of the narrative.

330. Mawochok ridge is called Five-Pointed Vajra Red Rock (Brag mar rdo rje rtse lnga),

as the destined treasure revealer, and since they are reproduced in every version of the *Copper Island* and the *Essence of Flowers* (whose figures have a *terminus ad quem* around the conclusion of Nyangrel's life), this is the most compelling evidence that Nyangrel was the source of this Padmasambhava narrative. Only he would gain from the articulation and distribution of this prophecy; it is critical to legitimating his treasure career and thus his legacy. Once the text was sufficiently well known and vaunted, his disciples would presumably garner some prestige by association as well, but it took time—perhaps centuries—for Nyangrel's Padmasambhava narrative to acquire such acceptance, recognition, and status, and several more centuries and new Padmasambhava biographies by subsequent treasure revealers for it to become normative. As evidenced by the evolution of its title, Nyangrel's biography of Padmasambhava required time and strategic repackaging to acquire broader acceptance and higher valuation in Tibet's cultural milieu.

Though it seems to have always been attributed to Nyangrel, this first complete biography of Padmasambhava acquired its treasure origin myth and ornamental title well after his death. Only two out of the five exemplars of the *Copper Island*'s earliest recension, the one that most resembles whatever was originally constructed by Nyangrel, actually include "the Copper Island" in their titles.[331] Another (H) makes no reference to that site within its title or colophon: the cover describes its contents as the *Extensive Testament of Padma* (*Padma bka' chems brgyas [rgyas] pa*) whereas the colophon refers to it as the *Great Summary: The Chronicle of the Great Master Padmasambhava* (*Slob dpon chen po padma 'byung gnas kyi lo rgyus / Spyi chings chen mo*). The title page of a more corrupted exemplar in the same recensional line (L) concurs that it is the *Testament of Urgyen Padmasambhava* (*Dbu rgyan pad ma 'byung gnas kyi bka' chems*), and it too makes no reference to its recovery from the Copper Island of the Three Realms, or any other site for that matter. Yet another exemplar (J) proposes a different recovery site altogether! Its title reads, *Biography of Urgyen Padmasambhava Revealed as Treasure by Ngadak Nyangrelpa from Lhodrak's Rock Bearing the Clawmarks of the Demoness* (*U rgyan padma 'byung gnas kyi rnam thar mnga' bdag nyang ral pas lho brag gi brag srin po'i sbar rjes 'dra ba nas gter nas ston pa*). While this identification of Drak Sinmo

---

and according to Dorje 2009, 249, the road from Trigu Lake south to Mawochok features "a remarkable canyon where the bare red hillsides are severely contorted and eroded." The region evidently has many striking red geological features.

331. I am grateful to Lewis Doney for sharing his twelve exemplars of Nyangrel's Padmasambhava biography, two of which (H and I) are reproduced in his 2014 monograph. I rely on the findings and designations of his "preliminary stemma" for the recensional process of the *Copper Island* (42).

Barjé as the recovery site demonstrates a degree of familiarity with Nyangrel's biographical traditions, the suggestion of a distinct site as the source of the text reflects a persistent uncertainty with regard to its provenance. Given the absence or substitution of the Copper Island within many exemplars of the earliest recension of the text, it is clear that Nyangrel's biography of Padmasambhava only became known as the *Copper Island* well after his introduction of it. He did not recognize his work by that name.

Likewise, he did not recover this treasure from the Copper Island of the Three Realms. Unattested among early sources, the traditional treasure-recovery narrative describes Nyangrel's retrieval of this text from beneath the foot of a Hayagrīva statue within the queen's palace, yet this bears an unmistakable resemblance to Ngödrup's recovery of the *Great Compassionate One* (a.k.a. the *Maṇi Kambum*) from beneath the foot of Hayagrīva in the Jokhang.[332] While the sites of these statues are distinct, the correlation suggests that the narrative for Nyangrel's recovery of his Padmasambhava narrative from the Copper Island of the Three Realms may have been derived from or conflated with the discovery of the *Great Compassionate One* by his mentor. Given that both the Copper Island recovery narrative and its ornamental title are founded solely on a later tradition, Nyangrel did not recover his Padmasambhava biography from the site that provides its renowned name.

As to when exactly Nyangrel's Padmasambhava biography acquired its discovery narrative and title, it is hard to say, but some codas to Urgyen Lingpa's fourteenth-century *Testament of Padmasambhava* likewise make reference to Nyangrel's text by its alleged place of origin. This material begins with a precise colophon describing the *Testament*'s discovery by Urgyen Lingpa, providing details down to the day of the week, though this does not conclude every exemplar and thus may not be original to the *Testament*. In those that preserve this recovery colophon, however, many versions of the *Testament* append an editorial coda stating that this biography of Padmasambhava was harmonized with "Ngadak Nyang's treasure renowned as the *Copper Island Biography*." In xylographs based on the Fifth Dalai Lama's redaction, this is most often followed by an additional coda signed by the Great Fifth himself, so the reference to the *Copper Island* is seventeenth century at the latest. Elsewhere Tselé Natsok Rangdröl, a contemporary of the Great Fifth who lived to the east of Lhasa as the hierarch of Tselé Monastery, a Kagyü-Nyingma institution, relies on nearly the exact same words to note that he too perused "Ngadak Nyang's

332. Compare traditional accounts of Ngödrup's discovery of the *Maṇi Kambum* (Kapstein 2000, 145–46) with those of Nyangrel's discovery of the *Copper Island* (Kunsang 1993, 3).

treasure renowned as the *Copper Island Biography*," so it was certainly designated and renowned as such by the seventeenth century at the latest.[333]

While investigation of the title uncovers variants that interject much uncertainty concerning the site of the text's retrieval, the colophons to the narrative are remarkably consistent. While an array of additions has been made across the various versions of Nyangrel's Padmasambhava biography, all of them share several lines as the core of the colophon:

> For the benefit of future generations, having transcribed into a single perspective the words of Master Padmasambhava's mindstream, the words of the testament of the sovereign Tri Songdetsen, and the words of the exalted qualities of the Great Compassionate One,[334] the sole mother Lady Tsogyal, the magical emanation of the goddess Sarasvatī, the one who attained the mnemonic retention of nonforgetting, concealed it as a precious treasure. It was placed for the benefit of those endowed with fortune and karmic connection, and entrusted by means of the three stages of seal: seal of treasure, seal of concealment, and seal of entrustment. Seal, seal, seal. *Īthi.*[335]

333. *Padma bka' thang*, 505.5–6. Concerning the Fifth Dalai Lama's use of *Zangs gling ma* in his redaction of *Padma bka' thang*, see van der Kuijp 2013a, 144–46. Rtse le Sna tshogs rang grol 1979, 423.1.

Also of note is Blondeau 1992, where she describes her analysis of a Padmasambhava biography revealed by Ratna Lingpa (1403–79) called the *Golden Rosary* (*Bka' thang gser phreng*). The colophon attests that it was found in Nyangrel's home region of Lhodrak, and given its content, this claim is especially cogent: most of the text replicates Nyangrel's *Copper Island* verbatim. The text is produced beneath a different title but one that is itself not new: the *Golden Rosary* most certainly was titled as such as an homage to the well-known exemplar by Sangyé Lingpa. Yet this process only underscores the Tibetan practice of tradency in the re/production of texts, whether via treasure recovery or more conventionally; again, the negative connotations of "plagiarism" are irrelevant here (Cf. Blondeau 1992, 69). Blondeau relates that she was tipped off to this reproduction because her unique *Golden Rosary* manuscript explicitly inscribed the *Copper Island* (*Zangs gling ma'o*) as a subtitle, but such is not apparent in published versions of the text. This being the case, it seems very unlikely that Ratna Lingpa himself made such a citation; instead it was inscribed by a later cataloger or copyist who correctly identified the source.

334. These three sources may be interpreted as indifferentiable: Padmasambhava is an emanation of the Great Compassionate One—Avalokiteśvara—and Tri Songdetsen is his foremost disciple, who bears witness to the same events. Furthermore, the emperor is destined to inherit his instructions and attain realization by means of them, thereby becoming equivalent to and inseparable from Padmasambhava and Avalokiteśvara. From this perspective it becomes difficult to distinguish how these sources could be anything but in agreement, and how they are three sources instead of one.

335. Despite Lady Tsogyal's critical role in this colophon that reflects her later elaboration as Padmasambhava's aide-de-camp, she garners nothing more than a couple of passing references

With little variation these lines appear in every version of Nyangrel's Padmasambhava biography presently available to us, including the one embedded within his *Essence of Flowers*, but there the last few lines are omitted. Following a concluding summary of the entire narrative that only appears in the *Essence of Flowers*, the standard colophon to Nyangrel's Padmasambhava biography begins but is then interrupted after "the testament of the sovereign Tri Songdetsen," which not only divorces these phrases from their final verb and grammatical function but also excises the treasure origins of the entire narrative that precedes it.

All textual evidence presently available to us indicates that the Padmasambhava biography existed independently first and was subsequently embedded as the core of the *Essence of Flowers*. The deliberate exclusion of its treasure origins in the *Essence of Flowers* perhaps reflects a concern that this history would be considered illegitimate by some if identified as a treasure. This would provide an impetus for its reproduction—without any reference to its treasure origins—within a historical genre. While there is little evidence that Nyangrel was the target of such critiques in his lifetime, his biographies do preserve a couple of episodes that reflect a similar concern. Moreover, within the Padmasambhava biography itself, the master warns that some of the emperor's future teachings will meet with skepticism as the karmic residue of imperial-era transgressions such as banishing Vairocana and other prominent Buddhists.

Given the repetition of this treasure colophon within all recensions of Nyangrel's Padmasambhava biography, and even the tactical omission of its treasure designation from the *Essence of Flowers*, Nyangrel most likely revealed his biography of Padmasambhava—or more accurately it "emerged" to him—as a treasure.[336] And yet despite its famous ornamental title and recovery narrative, Nyangrel certainly did not excavate this text from the Copper Island of the Three Realms. In retaining a skepticism toward his direct authorship of the *Essence of Flowers*, I suspect that Nyangrel framed his entire literary corpus without exception

in a single chapter of the *Copper Island* narrative itself, where she plays no role in treasure concealment. While she is listed among the disciples as possessing the ability to raise the dead, no mention is made of additional siddhis such as her mnemonic abilities that become so key to her role in treasure concealment. For some early threads of Yeshé Tsogyal and her elaboration within her hagiographies, see Gyatso 2006, passim.

336. Though this book grew out of my dissertation, it involved a thorough review and revision, and thus there are numerous differences between them, mostly minor but a few major as well. Among the latter is this conclusion, where I argued against its status as a treasure in my dissertation (cf. Hirshberg 2012, 253–56). As evidenced by my argument there, there is good reason to think that Nyangrel did not consider his biography of Padmasambhava to be a treasure text, but the argument above seems more cogent.

as treasures, as attested in his biographies. But what did the "emergence" of this Padmasambhava narrative signify for Nyangrel? How was it produced?

Second Hypothesis: Content

For Nyangrel treasure recovery was not one of textual discovery alone, where the document was brought forth whole and reintroduced *in situ*. Instead, discovery only initiated a process by which old sources or textual fragments were readied for reproduction and redistribution through compilation, augmentation, and emendation with original writing as needed. Cantwell and Mayer have identified instances within Nyangrel's *Eight Instructions* collection that strongly point to this exact process, and they also found a fragment of an imperial-era textual source within his Padmasambhava narrative as well. It is difficult to definitively identify the array of sources that contributed to the elaboration of Nyangrel's Padmasambhava narrative, yet its content strongly suggests his reliance on at least three distinct types: textual, oral, and mnemonic. As has been suggested if not demonstrated by others, Nyangrel replicated and expanded upon old texts as well as popular yarns and didactic songs for raw material, but I would like to forward a third, previously unconsidered element as the unifying principle and foremost source of this unprecedented text: it was the memory of his past life as Tri Songdetsen that empowered Nyangrel, like no other who preceded him, to produce a narrative starring Padmasambhava in Tibet's golden age.

As surveyed in the introduction, mentions of Padmasambhava are found throughout a number of post-imperial if not late-imperial texts, some of which already hail him with devotional epithets that prefigure the extensive guru-yoga literature that would focus on him,[337] so Nyangrel likely read about the master and found some references and episodes among the folios of old manuscripts he deemed treasure. In fact, attributed to Nyangrel, his contemporary Lama Shang, and his reincarnation Guru Chöwang are elaborate Padmasambhava guru yogas that "seek to embed the entire Nyingma ritual path within a particular narrative of Padmasambhava," so Robert Mayer identifies this genre as an especially promising area to investigate for the development of his biography.[338] Indeed, since a goal of devotional guru yoga is to melt the rigidity of self-directed visualization for the natural fluidity of a visionary encounter with the object of one's devotion, guru yoga would seem to be a potent resource

337. Mayer 2015b, 342.

338. Mayer 2013a, citing a personal discussion with Dan Martin.

for the Precious Guru's many biographers, including Nyangrel. While Nyangrel may have been familiar with the *Testimony of Ba*, its relegation of Padmasambhava to a minor personage suffering an inglorious departure could not have jibed with his fervent devotion to him. Even though the *Testimony of Ba* does not share any text with the *Copper Island*, their plotlines recounting Padmasambhava's invitation to Tibet and his campaign through the landscape share several thematic correlates, and Nyangrel may have expanded those elements that fit his conception while omitting those that contradicted it.

One among the many issues in approaching the origins of the *Copper Island* has been the absence of corresponding source texts from which it was drawn. While old textual fragments have been hypothesized among its sources, none had been confirmed until recently, thereby inviting further skepticism concerning the significance of its treasure origins: did revelation really signify the discovery and reproduction of old texts, or were treasures merely the original inventions of their revealers? As evidence of the former and repudiation of the latter we now have Cantwell and Mayer's recently discovered example of textual correspondence between an ancient manuscript and Nyangrel's Padmasambhava biography. A single verse of praise to "the Lotus King" from *A Noble Noose of Methods*, a text recovered from the cache near Dunhuang, is replicated in the fourth chapter of the *Copper Island*. Following their translation:

> *A Noble Noose of Methods*:
> [I] prostrate to he who has attained the supreme siddhi of great wonder,
> the Lotus King who is not worldly,
> who unravels from the expanse
> the Tathāgata's great secret pith instructions.
>
> Nyangrel's *Extensive Testament of Padma*:
> [I] prostrate to and praise the exalted form who has attained the supreme siddhi of great wonder,
> the exalted form of incomparable realization, the Lotus King,
> you who unravels from the expanse
> the Tathāgata's great secret pith instructions.[339]

Mayer reiterates that the *Noble Noose of Methods* manuscript is at least two copyings past the original and so could have originated in the late-imperial era

339. Cantwell and Mayer 2012, 93.

not long after Padmasambhava's visit.[340] Thanks to Cantwell and Mayer's discovery, there can be little doubt that Nyangrel drew at least some elements of his Padmasambhava narrative from old manuscripts deemed treasure. While additional correspondences have yet to be revealed, it is highly unlikely that this is the only instance; instead, such replication would be the rule rather than the exception in my thesis concerning the postproduction involved in Nyangrel's treasure recoveries. Furthermore, despite the absence of concrete textual evidence indicating an earlier provenance of Padmasambhava's biographical literature, it is likely that the proto-Nyingma clans of the eleventh century contributed much to its development and transmission. An affinity for Padmasambhava may have been passed down the line of Nyangrel's own Nyang clan, and Matthew Kapstein relates that "in the case of the Zur, the fortuitous survival of the *Paṇ sgrub snying gi nyi ma* (*Heart-Sun of the Scholars and Siddhas*) assures us that a developed narrative of Vairocana, which formed the kernel of the later *Bai ro 'dra 'bag* (*Likeness of Vairocana*) texts, was already in existence."[341] It is safe to assume that some clans preserved, elaborated, and transmitted the devout interest in Padmasambhava as witnessed in post-imperial literature and contributed much to the life of Padmasambhava in various media, both textual and oral, throughout the renaissance.

In addition to mentions of Padmasambhava that were committed to the page, it has been suggested that his role in Tibet's conversion to Buddhism developed in Tibetan folklore as it was threaded into the yarns of wandering storytellers.[342] Based on the content of the *Copper Island*, it seems that a vibrant tradition of didactic songs attributed to him, lyrical instructions for the practice of esoteric Buddhism, circulated as well. While the various codas in the addendum to the *Essence of Flowers* cannot be attributed to Nyangrel, their repeated insistence on the validity of oral sources indicates that many were available and considered historical at their times of writing. Oral sources may have contributed some episodes, themes, and details to the plotline itself, but Padmasambhava's versified advice to various groups of his Tibetan disciples fills all but three of the *Copper Island*'s last twenty-one chapters, few of which include any narrative content. Incorporating a lyrical anthology as part of his compilation process, Nyangrel may have adapted some of these verses from the songs of bards.

340. Mayer 2011b, translating IOL Tib J 321, 84a, and *Zangs gling ma* H, 16a5–b1.

341. Kapstein, personal communication, March 18, 2015. *Paṇ sgrub rnams kyi thugs bcud snying gi nyi ma*, the *Heart-Sun Which Is the Essential Mind of the Scholars and Siddhas*, is the first text in the *Bai ro rgyud 'bum*.

342. Sørensen 1994, 1; Davidson 2005, 243.

Recent theorists such as Wulf Oestereicher have clarified the "transcoding" of oral sources into text where the inclusion of these didactic songs throughout the latter half of the *Copper Island* would represent "the mimesis of immediacy or simulated orality." Alleged to be transcribed by perfect recall, these songs attempt to recreate the immediacy of direct aural experience in written form—the reader is transported to the court and joins the audience of these instructions. This functions quite effectively in the *Copper Island*, as these songs "feature the characteristics of people and their affective dispositions; mark communicative and dramatic constellations; and provoke attention,"[343] all of which aid the primary objective of the narrative, which is the construction of Padmasambhava as the Second Buddha. Lauri Honko argues that oral perfomers and textual authors alike are fluent in the same "pool of tradition," the "generic rules, storylines, mental images of epic events, linguistically preprocessed descriptions of repeatable scenes, sets of established terms and attributes, phrases and formulas,"[344] which symbiotically informs and influences both the creators of content and their intended audience. In Tibetan biographical literature in general and the *Copper Island* in particular, the diverse elements extracted from this pool are synthesized into a compelling narrative that redefines, rehabilitates, and apotheosizes its protagonist and era. With these textual fragments from old sources deemed treasure, and the inspirational stories and songs propagated and elaborated by the ancient clans, storytellers, and bards amid the local populace of Lhodrak especially, Nyangrel would have had much material to knit into a complete narrative featuring Padmasambhava, but so did his treasure-revealing contemporaries: why was Nyangrel the one who introduced this unprecedented document?

Twelfth-century Tibet saw a unique coalescence of conditions: in this fragmented era when clan influence had diminished, a popular nostalgia for the stability and grandeur of the empire persisted as expressed in part by the emergence of old manuscripts as treasure and the oral transmission of Padmasambhava lore. While these conditions were shared by other treasure revealers of the era, Nyangrel stands out as an especially gifted author and tradent, and one with a fervent devotion to Padmasambhava. His talents made him the foremost architect of Buddhist treasure recovery. And in claiming to be the reincarnation of Tri Songdetsen, Nyangrel constructed a precise karmic pretext for his contributions, one that hinged on an omniscient Padmasambhava as the treasure concealer *par excellence* who guaranteed their later recovery. In the *Copper Island*, the tantrika foretells the emperor's eventual rebirth as the great

343. Oesterreicher 1997, 205.

344. Honko 2000, 18, cited by Dotson 2013, 200–202.

treasure revealer, prophesying his enlightenment and literary activity in that lifetime, and promises to appear and guide him in all his lives. This prophecy is dutifully fulfilled in each of (Guru Chöwang's and) Nyangrel's preincarnation narratives, and while explicitly identified as Padmasambhava only in the *Clear Mirror*, Nyangrel's encounter with a young yogin bearing certificates in both biographies is a critical turning point in his ascension from impoverished tantrika to glorious treasure-revealing king.

Nyangrel was undoubtedly inspired, but I suspect that his inspiration was foremost characterized by the one source that superseded the authority of all others, textual and oral, historical or not, the one to which he had exclusive access and that thereby set him apart from all others, which was what he believed to be authentic personal memories of these events from his past life as Tri Songdetsen. That life was the karmic basis of his treasure recoveries, his enlightenment, and his legacy, and it served as the mandate for his revision of Tibet's conversion as well. If the colophon to his Padmasambhava narrative is original—and it appears to be given its repetition across all recensions—then Nyangrel quite explicitly cites himself among its three foremost sources. Nyangrel's own testimony is "the testament of the sovereign Tri Songdetsen" because he *is* Emperor Tri Songdetsen, "the sovereign" Ngadak Nyangrel, which he repeatedly attests by way of memory.

While both of Nyangrel's biographies present several instances where he remembers his past life as the emperor, only the primary biography of the *Clear Mirror* preserves four narrations of their content, each of which is in the first person. For Nyangrel these mnemonic episodes naturally arise in mind when provoked by a correlate reminder, a basic causative function of all human memory. For example, returning to an old childhood haunt after a long time, countless moments long forgotten resurface as remembrance across the spectrum of sensory experience; not just sights but sounds and smells and even tactile sensations of being in that body as that person return as momentary, fragmented phantoms that nevertheless are quite vividly revived.

In our time and our culture, we accept a restricted view of that range of experience: ordinarily we only remember the events of this life. And yet while we might recognize the subjectivity, selectivity, and fallibility inherent in those memories, they seem perfectly real, legitimate, and accurate as representations of the past unless contested and disproven. By contrast, in considering Nyangrel's time, culture, and beliefs, there seems little reason to doubt that Nyangrel operated on the conviction that his mnemonic context was far more expansive and irrefutably authentic. Just as he understood that his karmic continuum persisted throughout many lives, his enlightenment transcended the hapless constriction of memory to the life of a single physical body. He repeatedly claims to remember events from his past lives exactly as he does those of his present one. Given the degree of realization he claimed, he would have assumed that those memories were authentic, historically accurate representations of real past events. By means of such unique access to Tibet's history, he also may have assumed a uniquely authoritative editorial position for its revision, where discordant accounts such as the *Testimony of Ba* could be repudiated (and therefore omitted) as mistaken, biased, inaccurate, and incomplete. In the backwaters of Lhodrak, who among Nyangrel's retinue of disciples would have challenged the account of their enlightened guru? Some of these very disciples are cited as those to whom Nyangrel himself orally recounted his memories of the empire that they subsequently committed to the page within his biographies.

As Nyangrel proceeds to recount his present life in the *Clear Mirror*, recollections from his past life as the emperor arise as naturally and vividly as those from his own childhood. Nyangrel may have been fond of sharing these recollections with his disciples, sometimes as causal explanations for some challenging circumstances manifesting in his current life, another context borrowed from Indic Buddhist materials. These address the paradox of how an enlightened individual, who necessarily has purified all obscurations and accumulated an infinite store of merit and wisdom, may still experience suffering that is the fruition of negative karma by definition. Exactly along these lines in the *Clear Mirror*, Nyangrel explains his impoverishment in young adulthood by way of a memory:

> While there was enjoyment and favorable conditions in retreat, I was famished and had to earn a living by performing the thread-cross rites of the Mighty Weapon and Matram's Blood. In this way I came to ponder what conditions caused my poverty, and because I did [this memory arose]:
>
> Previously when I took birth as the king, I was distracted by wealth and did not apply myself to the practice of Buddhism. At that time I beseeched the master for a method that would decrease wealth, so Padmasambhava replied, "Step over my food bowl one time." Instead I disobeyed his instruction and stepped over his bowl three times, to which he said, "By the power of your aspiration, there will now be an equivalent decline of your wealth!"[345]

Padmasambhava thus prophesies that, at some point along the emperor's

345. *Gsal ba'i me long*, 334.6–335.3.

rebirth trajectory, he will become impoverished as a result of the ardent enthusiasm that compelled him to step over the bowl not just once as instructed by his guru but thrice, which would be considered an offensive and inherently negative act even when a correlate intent was absent. The omniscient Padmasambhava knows that the single performance of this action would produce Tri Songdetsen's desired result—a reduction of wealth and its attendant distractions such that the king could practice Buddhism and accomplish the path in the future—but his overzealous disobedience will produce not just a little reduction of wealth but three times that. This causes Nyangrel to endure poverty and hunger as a young man despite being the enlightened treasure revealer who enjoys the fruition of outstanding merit throughout most of his life.

The remaining three instances where Nyangrel confides a direct recollection from his life as Tri Songdetsen mostly provide insight into his impending future in the *Clear Mirror*. While the next memory initiates a convoluted genealogy of descendants from Tri Songdetsen and the progressive deterioration of the teachings until he reincarnates as Nyangrel, it also offers several prophecies concerning the decades after his death in 1192, which supports my hypothesis that his biographers began compiling the *Clear Mirror* in this period. In particular, Nyangrel warns of the coming incursion of foreign armies, which must be the Mongol invasions of central Tibet that began in 1240. Early in their campaigns the Mongols famously passed through Drigung Monastery, and the well-traveled pilgrimage route linking Drigung to Nyangrel's Mawochok hermitage likely carried such news south to Lhodrak. In designing a bulwark against these invasions to come, Nyangrel advises his disciples to construct and consecrate new representations of the Three Jewels, including four large stūpas in the four directions, and to inter treasure vases in specific locations as a means to safeguard the area. While this memory offers a glimpse of the anxieties pervading Tibet when the Mongols threatened, its content is more prophecy than memory and relates little to Nyangrel's preincarnation as the emperor.

The remaining two memories karmically contextualize the irrevocable certainty of Nyangrel's approaching death and cryptically address the degree of his involvement in the world thereafter. As such they are communicated at the very end of his life in response to the concerns of his intimate disciples, who supplicate him to remain in the world a bit longer. Nyangrel first replies, in effect, that there is nothing to be done because:

> The prophecy of my nirvāṇa is from a previous time: when I was Tri Songdetsen, Master Padmasambhava said, "King! In the last of your

> thirteen lives of training,[346] you will be known as Nyang Ralpachen. Having met with the treasures of my exalted mind at that time, you will benefit beings for sixty-nine human years."
>
> Since that moment has now arrived and it is time to go, there is no way to extend my life and I will depart for the Lotus-Arrayed Pure Realm of Great Bliss. The retinue of disciples, having fused aspiration to action and paying homage to me, will swiftly become bodhisattvas. Since there is no such thing as coming or going in actuality, make those supplications, and because I am an authentic guru, we will meet again and again.

Shifting back to a third-person narrator, this episode then concludes, "Having said that, Nyangrel gave his many last wills and testaments to the retinue of his disciples."[347] Once again, this mnemonic episode highlights the inerrancy of Padmasambhava's omniscience by prefiguring Nyangrel's inherited karmic context: these circumstances are inevitable. Nothing can delay his death since it was prophesied by Padmasambhava centuries ago. While the grief of his disciples cannot be allayed or delayed, Nyangrel reminds them that he also is the fulfillment of Padmasambhava's prophecy that Tri Songdetsen would become an enlightened treasure revealer, so his disciples should take comfort in the merit of their association and can expect high degrees of attainment as a result of it.

The fourth and final memory is divulged not long before Nyangrel's death, where he states that his departure for the western buddha realm of great bliss is imminent, and yet the *Clear Mirror* then proceeds to predict various sets of magical emanations. The ambiguities if not contradictions inherent in the final chapter of this biography, coupled with a closer analysis of its construction, suggests that its content was drawn from conflicting sources. Once again the memory is provoked in Nyangrel's mind due to questions forwarded by his disciples concerning his future emanations. Nyangrel recounts:

> In my previous life King Tri Songdetsen asked Guru Padmasambhava, "When I become a buddha, will my magical emanations arise to benefit sentient beings or not?" Master Padmasambhava

346. Recall that the modes of enumeration and final tallies of Nyangrel's incarnations varies in his biographies. In the *Clear Mirror* the first three are excluded from the tally. See Hirshberg forthcoming for the origination of these inconsistencies in Guru Chöwang's accounts of their shared incarnations, and how some were transferred into Nyangrel's biographies.

347. *Gsal ba'i me long*, 363.2–6; B, 145.2–7.

> replied, "Since the sovereign himself is a yogic practitioner of the Great Compassionate One, if you take to heart this doctrine of the Great Compassionate One, the vast benefit of beings will arise as if irreversibly."[348]

The details of this prophecy remain cryptic, but the *Clear Mirror* interjects a clear break by isolating "additionally" (*de yang*) between *shad* marks before proceeding with far more explicit prophecies for Nyangrel's future emanations. Whenever these proved to be insufficiently explicit, later interlocutors inserted resolutions interlineally to resolve any lingering questions concerning the identities of these emanations. Rather than beneficent appearances of Nyangrel as an enlightened entity in dreams and visions, several tap real historical persons as the reincarnations of Nyangrel. Just as Nyangrel appropriated Tri Songdetsen to karmically construct his present life, later treasure revealers invoked Nyangrel out of his intended retirement in the western buddha realm to legitimate their activities.

In sum, none of Nyangrel's memories allegedly transcribed verbatim into the *Clear Mirror* present historical content relevant to Tibet's conversion, and they neither were included in nor informed Nyangrel's Padmasambhava narrative directly. Yet they perform very specific functions within the biographical narrative that preserves them and, as such, appropriately relate to the life of Nyangrel rather than Padmasambhava. While Kapstein offers a systematic study of "mnemotechnic terminology" in a fourteenth-century Great Perfection treatise,[349] Nyangrel's biographies provide no such opportunity for analysis, since there are so few mnemic or even technical terms. The *Stainless Proclamations* states that he "recollected (*dran*) fifteen preincarnations like a reflection dawning in a mirror,"[350] but even this basic verb of remembrance is omitted in the recollection of past events confided elsewhere in his primary biographies. The *Clear Mirror* only prefaces these episodes with variants of "when I was Tri Songdetsen" in the exact same way that childhood episodes are prefaced by "when I reached the age of ten" and so forth. His memories of being Tri Songdetsen are presented as equivalent with his memories of being a ten-year-old child in his present life. Only the chronology is different; the mnemonic context is not. His recollections of experiences from three centuries prior are trace effects of past experience resurrected as thought, and neither questions of accuracy nor the creative capacity of the imagination are

348. *Gsal ba'i me long*, 372.3–5; B, 154.2–4.

349. Kapstein 2000, 178–96.

350. *Dri ma med pa*, 100.6.

raised as problematic. Nyangrel believed these memories to be true, and he lived as a charismatic figure claiming enlightenment within a time and context when that valuation was considered cogent and so rewarded.

In the long aftermath of the empire's collapse, chaos spread throughout the Tibetan cultural area as religious and political institutions crumbled, resulting in the dissolution of centralized authority. As the dust settled over the centuries that followed, formerly influential clans persevered with the material and spiritual relics of the empire while some of Tibet's splintered polities began to consolidate into larger entities. Their rulers knew of the empire and sought to model themselves on the emperors of old who invited peace, stability, glory, and legacy through their patronage of Buddhism. The empire thus cast a long wake on the collective memory of Tibetans, but with the relics of the imperium scattered and its history relegated to the limited contents of surviving inscriptions or narratives such as the *Testimony of Ba*, which was discordant given Tri Songdetsen's mistrust and vacillations, Padmasambhava's declaration that Buddhism was not properly established, and so forth, there was a popular yearning for media that evoked the grandeur of Tibet's collective past. Such may have been addressed in part by an economy of bards and storytellers who capitalized on the formulation and performance of songs and yarns that revived the glory of the empire, but it was Nyangrel who, having discovered the vestiges of empire reincarnated within himself, seized upon this need to weave the threads of history and memory into a new vision of the empire. Jan Assmann writes:

> [Collective memory] is a projection on the part of the collective that wishes to remember and of the individual who remembers in order to belong. Both the collective and the individual turn to the archive of cultural traditions, the arsenal of symbolic forms, the "imaginary" of myths and images, of the "great stories," sagas and legends, scenes and constellations that live or can be reactivated in the treasure stores of a people.[351]

As a scion of the imperial clans and their ancient transmissions, Nyangrel and his imperial-era lineages were in danger of being forgotten beneath a surge of newly imported doctrines, doxographies, and hierarchies during the New Translation period. In order to belong in a context that was swiftly leaving him behind, Nyangrel tapped into a popular nostalgia for the imperium to frame a new narrative that reenvisioned and revalidated the old. He presented

351. Assmann 2006, 7–8.

himself as someone capable of powerful, uncommon, irrefutable remembrance. While simultaneously legitimating his literary activities and his stature as an enlightened treasure revealer, Nyangrel navigated a vibrant pool of tradition to recover a treasure that truly was of the Tibetan people, reformulating their history as they wished to remember it.

Third Hypothesis: Transmission

Finally, based on the textual, oral, and mnemonic resources detailed above, Nyangrel compiled a single narrative starring Tri Songdetsen and Padmasambhava that became the basis for both the *Copper Island* and the *Essence of Flowers*, neither of which he knew by these titles. Subsequent redactors developed two distinct lines of textual transmission, one as much a treasure text as the other was not.

The *Copper Island* and the *Essence of Flowers* represent two distinct strategies for the distribution of Nyangrel's account of Tibet's conversion to Buddhism. The first celebrated and elaborated its status as a treasure text by fabricating a recovery narrative; the other systematically excised these treasure origins in order to clandestinely integrate it within a larger history of Buddhism as a legitimate source for the reign of Tri Songdetsen. Whereas the treasure text relied on Nyangrel's renown as a treasure revealer to verify its authenticity, the repetitive attribution of the history of Buddhism to Nyangrel remains the most explicit indication that his original treasure text was concealed within it. While there is no evidence that the core Padmasambhava narrative originated as something other than a treasure text, such a possibility cannot be ruled out either. As detailed above, every single exemplar includes at least the opening of the treasure colophon, and yet the absence of this narrative from the inventories of Nyangrel's recoveries is troubling. Based on the available evidence, it appears that Nyangrel indeed considered the Padmasambhava narrative to be a treasure text (albeit not from the Copper Island of the Three Realms at Samyé) that, for whatever reason, was ignored by his biographers and yet persisted in two distinct textual streams, one with the explicit hallmarks of a treasure and the other deliberately omitting them.

Whereas doctrinal treasures had become commonplace by the twelfth century as evidenced by the products of his mentors, such as Ngödrup's *Great Compassionate One*, Nyangrel's unprecedented treasure narrative presented new problems even if some of its content was already familiar to its audience. An unanswerable question is whether Padmasambhava's twelfth-century oral lore already placed him at the epicenter of Tibet's conversion or if Nyangrel was the one who introduced a radically new counternarrative. While the apotheosis of Padmasambhava has clearly been initiated in earlier documents, none ascribe to him the catalyzing role that distinguishes Nyangrel's account. This split into two distinct textual streams may signify the recognition and attempted resolution of a marketing and distribution issue confronted by Nyangrel, his lineal and familial descendants, and/or the later admirers who championed his account of Padmasambhava. Would its status as a treasure help or hurt its distribution? Or would it gain broader acceptance if concealed within a conventional history?

This likely changed over time: at first the treasure origins of an unprecedented textual narrative were a liability, thereby necessitating its nearly wholesale inclusion clandestinely within the *Essence of Flowers*. As the Padmasambhava narrative and treasure texts gained broader acceptance, however, its revelation by Nyangrel, the most renowned revealer of his age, became an asset, and later redactors sought to capitalize on that status by ascribing an ornamental title based on newly invented treasure origins. By contrasting the widespread distribution and influence of the *Copper Island* against the relative obscurity of the *Essence of Flowers*, it is clear which strategy proved more successful.

Conclusion: Myth, Culture, and Continuity

As Matthew Kapstein has written in relation to some of the same topics, "a myth is felt to be true whenever it functions in the discourse of a community to ground action that is itself felt to bring about the success of that community, or of its individual members."[352] In that, Nyangrel's account of Padmasambhava is a masterpiece that continues to resonate eight centuries later. The story of Padmasambhava and his conversion of Tibet persists as a wellspring of Tibetan identity: as first articulated by Nyangrel this is their origin narrative, their history that unites them as a collective, a single people by virtue of a shared past that sets Tibetans apart from all others.

Its constant relevance throughout these many centuries has been aided by a process of reinterpretation and revision that has been nearly as constant: the story of Padmasambhava has been told and retold, refashioned and re-revealed by a succession of visionaries. It is said that a new Padmasambhava narrative will emerge in every era, since it must be revised under the circumstances of each new present. This occurred not long after Nyangrel's time in

352. Kapstein 2000, 143.

a political context destabilized by foreign interventions as much as domestic conflicts. Two *Testaments of Padmasambhava* were discovered in quick succession in the fourteenth century: Sangyé Lingpa's *Golden Garland* in prose and Urgyen Lingpa's *Crystal Cave* in verse. Due to the terminological truncations and grammatical omissions of Tibetan poetry, even contemporary Tibetans admit that some stanzas of Urgyen Lingpa's *Testament of Padmasambhava* remain opaque, yet it remains the most famous version of Tibet's golden age, and arguably the most popular narrative Tibet ever produced.

While hand-scribed manuscripts and block-printed publications of the Padmasambhava story are fixed in ink, the actual text of Padmasambhava is never static: it constantly evolves as it is remembered and retold, incorporating countless details from previous versions while adding new content before it is committed to the page once again. Comparative analysis projects a sequence that portrays the *mouvance* of its recensional process,[353] noting differences incorporated in the textual scene from one frame to the next, but philology alone can neither record nor reveal the full expression of the living tradition that produces each text. Jan Assmann writes:

> Because the letter is "solid" and cannot be altered by a single iota, but because, on the other hand, the world of men is subject to continuous change, there is a gulf between the established text and the changing reality that can only be bridged by interpretation. In this way interpretation becomes the central principle of cultural coherence and identity. The normative and formative impulses of cultural memory can only be gleaned from the incessant, constantly renewed textual interpretation of the tradition through which identity is established. Interpretation becomes the gesture of remembering, the interpreter becomes a person who remembers and reminds us of a forgotten truth.[354]

For Nyangrel the established "texts," whether material or oral, offered only fragments of Padmasambhava. While some apotheosized Padmasambhava as an enlightened master, the inscriptions ignored him and the *Testimony of Ba* expelled him. Thus Nyangrel compiled a new interpretation in response to the immediate needs of himself and others. Even more literally than Assmann intended, Nyangrel truly was the interpreter who, by remembering a past life as Tri Songdetsen, reminded Tibetans of their unification under the

353. Assmann 2006, 108.

354. Assmann 2006, 43.

banner of Buddhism. In a fractured age now as then, the truth of a common Tibetan identity is at risk of being lost and forgotten. As the Chinese administration continues to severely restrict Tibetan cultural expression at its source, and as diaspora weakens the bonds of cultural coherence abroad, the memory of Padmasambhava's conversion of Tibet to Buddhism is a universal that Tibetans still share, a means to identify their selves and recognize their selves in each other.

As every cause is an effect and every effect a cause, Nyangrel was both the architect of his enlightened identity and the product of his time. He was at once an excavator of Tibet's past and the author of its future. From within Tibet's imperial-era sites, these *lieux de mémoire*, he uncovered the archive of Tibet's cultural traditions as caches of treasure texts and relics. In reliance upon the material fragments of the empire, the oral traditions of contemporaries, and his personal memory, Nyangrel discovered a truly unique treasure that not only defined his life and legacy but also articulated for the first time an emic history of Tibet's golden age that continues to resonate at the core of Tibetan collective identity to the present.

Appendix: Dating the Birth, Life, and Death of Nyangrel

THE YEARS OF Nyangrel's birth and death are problematic and a point of contention in both primary and secondary literature. In Western publications that mention Nyangrel, his dates are listed as 1124–92, 1136–1204, or both in acknowledging the issue, but a comparative analysis of the earliest sources and the forwarding of supporting evidence helps settle the debate, indicating that 1124–92 is the most likely span of Nyangrel's life. In the end, this analysis serves as a poignant example of the complications confronted when dating Tibetan historical persons and events, which tend to increase exponentially as one extends further into the past.

As elements of Nyangrel's two biographies were compiled within a generation of his death, these remain the best resources for his life and the main sources of confusion concerning it as well. By way of introducing Tibetan dates, the sexagenary Tibetan calendric system is drawn from both Indian and Chinese exemplars, where a complete *rabjung* (*rab byung*) consists of sixty years, but it is designated by only twelve animals that run cyclically in sequence. There are thus five possibilities for any animal year within a specific *rabjung* (60/12=5) and an equal degree of ambiguity as well. While there is evidence that the five elements were introduced in Tibet as early as the ninth century to resolve such ambiguities,[355] they do not appear to have become widespread until at least the thirteenth century. Since Nyangrel's primary biographies were composed in the time of this system's popularization, it comes as no surprise that the *Stainless Proclamations* lacks elements for its dates. It simply states that Nyangrel was born in a dragon year such that the year of his birth could have been 1088, 1100, 1112, 1124, or 1136, the five dragon years of the second *rabjung*, though the dates of other figures and events in this biography certainly help narrow the field. Conversely, the *Clear Mirror* provides elements and thus specific years for Nyangrel's birth and death but introduces a discrepancy as well,

355. The dates on the east face of the Lhasa Treaty pillar of 821–22 are precise in reliance upon the five elements as well as gender and reign years. See Richardson 1985, 110–17.

which seems to reflect a miscalculation of the elemental system as it became standard. As can happen when new systems are not yet widespread or well understood, the *Clear Mirror* got at least one of the elements wrong and so introduced further confusion rather than a resolution of Nyangrel's dates.

The *Clear Mirror* states that Nyangrel was born in a wood-dragon year (1124) and died in a wood-mouse year (1204), yet these dates conflict with another important piece of data.[356] The *Stainless Proclamations*, the *Clear Mirror*, and the biography of Nyangrel's younger son and primary heir, Namkhapel, all concur that Nyangrel lived sixty-nine years according to the Tibetan lunisolar calendar and not eighty-one as the dates in the *Clear Mirror* imply.[357] With all three sources in explicit agreement on Nyangrel's age at his time of death, that lifespan is given precedence in determining the dates of his life; thus one of the elements in the *Clear Mirror* must be mistaken and in need of revision.

Since the *Stainless Proclamations* only attests that Nyangrel was born in a dragon year and fails to include an account of his death altogether, it remains silent on the matter, but the corroboration of the animal year suggests that the margin of error is limited to one twelve-year cycle. The year of his birth is thus isolated as either 1124 (wood-dragon, as stated in the *Clear Mirror*) or 1136 (fire-dragon, revising the *Clear Mirror*)[358] and the year of his death must be either 1192 (water-mouse, revising the *Clear Mirror*) or 1204 (wood-mouse, as stated in the *Clear Mirror*). With these possibilities, his sixty-nine-year lifespan indicates that Nyangrel lived from either 1124–92 or 1136–1204, though

356. Birth: *Gsal ba'i me long*, 325.3; B, 109.1. Death: 377.1; B, 158.4.

357. *Yid bzhin nor bu'i 'phreng ba*, 390.6. Among available sources, the *Garland of Wish-Fulfilling Jewels* had the most potential for corroborating Nyangrel's dates, but the details it provides, which include the animal year of Namkhapel's birth and his age at the time of his father's death, are contradictory. Both recensions of the *Clear Mirror* (*Gsal ba'i me long*, 354.6; B, 137.2) and all three recensions of the *Garland of Wish-Fulfilling Jewels* (*Yid bzhin nor bu'i 'phreng ba* A, 387.1; B, 168.2; C, 16.1) specify that Namkhapel was born in a monkey year and the *Garland of Wish-Fulfilling Jewels* attests that Nyangrel died when Namkhapel was twenty-three (390.6; B, 171.7; C, 19.4), but one of these details is necessarily mistaken. Mathematically, he could not have been born in a monkey year *and* twenty-three at the time of Nyangrel's death. If Namkhapel was born in a monkey year, this would most likely be either 1164–65 or 1176–77, which means he would have been either sixteen or twenty-eight years of age in 1192. If he were twenty-three, then he would have been born in the tiger year, 1169–70. For a similar analysis with slightly different conclusions, see Sørensen 2007, 473n117.

358. One additional complication must be mentioned in that the *Clear Mirror* states that Nyangrel was conceived in an earth-rabbit year, which would be 1099. Perhaps this is so blatantly incorrect as to be immediately dismissed, but it reiterates that his biographers had difficulty with calendric calculations or perhaps relied on a nonstandard system.

there is one additional piece of historical evidence that has been applied more recently in an attempt to resolve this ambiguity.

Having replicated the conflicting dates from the *Clear Mirror* for centuries, the Tibetan historical tradition remained unresolved until Dudjom Rinpoché's twentieth-century *Nyingma History* (*Rnying ma'i chos 'byung*), in which he revised Nyangrel's dates to 1124–92.[359] When that history was first translated into English, however, its editors elected to revise the Tibetan source text by inserting 1136–1204 into the translation of that work. In the endnotes they explain that the eminent Tibetologist R. A. Stein first revised Nyangrel's birth year to 1136 and, in agreeing with his revision, they add that the great Kaśmīri paṇḍita, Śākyaśrībhadra (d. ca. 1225), is widely reported to have arrived in Tibet in the wood-mouse year of 1204, which they assume concurred with Nyangrel's death and Śākyaśrī's subsequent consecration of Nyangrel's funerary reliquary at Mawochok.[360] While the time that elapsed between Nyangrel's death and the consecration of his reliquary remains unknown, since Nyangrel's Mawochok hermitage lies in relatively close proximity to where Śākyaśrī entered Tibet, the editors suggest that he may have visited Mawochok in the same year that he arrived, which concurs with the year of Nyangrel's death as attested in the *Clear Mirror* (1204), or otherwise they assume that Śākyaśrī must have consecrated the reliquary within a few years of it. The brief biography of Nyangrel in Jamgön Kongtrul's *Garland of Precious Beryl* describes the arrival of Śākyaśrī in 1204 directly after Nyangrel's death, which itself is undated, and therefore may imply that Nyangrel died in that same year as well.[361] Yet it is critical to note that neither this argument nor its shift in dates is explicitly attested in Tibetan sources.

The date that Śākyaśrī consecrated Nyangrel's reliquary is not specified in any source, but Śākyaśrī's earliest biographies trace his route into Tibet as well as his travels in the decade he spent there (see figure 17). He entered via Phakri in 1204, which lies near the conjunction of modern day Sikkim, Bhutan, and Tibet, then first traveled north toward Shigatsé in the region of southern Nyang. He completed his first rainy season retreat at the monastery of his host, Trophu, in the summer of 1204, and his second near Chumik Ringmo in 1205. He then accepted an invitation to Lhasa and traveled there via Tsurphu Monastery before spending a third rainy season in retreat at Sinmori near the confluence of the Yarlung Tsangpo and Kyichu rivers to the southwest of

359. *Rnying ma'i chos 'byung*, 585.3.

360. Dorje and Kapstein 1991, 70n989, cite Stein 1972, 74, but Stein does not explain his dating of Nyangrel, which he lists as 1136–1203.

361. *Rin chen baiḍūrya'i phreng ba*, 388.1–2.

Lhasa. After his retreat there in 1206, Śākyaśrī made pilgrimages from Sinmori to Samyé, Chimphu, Lhasa, and Radreng but was thwarted by Kadam and Denchik monks when attempting to visit Drigung. He returned to Sinmori after each of these treks, as it remained his home base for several years, and only after the completion of these shorter pilgrimages did he set out on the longer journey through Lhodrak.[362] Since Śākyaśrī did not go to Lhodrak until after at least three annual rainy-season retreats and several shorter pilgrimages, and since he returned to southern Nyang after four years in central Tibet, his consecration of Nyangrel's reliquary occurred no earlier than 1207 and no later than 1210. It is therefore certain that the consecration did not occur in the same year that Nyangrel died; Nyangrel's death and Śākyaśrī's consecration of his funeral reliquary did not concur in 1204. In sum, the revision of Nyangrel's dates to 1136–1204 appears to be a uniquely Western hypothesis based on the conflation of Śākyaśrī's arrival in Tibet with his visit to Mawochok, and the translators and editors of Dudjom's *History* address this discrepancy in the second edition.[363] Having refuted the hypothesis that Nyangrel died in the same year that Śākyaśrī entered Tibet, we may now return to the original conundrum anew.

According to Namkhapel's biography, after seventeen days of continuous recitation, Nyangrel's funerary rites continued periodically into the summer, when Namkhapel hosted Chak Lotsāwa Drachom (1153–1216) at Mawochok.[364] Later sources add that Chak Lotsāwa presided over Nyangrel's cremation, attesting that when he could not light the funeral pyre it miraculously ignited on its own.[365] There are thus two distinct events described: Nyangrel's funeral and the consecration of his reliquary, which seem to be separated by several years. Namkhapel's biography portrays him as being very busy after the death of his father, where the construction of dikes in Lhasa was but one of several long-term, labor-intensive, and significantly expensive projects. These

362. Jackson 1990, 13–15.

363. Kapstein later revised Nyangrel's dates to 1124–92 following van der Kuijp's review of Śākyaśrī's activities in Tibet (Kapstein 2000, 261n24; van der Kuijp 1994, 612). Discrepancy noted in Dorje and Kapstein 2002, 70–71n995.

364. His more renowned nephew, Chak Lotsāwa Chöje Pal (1196–1263/64), would have been a child and thus too young to preside over such ceremonies even if they had occurred in 1204. There is some additional data about Chak Drachom in *Yid bzhin nor bu'i 'phreng ba*, 392, where he confronts a number of plagues in the region.

365. *Chos 'byung mkhas pa'i dga' ston*, 632. Also recounted in the recent article by Mawochok's current abbot, Smra bo lcog kun bzang bstan 'dzin rgya mtsho 1994, 30.

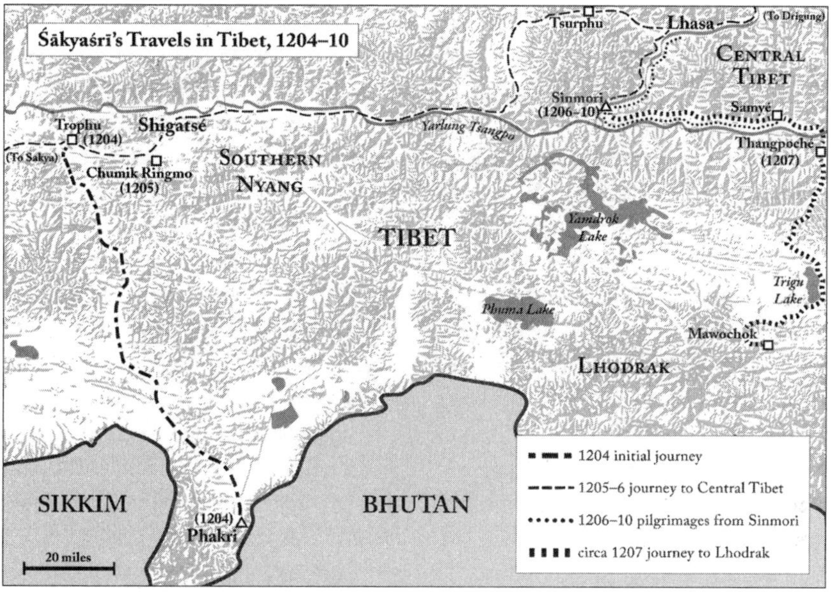

Figure 17. Estimation of Śākyaśrī's route in Tibet based on the major sites that punctuate his itinerary in his biographies and well-established paths through the topography. He entered via Phakri in 1204 and traveled north to the region of southern Nyang. He remained in this area through 1205 and then went on to Sinmori via Tsurphu and Lhasa in 1206. Based out of Sinmori he made a number of pilgrimages over the next several years. He departed for Lhodrak some time after 1206 and spent four years in central Tibet before returning to southern Nyang circa 1210. It is unclear whether he returned to southern Nyang by the same route or whether he completed a circle by continuing his pilgrimage to the major Kagyü sites in Lhodrak. Given the clockwise trajectory of his total pilgrimage and the significance of the sites, I would suspect that he completed a circumambulation of central Tibet, though I am not aware of any historical evidence to confirm it.

preoccupied Namkhapel while he built his father's massive reliquary, which may have taken some years to complete before Śākyaśrī's consecration.[366]

In both the *Clear Mirror* and the *Stainless Proclamations*, Shikpo Dütsi (1149–99) is prominently listed among Nyangrel's primary disciples as the heir to his treasures concerning Emperor Songsten Gampo's lineage of the Great

366. It must have required ample resources, which is testament to the donations and renown Nyangrel received by the end of his life.

Compassionate One, Avalokiteśvara, which became renowned in subsequent treasures as the *Maṇi Kambum*. While neither biography preserves a complete list of mourners who attended Nyangrel's funerary rites, the definition and primary function of an heir is that s/he outlives the one who bequeaths an inheritance, which is all the more paramount in Buddhist lineages, since they generally must be transmitted personally from master to student in an unbroken succession. Unlike material wealth that may easily be redirected to another in the event that an heir dies before their benefactor, practice lineages should be entrusted completely and properly to specially designated disciples. Masters select and verify their spiritual heirs as authentic lineage holders such that the transmissions may continue when s/he dies.

If Nyangrel died in 1204, the question then is this: how could Shikpo Dütsi inherit and transmit Nyangrel's cycle of Avalokiteśvara when he died in 1199 and thus five years *before* Nyangrel? If Nyangrel died in 1204, he would have had those five years to empower, train, and appoint a replacement to continue that cycle, which ranks among his most important treasures and certainly would have been a priority. Since Nyangrel did not appoint another heir for this lineage of the Great Compassionate One and Shikpo Dütsi remains listed among Nyangrel's primary heirs in both biographies, Nyangrel must have died before his disciple and heir and not after him. One could rightly argue that Shikpo Dütsi's dates are derived from few sources and may too be inaccurate, but at least there is no evidence to contradict them. In sum, based on his dates and all of the evidence presented above, Nyangrel's death may be conclusively revised to 1192, and since the sources concur that Nyangrel was born in a dragon year and lived for sixty-nine years, 1124–92 is the most likely span of Nyangrel's life.

List of Tibetan Title Abbreviations

Bka' rgya brgyad ma (*Eight Pronouncements*)

Gu ru Chos kyi dbang phyug. "Ghu ru chos dbang gis rnam mthar bka' rgya brgyad ma." In *Gu ru chos dbang gi rang rnam dang zhal gdams*, 1: 65–151. Paro: Ugyen Tempai Gyaltsen, 1979.

Bka' brgyad bde gshegs 'dus pa (*Eight Instructions: Gathering of the Ones Gone to Bliss*)

Mnga' bdag Nyang ral Nyi ma 'od zer. *Bka' brgyad bde gshegs 'dus pa'i chos skor.*

A: 13 volumes. Gangtok: Sonam Topgay Kazi, 1978–81.

B: 13 volumes. Paro: Ngodrub, 1979–80.

C: 2 volumes. *A Collection of Rare Teachings from the Gter-ma Rediscovered by Mnga' bdag Nyang ral Nyi ma 'od zer.* New Delhi: B. Jamyang Norbu, 1971.

D: 4 volumes. Dalhousie: Damchoe Sangpo, 1977.

Skabs brgyad ma (*Eight Chapters*)

Gu ru Chos kyi dbang phyug. "Ghu ru chos dbang gis sku'i rnam thar skabs brgyad ma." In *Gu ru chos dbang gi rang rnam dang zhal gdams*, 1: 1–53. Paro: Ugyen Tempai Gyaltsen, 1979.

Gter 'byung chen mo (*Great History of Treasure*)

Gu ru Chos kyi dbang phyug. "Gu ru chos dbang gis gter 'byung chen mo." In *Gu ru chos dbang gi rang rnam dang zhal gdams*, 2: 75–193. Paro: Ugyen Tempai Gyaltsen, 1979.

Dri ma med pa (*Stainless Proclamations*)

Chos kyi 'od zer, Myang ston Bsod nams seng ge, and Mi 'gyur rdo rje. "Sprul sku mnga' bdag chen po'i skyes rabs rnam thar dri ma med pa'i bka' rgya can la ldeb." In *Bka' brgyad bder gshegs 'dus pa'i chos skor*, 1: 1–163. Gangtok: Lama Sonam Tobgay Kazi, 1978.

Dba'/Rba/Sba bzhed (*Testimony of Ba*)

Sba Gsal snang Ye shes dbang po.

A: Pasang Wangdu, and Hildegard Diemberger, eds. and trans. *dBa' bzhed: The Royal Narrative Concerning the Bringing of the Buddha's Doctrine to Tibet.* Vienna: Verlag der Österreichischen Akademie der Wissenschaften, 2000.

B: Bde skyid, ed. *Rba bzhed phyogs sgrigs.* Beijing: Mi rigs dpe skron khang, 2009.

C: *Btsan po khri srong lde btsan dang mkhan po slob dpon padma'i dus mdo sngags so sor mdzad pa'i sba bzhed zhabs btags ma.* Dharamsala: Shes rig par khang, 1968.

G: Mgon po rgyal mtshan, ed. *Sba bzhed ces bya ba las sba bsal snang gi bzhed pa bzhugs*. Beijing: Mi rigs dpe skrun khang, 1982.

S: R. A. Stein, ed. *Une Chronique Ancienne de bSam-yas, sBa bźed*. Paris: Institut des Hautes Études Chinoises, 1961.

Maṇi bka' 'bum (*Maṇi Kambum*)

Mnga' bdag Nyang ral Nyi ma 'od zer. *Ma ṇi bka' 'bum: A Collection of Rediscovered Teachings Focussing upon the Tutelary Deity Avalokiteśvara (Mahākaruṇika)*, 2 vols. New Delhi: Trayang and Jamyang Samten, 1975.

Me tog snying po (*Essence of Flowers*)

Mnga' bdag Nyang ral Nyi ma 'od zer. *Chos 'byung me tog snying po sbrang rtsi'i bcud*.

A: Manuscript A. Paro: Ugyen Tempai Gyaltsen, 1979.

B: Manuscript B. Paro: Ugyen Tempai Gyaltsen, 1979.

K: Nyan shul Mkhyen rab 'od gsal, ed. Gangs can rig mdzod series no. 5. Lhasa: Bod ljongs mi dmangs dpe skrun khang, 1988. Reprinted in 2010.

M: R. O. Meisezahl. *Die Große Geschichte des Tibetischen Buddhismus nach Alter Tradition*. Sankt Augustin: VGH Wissenschaftsverlag, 1985.

Zangs gling ma (*Copper Island*)

Mnga' bdag Nyang ral Nyi ma 'od zer.

A: *Slob dpon padma 'byung gnas kyi skyes rabs chos 'byung nor bu'i phreng ba, rnam thar zangs gling ma*. In *Rin chen gter mdzod chen mo*, vol. ka/1, ed. 'Jam mgon Kong sprul Blo gros Mtha' yas, 1–219. Paro: Ngodrub and Sherab Drimay, 1976.

H: *Pad ma bka' chems brgyas pa*. NGMCP E 2703/10.

I: *Bka' thang zangs gling ma*. NGMCP E 1217/02.

J: *U rgyan padma 'byung gnas kyi rnam thar mnga' bdag nyang ral pas lho brag gi brag srin po'i sbar rjes 'dra ba nas gter nas ston pa*. Gangtey: Karma Phuntso, Thorbu no. 196.

K: *Urgyan gyi slob dpon chen po padma 'byung gnas kyi rnam par thar pa nyang gter zangs gling mar grags pa*, 1–79. Gangtey: Karma Phuntso, Thorbu no. 288.

L: *Dbu rgyan pad ma 'byung gnas kyi bka' chems*, 1–218. Sumra HP: Urgyan Dorje, 1977.

Yid bzhin nor bu'i 'phreng ba (*Garland of Wish-Fulfilling Jewels*)

So ston and Dpon yes. *Sras mnga' bdag chos rje 'gro ba'i dgon po'i rnam thar yid bzhin nor bu'i phreng ba*.

A: In *Bka' brgyad bde gshegs bsdus pa'i chos skor*, 2: 383–465. Paro: Ngodrub, 1979–80.

B: In *Mnga' bdag bla ma brgyud pa'i rnam thar: The Biographies of the Early Masters in the Transmission Lineage of the Bka' brgyad bde gshegs 'dus pa Teachings Revealed by Mnga' bdag myang ral nyi ma 'od ze*, 66–245. Mandi: Sherab Gyaltsen Lama and Acharya Shedub Tenzin, 1985.

C: In *Bka' brgyad bde gshegs bsdus pa'i chos skor*, 1: 13–85. Dalhousie: Damchoe Sangpo, 1977.

Rin chen baiḍūrya'i phreng ba (*Garland of Precious Beryl*)

Kong sprul Lo gros mtha' yas. "Zab mo'i gter dang gter ston grub thob ji ltar byon pa'i lo rgyus mdor bsdus bskod pa rin chen baiḍūrya'i phreng ba." In *Rin chen gter mdzod chen mo*, 1: 291–645. Paro: Ngodrup and Sherab Drimay, 1976–80.

Gsal ba'i me long (*Clear Mirror*)
Myang ston Rig 'dzin lhun grub 'od zer.

A: "Bka' brgyad bde gshegs 'dus pa'i gter ston myang sprul sku nyi ma 'od zer gyi rnam thar gsal ba'i me long." In *Bka' brgyad bde gshegs 'dus pa'i chos skor,* 2:199–381. Paro: Lama Ngodrup, 1979.

B: "Mnga' bdag myang nyi ma 'od zer gyi rnam thar gsal ba'i me long." In *Mnga' bdag bla ma brgyud pa'i rnam thar: The Biographies of the Early Masters in the Transmission Lineage of the Bka' brgyad bde gshegs 'dus pa Teachings Revealed by Mnga' bdag myang ral nyi ma 'od zer,* 1–163. Mandi: Sherab Gyaltsen Lama and Acharya Shedub Tenzin, 1985.

Bibliography

Primary Sources

Dkar chag 'phang thang ma / Sgra sbyor bam po gnyis pa. Lhasa: Mi rigs dpe skrun khang, 2003.

Bka' 'gyur (*dpe bsdur ma*), 109 volumes. Beijing: Krung go'i bod rig pa dpe skrun khang, 2006–9. TBRC W2MS25207.

Bka' chems ka khol ma (attributed to Srong btsan sgam po).

A: Lanzhou: Kan su'u mi rigs dpe skrun khang, 1989.

B: Manuscript: TBRC W00KG010083.

C: In *The Literary Arts of Ladakh*, 1: 363–481. Darjeeling: Kargyud Sungrab Nyamso Khang, 1972.

Karma pa III Rang byung rdo rje. *The Tibetan Rendering of the Jātakamāla of Āryaśūra, Supplemented with 67 Additional Jātaka Stories by the Third Karma pa Rang byung rdo rje. Reproduced from a Rare Manuscript Preserved in the Library of the Stog rgyal po of Ladakh*, 2 volumes. Darjeeling: Kargyud Sungrab Nyamso Khang, 1974.

Kong sprul Lo gros mtha' yas. "Zab mo'i gter dang gter ston grub thob ji ltar byon pa'i lo rgyus mdor bsdus bskod pa rin chen baiḍūrya'i phreng ba." In *Rin chen gter mdzod chen mo*, 1: 291–645. Paro: Ngodrup and Sherab Drimay, 1976–80.

Khro phu Lo tsā ba Byams pa dpal. *Byams pa dpal gyi rnam thar 'khri shing ma*. TBRC W1CZ1880.

———. *Khro phu lo tsa+tsha ba'i rnam thar yab sras mjal ba*. TBRC W1CZ1879.

———. *Paṇ chen shākya shrī'i rnam thar*, edited by David. P. Jackson. Stuttgart: Franz Steiner Verlag, 1990.

Klong chen rab 'byams pa. "Gter 'byung rin po che'i lo rgyus." In *Snying thig ya bzhi*, 7: 15–499. Delhi: Sherab Gyaltsen Lama, 1975.

Mkhas pa lde'u. *Mkhas pa lde'us mdzad pa'i rgya bod kyi chos 'byung rgyas pa*. Lhasa: Bod ljongs sa bod yig dpe rnying dpe skrun khang, 1987.

Gu ru Bkra shis stag sgang mkhas mchog ngag dbang blo gros. *Bstan pa'i snying po gsang chen snga 'gyur nges don zab mo'i chos kyi 'byung ba gsal bar byed pa'i legs bshad mkhas pa dga' byed ngo mtshar gtam gyi rol mtsho*, 4 volumes. Paro: Ugyen Tempai Gyaltsen, 1979.

Gu ru Chos kyi dbang phyug. *Bka' brgyad gsang ba yongs rdzogs*, 4 volumes. Paro: Lama Ngodrub and Sherab Drimey, 1979.

———. *Gu ru chos dbang gi rang rnam dang zhal gdams*, 2 volumes. Paro: Ugyen Tempai Gyaltsen, 1979.

———. *Maṇi bka' 'bum chen mo*.

A: Redaction A. Paro: Ugyen Tempai Gyaltsen, 1981.

B: Redaction B. Paro: Ugyen Tempai Gyaltsen, 1981.

C: With *Thugs rje chen po'i rgyud rang byung ye shes*, revealed by Mnga' bdag Nyang ral Nyi ma 'od zer. Paro: Ugyen Tempai Gyaltsen, 1981.

Mnga' bdag Nyang ral Nyi ma 'od zer. *Bka' brgyad bde gshegs 'dus pa'i chos skor*.

A: 13 volumes. Gangtok: Sonam Topgay Kazi, 1978–81.

B: 13 volumes. Paro: Ngodrub, 1979–80.

C: 2 volumes. *A Collection of Rare Teachings from the gter-ma Rediscovered by Mnga' bdag Nyang ral Nyi ma 'od zer*. New Delhi: B. Jamyang Norbu, 1971.

D: 4 volumes. Dalhousie: Damchoe Sangpo, 1977.

———. *Chos 'byung me tog snying po sbrang rtsi'i bcud*.

A: Manuscript A. Paro: Ugyen Tempai Gyaltsen, 1979.

B: Manuscript B. Paro: Ugyen Tempai Gyaltsen, 1979.

K: Edited by Nyan shul Mkhyen rab 'od gsal. Gangs can rig mdzod series no. 5. Lhasa: Bod ljongs mi dmangs dpe skrun khang, 1988. Reprinted in 2010.

M: Meisezahl, R. O. 1985. *Die Große Geschichte des Tibetischen Buddhismus nach Alter Tradition*. Sankt Augustin: VGH Wissenschaftsverlag.

———. *Jo mo la gdams pa'i chos skor*. Paro: Konchhog Lhadripa, 1983.

———. *Thugs rje chen po'i rgyud rang 'byung ye shes*. Paro: Ugyen Tempai Gyaltsen, 1981.

———. *Ma ṇi bka' 'bum: A Collection of Rediscovered Teachings Focussing upon the Tutelary Deity Avalokiteśvara (Mahākaruṇika)*, 2 volumes. New Delhi: Trayang and Jamyang Samten, 1975.

———. *Zangs gling ma*.

A: *Slob dpon padma 'byung gnas kyi skyes rabs chos 'byung nor bu'i phreng ba, rnam thar zangs gling ma*. In *Rin chen gter mdzod chen mo*, ed. 'Jam mgon Kong sprul Blo gros Mtha' yas, 1: 1–219. Paro: Ngodrub and Sherab Drimay, 1976.

H: *Pad ma bka' chems brgyas pa*. NGMCP E 2703/10.

I: *Bka' thang zangs gling ma*. NGMCP E 1217/02.

J: *U rgyan padma 'byung gnas kyi rnam thar mnga' bdag nyang ral pas lho brag gi brag srin po'i sbar rjes 'dra ba nas gter nas ston pa*. Gangtey: Karma Phuntso, Thorbu no. 196.

K: *Urgyan gyi slob dpon chen po padma 'byung gnas kyi rnam par thar pa nyang gter zangs gling mar grags pa*, 1–79. Gangtey: Karma Phuntso, Thorbu no. 288.

L: *Dbu rgyan pad ma 'byung gnas kyi bka' chems*, 1–218. Sumra HP: Urgyan Dorje, 1977.

Chag lo tsā ba Chos kyi dpal. *Snags log sun 'byin gyi skor*. Thimpu: Kunsang Topgyel and Mani Dorji, 1979.

Chos kyi grags pa. "Sgrub chen bka' brgyad kyi spyi dang bye brag bde gshegs 'dus pa'i chos kyi byung tshul 'khrul med yid ches drug ldan." In *The Collected Works (gsung 'bum) of Kun-mkhyen Rig-pa 'dzin-pa Chen-po Chos-kyi-grags-pa*, 10: 305–62. Dehradun: Drikung Kagyu Institute, 1999.

Chos kyi 'od zer, Myang ston Bsod nams seng ge, and Mi 'gyur rdo rje. "Sprul sku mnga' bdag chen po'i skyes rabs rnam thar dri ma med pa'i bka' rgya can la ldeb." In *Bka' brgyad bder gshegs 'dus pa'i chos skor*, 1: 1–163. Gangtok: Lama Sonam Tobgay Kazi, 1978.

Jo bo rje dpal ldan Atiśa. *'Brom ston pa rgyal ba'i 'byung gnas kyi skyes rabs bka'gdams bu chos*. Ziling: Mtsho-sngon mi rigs dpe skrun khang, 1993.

Thub bstan rgyal mtshan, ed. *Rnying ma'i gsung 'bum dkar chag*. Lhasa: Bod ljongs gsar dpe tho gzhung, 1992.

Don grub rgyal po. "Rig 'dzin chen po ratṇa gling pa'i rnam thar skyes rabs 'bring po tshigs su bcad pa." In *Gsung thor bu/ ratṇa gling pa*, 1: 217–65. Tezu: Tibetan Nyingmapa Monastery, 1973.

Bdud 'joms rin po che, 'Jigs bral ye shes rdo rje. *Rnying ma'i chos 'byung*. Bylakuppe: Ngagyur Nyingma Institute, 2002.

Nor brang o rgyan, ed. *Gangs can rig brgya'i chos kyi rnam grangs mthong tshad kun las btus pa ngo mtshar 'phrul gyi lde mig chen po*, 3 volumes. Beijing: Krung go'i bod rig pa dpe skrun khang, 2008.

Padma las 'brel rtsal. *Mkha' 'gro snying thig gi chos skor: Collected Revelations of Rdzogs chen Practice by Padma las 'brel rtsal. Reproduced from an Ancient but Perhaps Incomplete and Disordered Manuscript from the Library of Bla ma Nyi ma of Glang phrang*. Gangtok: Lama Dawa and Sherab Gyaltsan, 1984.

Dpa' bo Gtsug lag phreng ba. *Chos 'byung mkhas pa'i dga' ston*. Varanasi: Vajra Vidhya Library, 2003.

Spyan snga rdo rje shes rab, ed. *Chos rje 'jig rten mgon po'i rnam thar rdo rje 'bar ba dang/ spyan snga 'bri gung gling pa'i rnam thar snyan pa'i 'brug sgra/ dgongs gcig 'grel lchen snang mdzad ye shes sgron me bcas*. Shang kang: Ahang kang then mā dpe skrun khang gis bskrun zhing bkram, 2006.

'Phags pa dpa' bo (Āryaśūra). *Skyes pa 'i rabs kyi rgyud (Jātakamāla)*.

A: Sde dge bstan 'gyur, 168: 4–271.

B: Snar thang bstan 'gyur, 179: 1–296.

C: Co ne bstan 'gyur, 168: 6–269.

D: Spe bsdur ma bstan 'gyur, 94: 19–405.

E: *The Tibetan Rendering of the* Jātakamāla *of Āryaśūra, Supplemented with 67 Additional Jātaka Stories by the Third Karma-pa Raṅ-byuṅ-rdo-rje*. Darjeeling: Kargyud Sungrab Nyamso Khang, 1974.

F: Thimphu: Kunsang Tobgay, 1975.

Brag sgon pa dkon mchog bstan pa rab rgyas. *Mdo smad chos 'byung*. Lanzhou: Kun su'u zhing chen zhin hrwa dpe khang, 1982.

Sba Gsal snang Ye shes dbang po. *Dba'/Rba/Sba bzhed*.

A: Wangdu, Pasang and Hildegard Diemberger, eds. and trans. 2000. *dBa' bzhed: The Royal Narrative Concerning the Bringing of the Buddha's Doctrine to Tibet*. Vienna: Verlag der Österreichischen Akademie der Wissenschaften.

B: Bde skyid, ed. *Rba bzhed phyogs sgrigs*. Beijing: Mi rigs dpe skron khang, 2009.

C: *Btsan po khri srong lde btsan dang mkhan po slob dpon padma'i dus mdo sngags so sor mdzad pa'i sba bzhed zhabs btags ma*. Dharamsala: Shes rig par khang, 1968.

G: Mgon po rgyal mtshan, ed. *Sba bzhed ces bya ba las sba bsal snang gi bzhed pa bzhugs*. Beijing: Mi rigs dpe skrun khang, 1982.

S: Stein, R.A., ed. *Une Chronique Ancienne de bSam-yas, sBa bźed*. Paris: Institut des Hautes Études Chinoises, 1961.

Mi pham rgya mtsho. *Gsung 'bum*. Paro: Lama Ngodrup and Sherab Drimey, 1993.

Myang ston Rig 'dzin lhun grub 'od zer. *Gsal ba'i me long*.

A: "Bka' brgyad bde gshegs 'dus pa'i gter ston myang sprul sku nyi ma 'od zer gyi rnam thar gsal ba'i me long." In *Bka' brgyad bde gshegs 'dus pa'i chos skor*, 2: 199–381. Paro: Lama Ngodrup, 1979.

B: "Mnga' bdag myang nyi ma 'od zer gyi rnam thar gsal ba'i me long." In *Mnga' bdag bla ma brgyud pa'i rnam thar: The Biographies of the Early Masters in the Transmission Lineage of the Bka' brgyad bde gshegs 'dus pa Teachings Revealed by Mnga' bdag myang ral nyi ma 'od zer*, 1–163. Mandi: Sherab Gyaltsen Lama and Acharya Shedub Tenzin, 1985.

C: Manuscript (vol. 01306, kha) held in the Potala Palace collection.

Smra bo lcog kun bzang bstan 'dzin rgya mtsho. "Mnga' bdag nyang nyi ma 'od zer gyi mdzad rnam gdung rabs dang/ smra bo lcog dgon gyi dkar chag mdor bsdus." *Bod ljongs nang bstan*, 1.1 (1994): 27–35.

Rtse le sna tshogs rang grol. "Slob dpon pad ma'i rnam thar chen mo las brtsam te dri ba'i lan nges don gsal byed."

A: In *Rtse le sna tshogs rang grol gyi gsung 'bum*, 3: 397–492. Gangtok: Mgon po tshe brtan, 1979.

B: In *The Collected Works (gsung 'bum) of Rtse le sna tshogs rang grol*, 3: 271–343. Delhi: Sanje Dorji, 1974.

Ratna gling pa. "Gter 'byung chen mo gsal ba'i sgron me."

A: In *Gsung thor bu*, 1: 1–215. Tezu: Tibetan Nyingmapa Monastery, 1973.

B: In *Raṭna gling pa'i gter chos*, 2: 253–309. Darjeeling: Taklung Tsetrul Pema Wangyal, 1977–79.

———. "O rgyan Padma 'byung gnas kyi rnam thar gser gyi phreng ba." In *Raṭna gling pa'i gter chos*, 15: 15–344. Darjeeling: Taklung Tsetrul Pema Wangyal, 1977–79.

Rog ban dhe shes rab 'od. *Grub mtha' so so'i bzhed tshul gzhung gsal bar ston pa chos 'byung grub mtha' chen po bstan pa'i sgron me: A Detailed Survey of Comparative Siddhānta in the Context of Mahāyāna Buddhism and in Particular the Rnying ma pa.* Nemo, Ladakh: Tshul khrims Jam dbyangs, 1977.

Sa skya pa Bla ma dam pa Bsod nams rgyal mtshan. *Rgyal rabs gsal ba'i me long: The History of the Royal Lha Dynasty of Tibet, With an Account of the Mnga' bdag pa Lineage and its Descendants in Sikkim.* Gangtok: Indo-Tibetan Buddhist Literature Series, (unknown).

Sangs rgyas gling pa. "Gter 'byung chen mo." In *Bla ma dgongs 'dus*, 1: 21–116. Gangtok: Sonam Topgay Kazi, 1972.

———. *O rgyan gu ru pad ma 'byung gnas kyi rnam thar rgyas pa gser gyi phreng ba thar lam gsal byed.* Lhasa: Bod ljongs mi dmangs dpe skrun khang, 2007.

So ston and Dpon yes. *Sras mnga' bdag chos rje 'gro ba'i dgon po'i rnam thar yid bzhin nor bu'i phreng ba.*

A: In *Bka' brgyad bde gshegs bsdus pa'i chos skor*, 2: 383–465. Paro: Ngodrub, 1979–80.

B: In *Mnga' bdag bla ma brgyud pa'i rnam thar: The Biographies of the Early Masters in the Transmission Lineage of the Bka' brgyad bde gshegs 'dus pa Teachings Revealed by Mnga' bdag myang ral nyi ma 'od zer*, 66–245. Mandi: Sherab Gyaltsen Lama and Acharya Shedub Tenzin, 1985.

C: In *Bka' brgyad bde gshegs bsdus pa'i chos skor*, 1:13–85. Dalhousie: Damchoe Sangpo, 1977.

D: Manuscript (vol. 01306, *ga*) held in the Potala Palace collection.

Bsod nams dpal bzang po. *Sa'i steng na 'gran zla dang bral ba kha che paṇḍi ta shākya shrī bhadra'i rnam thar*, edited by David. P. Jackson. Stuttgart: Franz Steiner Verlag, 1990.

Shākya rin chen (misattributed to Mnga' bdag nyang ral nyi ma 'od zer). *Chos rgyal mes dpon rnam gsum gyi rnam thar rin po che'i 'phreng ba.* Paro: Ugyen Tempai Gyaltsen, 1980.

O/U rgyan gling pa. *Padma bka' thang.* Gangtok: Rumtek Monastery, 1966.

———. *Bka' thang sde lnga*, edited by Rdo rje rgyal po. Beijing: Mi rigs dpe skrun khang, 1986.

Secondary Sources

Achard, Jean-Luc. 1999. *L'Essence Perlée du Secret: Recherches Philologiques et Historiques sur l'Origine de la Grande Perfection dans la Tradition rNying ma pa*. Turnhout: Brepols.

———. 2004. *Bon Po Hidden Treasures: A Catalogue of Gter ston bde chen gling pa's* Collected Revelations. Leiden: Brill.

———. 2010. "Mesmerizing with the Useless? A Book-Review Inquiry into the Ability to Properly Reprint Older Worthy Material. *Revue d'Etudes Tibétaines* 19: 133–43.

Almogi, Orna. 2002. "Sources on the Life and Works of the Eleventh-Century Tibetan Scholar Rong zom chos kyi bzang po: A Brief Survey." In *Tibet, Past and Present*, edited by Henk Blezer, 67–80. Leiden: Brill.

Akagi, Takatoshi. 2011. "Six 10th Century Royal Seals of the Khotan Kingdom." In *New Studies of the Old Tibetan Documents: Philology, History and Religion*, 217–29. Tokyo: Tokyo University of Foreign Studies.

Aris, Michael. 1989. *Hidden Treasures and Secret Lives: A Study of Pema Lingpa 1450–1521, and the Sixth Dalai Lama 1683–1706*. London: Kegan Paul International Limited.

Assmann, Jan. 1997. *Moses the Egyptian: The Memory of Egypt in Western Monotheism*. Cambridge: Harvard University Press.

———. 2006. *Religion and Cultural Memory*, translated by Rodney Livingstone. Stanford, CA: Stanford University Press.

Beal, Samuel, trans. 1884. *Buddhist Records of the Western World, Translated from the Chinese of Xuan Tsang (A.D. 629)*. London: Trübner & Co.

Beckwith, Christopher I. 1977. *A Study of the Early Medieval Chinese, Latin, and Tibetan Historical Sources on Pre-Imperial Tibet*. Ph.D. dissertation at Indiana University.

———. 1987. *The Tibetan Empire in Central Asia*. Princeton: Princeton University Press.

Beer, Robert. 2003. *The Handbook of Tibetan Symbols*. Boston: Shambhala Publications.

Behrendt, Kurt A. 2004. *The Buddhist Architecture of Gandhāra*. Leiden: Brill.

Bertsch, Wolfgang. 2001. *The Currency of Tibet*. Dharamsala: Library of Tibetan Works and Archives.

Bischoff, F. A. 1978. "Padmasambhava Est-Il un Personnage Historique?" In *Proceedings of the Csoma de Kőrös Symposium*, edited by Louis Ligeti, 27–33. Budapest: Akadémiai Kiadó.

Bischoff, F. A., and Charles Hartman. 1971. "Padmasambhava's Invention of the Phur-bu: Ms. Pelliot Tibétain 44." In *Études Tibétaine, Dédiées à la Mémoire de Marcelle Lalou*, 11–28. Paris: Librairie d'Amérique et d'Orient.

Bjerken, Zeff. 2002. "Hall of Mirrors: Tibetan Religious Histories as Mimetic Narratives." *Acta Orientalia* 64: 177–223.

Blezer, Henk. 2001. "Karma gling pa: Treasure Finder or Creative Editor." In *Reading Asia: New Research in Asian Studies*, edited by Frans Hüsken and Dick van der Meij, 292–338. Richmond: Curzon.

Blondeau, Anne-Marie. 1980. "Analysis of the Biographies of Padmasambhava According to the Tibetan Tradition: Classification of Sources." In *Tibetan Studies in Honor of Hugh Richardson*, edited by Michael Aris and Aung San Suu Kyi, 45–58. New Delhi: Vikas.

———. 1984. "Le 'Découvreur' du *Maṇi bka' 'bum*: Était-Il Bon po?" In *Tibetan and Buddhist Studies Commemorating the 200th Anniversary of the Birth of Alexander Csoma de Kőrös*, edited by Louis Ligeti, 1: 77–123. Budapest: Akadémiai Kiadó.

———. 1987. "Une Polémique sur L'authenticité des Bka'-thaṅ au 17e Siècle." In *Silver on Lapus: Tibetan Literary Culture and History*, edited by Christopher I. Beckwith, 125–60. Bloomington: Tibet Society.

———. 1990a. "Identification de la Tradition Appelée *bsGrags pa bon lugs*." In *Indo-Tibetan Studies: Papers in Honour and Appreciation of Professor David L. Snellgrove's Contribution to Indo-Tibetan Studies*, edited by Tadeusz Skorupski, 37–54. Tring: The Institute of Buddhist Studies.

———. 1990b. "Questions Préliminaires sur les Rituals *mDos*." In *Actes du Colloque Tibet, Civilisation et Société*, 91–107. Paris: éditions de la Fondation Singer-Polignac/ éditions de la Maison des Sciences de l'homme.

———. 1992. "Conférence de Mme Anne Marie Blondeau: Religions tibétaines." *École Pratique des Hautes Études, Section des Sciences Religieuses* 101: 67–72.

———. 1997. "Que Notre Enfant Revienne! Un Ritual Méconnu Pour les Enfants Morts en Bas-Âge." In *Les Habitants du Toit du Monde: Hommage à Alexander W. Macdonald*, edited by Samten G. Karmay and Philippe Sagant, 193–220. Nanterre: Société d'ethnologie.

Bogin, Benjamin. 2008. "The Dreadlocks Treatise: On Tantric Hairstyles in Tibetan Buddhism." *History of Religions* 48.2: 85–109.

Boord, Martin J. 1993. *The Cult of the Deity Vajrakīla: According to the Texts of the Northern Treasures Tradition of Tibet (Byang-gter phur-pa)*. Tring: The Institute of Buddhist Studies.

Burchardi, Anne. 2002. "Towards an Understanding of Tathāgatagarbha Doctrine in Tibet, with Reference to the *Ratnagotravibhāga*." In *Religion and Secular Culture in Tibet*, edited by Henk Blezer, 59–78. Leiden: Brill.

Buswell Jr., Robert E., and Donald S. Lopez Jr. 2014. *The Princeton Dictionary of Buddhism*. Princeton: Princeton University Press.

Cantwell, Cathy. 1995. "The Dance of the Guru's Eight Aspects." *Tibet Journal* 20.4: 47–63.

Cantwell, Cathy, and Robert Mayer. 2007. *The Kīlaya Nirvāṇa Tantra and the Vajra Wrath Tantra: Two Texts from the Ancient Tantra Collection*. Vienna: Verlag der Österreichischen Akademie der Wissenschaften.

———. 2008a. *Early Tibetan Documents on Phur ba from Dunhuang*. Vienna: Verlag der Österreichischen Akademie der Wissenschaften.

———. 2008b. "Enduring myths: *Smrang, Rabs*, and Ritual in the Dunhuang Texts on Padmasambhava." *Revue d'Etudes Tibétaines* 15: 289–312.

———. 2010. "The Creation and Transmission of a Textual Corpus in the Twentieth Century: The *'Chi med srog thig*." In *Edition, Editions: l'Écrit au Tibet, Evolution et Devenir*, edited by Anne Chayet, Cristina Scherrer-Schaub, Françoise Robin, and Jean-Luc Achard, 65–84. Munich: Indus Verlag.

———. 2012. *A Noble Noose of Methods, The Lotus Garland Synopsis: A Mahāyoga Tantra and Its Commentary*. Vienna: Österreichische Akademie der Wissenschaften.

———. 2013. "Representations of Padmasambhava in Early Post-Imperial Tibet." In *Tibet after Empire: Culture, Society and Religion Between 850–1000*, edited by Christoph Cuppers, Robert Mayer, and Michael Walters, 19–50. Lumbini: Lumbini International Research Institute.

———. 2015. "The Winged and the Fanged." In *From Bhakti to Bon: Festschrift for Per Kvaerne*, edited by Hannah Havnevik and Charles Ramble, 153–70. Oslo: The Institute for Comparative Religion in Human Culture, Novus Forlag.

Csoma de Kőrös, Alexander. 1838. "Enumeration of Historical and Grammatical Works to be Met With in Tibet." *Journal of the Asiatic Society of Bengal* 7: 147ff.

Cuevas, Brian. 2003. *The Hidden History of* The Tibetan Book of the Dead. New York: Oxford University Press.

———. 2006. "Some Reflections on the Periodization of Tibetan History." *Revue d'Etudes Tibétaines* 10: 44–55.

———. 2010. "The 'Calf's Nipple' (Be'u bum) of Ju Mipham ('Ju Mi pham)." In *Tibetan Ritual*, edited by José Ignatio Cabezón, 165–86. New York: Oxford University Press.

Dalton, Jacob P. 2002. *The Uses of the Dgongs pa 'dus pa'i mdo in the Development of the Rnying-ma School of Tibetan Buddhism*. Ph.D. dissertation at the University of Michigan.

———. 2004. "The Early Development of the Padmasambhava Legend in Tibet: A Study of IOL Tib J 644 and Pelliot Tibétain 307." *Journal of the American Oriental Society* 124.4: 759–72.

———. 2011. *The Taming of the Demons: Violence and Liberation in Tibetan Buddhism*. New Haven: Yale University Press.

Dalton, Jacob, and Sam van Schaik. 2006. *Tibetan Tantric Manuscripts from Dunhuang: A Descriptive Catalogue of the Stein Collection at the British Library*. Leiden: Brill.

Davidson, Ronald M. 2002. "Gsar ma Apocrypha: The Creation of Orthodoxy, Gray Texts, and the New Revelation." In *The Many Canons of Tibetan Buddhism*, edited by Helmut Eimer and David Germano, 203–24. Leiden: Brill.

———. 2003. *Indian Esoteric Buddhism: A Social History of the Tantric Movement*. New York: Columbia University Press.

———. 2005. *Tibetan Renaissance: Tantric Buddhism in the Rebirth of Tibetan Culture*. New York: Columbia University Press.

———. 2006. "Imperial Agency in the Gsar ma Treasure Texts during the Tibetan Renaissance: the Rgyal po bla gter and Related Literature." In *Tibetan Buddhist Literature and Praxis: Studies in Its Formative Period (900–1400)*, edited by Ronald M. Davidson and Christian K. Wedemeyer, 125–47. Leiden: Brill.

Denwood, Phillip. 1990. "Some Remarks on the Status and Dating of the Sba bzhed." *Tibet Journal* 15.4: 135–48.

Doctor, Andreas. 2005. *Tibetan Treasure Literature*. Ithaca, NY: Snow Lion Publications.

Doney, Lewis J. A. 2011. *Transforming Tibetan Kingship: The Portrayal of Khri Srong lde brtsan in the Early Buddhist Histories*. Ph.D. thesis at the School of Oriental and African Studies, University of London.

———. 2014. *The Zangs gling ma: The First Padmasambhava Biography. Two Exemplars of Its Earliest Attested Recension*. Andiast, Switzerland: International Institute for Tibetan and Buddhist Studies.

Dorje, Gyurme. 1987. *The Guhyagarbhatantra and Its XIVth Century Commentary Phyogs-bcu mun-sel*. Ph.D. thesis at the School of Oriental and African Studies, University of London.

———. 2009. *Tibet Guidebook*, 4th edition. Bath, Somerset: Footprint Publications.

Dorje, Gyurme, and Matthew Kapstein. 1991 (Rev. ed. 2002). *The Nyingma School of Tibetan Buddhism, Vol. II: Reference Materials*. Boston: Wisdom Publications.

Dotson, Brandon. 2007. "'Emperor' Mu rug btsan and the *'Phang thang ma Catalogue*." *Journal of the International Association of Tibetan Studies* 3: 1–25.

———. 2008. "Complementarity and Opposition in Early Tibetan Ritual." *Journal of the American Oriental Society* 128.1: 41–67.

———. 2009. *The Old Tibetan Annals: An Annotated Translation of Tibet's First History. With an Annotated Cartographical Documentation by Guntram Hazod*. Vienna: Austrian Academy of Sciences.

———. 2013. "The Unhappy Bride and Her Lament." *Journal of the International Association for Bon Research* 1: 199–225.

Douglas, Kenneth, and Gwendolyn Bays, trans. 1978. *The Life and Liberation of Padmasambhava* (*Le Dict de Padma, Padma Thang Yig*, translated by Gustave-Charles Touissant). Emeryville, CA: Dharma Publishing.

Dowman, Keith, trans. 1973. *The Legend of the Great Stupa of Boudhanath*. Kathmandu: Diamond Sow.

Dudjom Rinpoche. 1991 (Rev. ed. 2002). *The Nyingma School of Tibetan Buddhism*, edited and translated by Gyurme Dorje. Boston: Wisdom Publications.

Ehrhard, Franz-Karl. 2015. "'An Ocean of Marvelous Perfections': A 17th-Century *Padma bka' thang yig* from the Sa skya pa School." In *Tibetan Literature: Genre, Text and Textual Types*, edited by Jim Rheingans, 139–81. Leiden: Brill.

Everding, Karl-Heinz. 2014. *Verzeichnis der Orientalischen Handschriften in Deutschland, Band XI, 18*. Stuttgart: Franz Steiner Verlag.

Faber, Flemming. 1986. "The Council of Tibet According to the *sBa bzhed*." *Acta Orientalia* 46: 33–61.

Filigenzi, Anna. 2003. "A Vajrayanic Theme in the Rock Sculpture of Swat." *Buddhist Asia* 1: 37–55.

Fitzgerald, Timothy. 2000. *The Ideology of Religious Studies*. Oxford: Oxford University Press.

Foley, John Miles. 2010. "Plenitude and Diversity: Interactions between Orality and Writing." In *The Interface of Orality and Writing: Speaking, Seeing, Writing in the Shaping of New Genres*, edited by Annette Weissenrieder and Robert Coote, 103–18. Tübingen: Mohr Siebeck Verlag.

Foucault, Michel. 1972. *The Archaeology of Knowledge & The Discourse on Language*, translated by A. M. Sheridan Smith. New York: Pantheon Books.

———. 1984. "What Is an Author?" In *The Foucault Reader*, edited by Paul Rabinow, 101–20. New York: Pantheon Books.

Gamble, Ruth. 2013. *The View from Nowhere: The Travels of the Third Karmapa, Rang byung rdo rje in Story and Songs*. Ph.D. thesis at The Australian National University.

Gardner, Andrew Patten. 2006. *The Twenty-Five Great Sites of Khams: Religious Geography, Revelation, and Nonsectarianism in Nineteenth-Century Eastern Tibet*. Ph.D. dissertation at the University of Michigan.

Gayley, Holly. 2003. "Introduction." In *The Life and Revelations of Pema Lingpa*, translated by Sarah Harding, 1–28. Ithaca, NY: Snow Lion Publications.

———. 2007. "Ontology of the Past and Its Materialization in Tibetan Treasures." In *The Invention of Sacred Tradition*, edited by James R. Lewis and Olav Hammer, 213–40. Cambridge: Cambridge University Press.

Germano, David. 1994. "Architecture and Absence in the Secret Tantric History of rDzogs Chen." *Journal of the International Association of Buddhist Studies* 17.2: 203–335.

———. 1998. "Re-Membering the Dismembered Body of Tibet: Contemporary Tibetan Visionary Movements in the People's Republic of China." In *Buddhism in Contemporary*

Tibet, edited by Melvyn C. Goldstein and Matthew Kapstein, 53–94. Berkeley: University of California Press.

———. 2002a. "A Brief History of Nyingma Literature." http://www.thlib.org/collections/literature/nyingma.html. Accessed August 14, 2008.

———. 2002b. "History and Nature of the Collected Tantras of the Ancients." http://www.thdl.org/collections/literature/ngb/ngb-history.html. Accessed April 14, 2007.

———. 2002c. "Introduction" to "Canons at the Boundaries: The Rnying ma Tantras and Shades of Gray Between the Early and Late Translations." In *The Many Canons of Tibetan Buddhism*, edited by Helmut Eimer and David Germano, 199–202. Leiden: Brill.

———. 2002d. "The Seven Descents and the Early History of Rnying ma Transmissions." In *The Many Canons of Tibetan Buddhism*, edited by Helmut Eimer and David Germano, 225–64. Leiden: Brill.

———. 2005. "The Funerary Transformation of the Great Perfection (*Rdzogs chen*)." *Journal of the International Association of Tibetan Studies* 1: 1–54.

Gyamtso, Yeshe, trans. 2011. *The Hundred Tertöns*, by Jamgön Kongtrul Lodrö Taye. Woodstock, NY: KTD Publications.

Gyatso, Janet. Unpublished. "The Relic Text as Prophecy: The Semantic Drift of *Byang bu* and Its Appropriation in the Tibetan Treasure Tradition."

———. 1986. "Signs, Memory and History: A Tantric Buddhist Theory of Scriptural Transmission." *Journal of the International Association of Buddhist Studies* 9.2: 7–35.

———. 1992. "Genre, Authorship, and Transmission in Visionary Buddhism." In *Tibetan Buddhism: Reason and Revelation*, edited by Ronald Davidson and Stephen Goodman, 95–106. Albany: State University of New York Press.

———. 1993. "The Logic of Legitimation in the Tibetan Treasure Tradition." *History of Religions* 33.2: 97–134.

———. 1994. "An Early Survey of the Treasure Tradition and Its Strategies in Discussing Bon Treasure." In *Tibetan Studies* 1, edited by Per Kvaerne, 275–87. Oslo: Institute for Comparative Research in Human Culture.

———. 1996. "Drawn from the Tibetan Treasury: The *gTer ma* Literature." In *Tibetan Literature: Studies in Genre*, edited by José I. Cabezón and Roger R. Jackson, 147–69. Ithaca, NY: Snow Lion Publications.

———. 1998. *Apparitions of the Self: The Secret Autobiographies of a Tibetan Visionary*. Princeton: Princeton University Press.

———. 2006. "A Partial Genealogy of the Life-Story of Ye shes mtsho rgyal." *Journal of the International Association of Tibetan Studies* 2: 1–27.

Haarh, Eric. 1969. *The Yar luṅ Dynasty*. Copenhagen: G.E.C. Gad.

Halkias, Georgios T. 2004. "Tibetan Buddhism Registered: An Imperial Catalogue from the Palace Temple of 'Phang-thang." *The Eastern Buddhist* 36.1–2: 46–105.

Harrison, Paul M. 1978. *The Tibetan Text of the Pratyutpanna-buddha-saṃmukhāvasthita-samādhi-nāma-mahāyāna-sūtra*. Tokyo: The Reiyukai Library.

———. 1990. *The Samādhi of Direct Encounter with the Buddhas of the Present: An Annotated English Translation of the Tibetan Version of the Pratyutpanna-Buddha-Saṃmukhāvasthita-Samādhi-Sūtra*. Tokyo: The International Institute for Buddhist Studies.

———. 2003. "Mediums and Messages: Reflections on the Production of Mahāyāna Sūtras." *Eastern Buddhist* 35.1–2: 115–51.

Hatchell, Christopher. 2014. *Naked Seeing: The Great Perfection, the Wheel of Time, and Visionary Buddhism in Renaissance Tibet*. New York: Oxford University Press.

Helman-Wazny, Agnieszka. 2010. "Historical, Art-Historical, and Natural Science Approaches to Dating Tibetan Books—Possibilities and Limitations." In *Tibetan Studies: An Anthology*, edited by Saadet Arslan and Peter Schwieger, 279–95. Andiast, Switzerland: International Institute for Tibetan and Buddhist Studies GmbH.

Hirshberg, Daniel A. 2009. "Karmic Foreshadowing on the Path of Fruition: Narrative Devices in the Early Biographies of Nyang ral nyi ma 'od zer." *Bulletin of Tibetology*, 45.1: 53–78.

———. 2012. *Delivering the Lotus-Born: Historiography in the Tibetan Renaissance*. Ph.D. dissertation at Harvard University.

———. Forthcoming. "A Post-Incarnate Usurper? Inheritance at the Dawn of Catenate Reincarnation in Tibet." In *The Reincarnation Institution in Tibetan Buddhism*, edited by Tsering Wangchuk and Derek Maher. Boston: Wisdom Publications.

Hodge, Stephen. 2003. *The Mahā-Vairocana-Abhisaṃbodhi Tantra with Buddhaguhya's Commentary*. New York: RoutledgeCurzon.

Honko, Lauri. 2000. "Text as Process and Practice: The Textualization of Oral Epics." In *Textualization of Oral Epics*, edited by Lauri Honko, 3–54. Berlin: Mouton de Gruyer.

Ishikawa, M. 1990. *A Critical Edition of the Sgra sbyor bam po gnyis pa: An Old and Basic Commentary on the Mahāvyutpatti*. Tokyo: Tōyō Bunko.

Jackson, David P. 1990. *Two Biographies of Śākyaśrībhadra: The Eulogy by Khro-phu lo-tsā-ba and Its "Commentary" by Bsod-nams-dpal-bzang-po: Texts and Variants from Two Rare Exemplars Preserved in the Bihar Research Society, Patna*. Stuttgart: Franz Steiner Verlag.

Jaffee, Martin S. 2007. "Rabbinic Authorship as a Collective Enterprise." In *The Cambridge Companion to the Talmud and Rabbinic Literature*, edited by Charlotte Elisheva Fonrobert and Martin S. Jaffee, 17–37. New York: Cambridge University Press.

Jinpa, Thupten, trans. 2008. *The Book of Kadam: The Core Texts*. Boston: Wisdom Publications.

Kapstein, Matthew T. 2000. *The Tibetan Assimilation of Buddhism*. New York: Oxford University Press.

———. 2003. "The Indian Literary Identity in Tibet." In *Literary Cultures in History: Reconstructions from South Asia*, edited by Sheldon Pollock, 747–802. Berkeley: University of California Press.

———. 2006. *The Tibetans*. Malden: Blackwell Publishing.

———. 2008. "The *Son of the Heart* and the *Bai-ro-rgyud-'bum*." *Revue d'Etudes Tibétaines*, 15: 275–88.

———. 2015. "*Gter-ma* as Imperial Treasure: The 1755 Beijing Edition of the *Padma bka' thang*." In *Trails of the Tibetan Tradition: Papers for Elliot Sperling*, edited by Roberto Vitali, 167–87. Dharamsala: Amnye Machen.

Karmay, Samten G. 1972. *The Treasury of Good Sayings: A Tibetan History of Bon*. London: Oxford University Press.

———. 1988. *The Great Perfection (rDzogs chen): A Philosophical and Meditative Teaching of Tibetan Buddhism*. Leiden: Brill.

———. 1998. *The Arrow and the Spindle: Studies in History, Myths, Rituals and Beliefs in Tibet*, vol. 1. Kathmandu: Mandala Book Point.

———. 2000. "Dorje Lingpa and His Rediscovery of the 'Gold Needle' in Bhutan." *Journal of Bhutan Studies* 2.2: 1–35.

Khoroche, Peter, trans. 1989. *Once the Buddha Was a Monkey: Ārya Śūra's Jātakamāla*. Chicago: University of Chicago Press.

Kunsang, Erik Pema, trans. 1990. *Dakini Teachings*. Boston: Shambhala Publications.

———. 1993. *The Lotus Born*. Boston: Shambhala Publications.

———. 1994. *Advice from the Lotus Born*. Hong Kong: Rangjung Yeshe Publications.

———. 2008. *Treasures from Juniper Ridge*. Hong Kong: Rangjung Yeshe Publications.

Kuwayama, Shoshin. 1991. "L'Inscription du Gaṇeśa de Gardez et la Chronologie des Turki-Ṣāhis." *Journal Asiatique* 279.3–4: 267–87.

Kvaerne, Per. 1972. "Aspects of the Origin of the Buddhist Tradition of Tibet." *Numen* 19.1: 22–40.

Lalou, Marcelle. 1953. "Les Textes Bouddhiques au Temps du Roi Khri-srong-lde-bcan." *Journal Asiatique* 241: 313–53.

Lamotte, Étienne. 1976. *The Teaching of Vimalakīrti (Vimalakīrtinirdeśa)*, translated by Sara Boin. London: Pali Text Society.

Li Fang Kuei and W. South Coblin. 1987. *A Study of the Old Tibetan Inscriptions*. Taipei: Institute of History and Philology Academia Sinica.

Lopez Jr., Donald S. 1992. "Memories of the Buddha." In *In the Mirror of Memory: Reflections on Mindfulness and Remembrance in Indian and Tibetan Buddhism*, edited by Janet Gyatso, 21–45. New York: State University of New York.

———. 1998. *Prisoners of Shangri-la*. Chicago: The University of Chicago Press.

———. 2011. *The Tibetan Book of the Dead: A Biography*. Princeton, NJ: Princeton University Press.

López, Manuel. 2014. *Bringing Light into the Darkness: An Intellectual History of Tibet's Dark Age*. Ph.D. dissertation at the University of Virginia.

Macdonald, Alexander. 1984. "Religion in Tibet at the Time of Srong-btsan sgam-po: Myth as History." In *Tibetan and Buddhist Studies Commemorating the 200th Anniversary of the Birth of Alexander Csoma de Kőrös*, edited by Louis Ligetti, 129–40. Budapest: Akadémiai Kiadó.

Manson, Charles E. 2009. "An Introduction to the Life of Karma Pakshi (1204/6–1283)." *Bulletin of Tibetology* 45.1: 25–52.

———. Forthcoming. "Elastic Time, Magical Memories: Multifarious Lives of Karmapas." In *The Reincarnation Institution in Tibetan Buddhism*, edited by Tsering Wangchuk and Derek Maher. Boston: Wisdom Publications.

Martin, Dan. 1996a. "The Star King and the Four Children of Pehar: Popular Religious Movements in 11th–12th-Century Tibet." *Acta Orientalia Hungarica* 46: 171–95.

———. 1996b. "Lay Religious Movements in 11th- to 12th-Century Tibet: A Survey of Sources." *Kailash* 18: 23–55.

———. 2001. *Unearthing Bon Treasures: Life and Contested Legacy of a Tibetan Scripture Revealer*. Leiden: Brill.

Mayer, Robert. 1994. "Scriptural Revelation in India and Tibet: Indian Precursors of the gTer ma Tradition." In *Tibetan Studies 6*, edited by Per Kvaerne, 533–44. Oslo: The Institute for Comparative Research in Human Culture.

———. 1996. *A Scripture of the Ancient Tantra Collection: The Phur pa bcu gnyis*. Oxford: Kiscadale Publications.

———. 2007. "The Importance of the Underworlds: Asuras' Caves in Buddhism, and Some Other Themes in Early Buddhist Tantras Reminiscent of the Later Padmasambhava Legends." *Journal of the International Association of Tibetan Studies* 3: 1–30.

———. 2010a. "Early Terma as Found Manuscripts." *Kīli Kīlaya*. http://blogs.orient.ox.ac.uk/kila/2010/09/17/early-terma-as-found-manuscripts/. Accessed October 1, 2010.

———. 2010b. "Authors, Plagiarists, or Tradents?" *Kīli Kīlaya*. http://blogs.orient.ox.ac.uk/kila/2010/10/09/authors-plagiarists-or-tradents/. Accessed December 17, 2010.

———. 2011a. "Padmasambhava in Early Tibetan Myth and Ritual: Part 1, Introduction." http://blogs.orient.ox.ac.uk/kila/2011/05/06/padmasambhava-in-early-tibetan-myth-and-ritual-part-1/. Accessed March 7, 2012.

———. 2011b. "Padmasambhava in Early Tibetan Myth and Ritual, Part 2: IOLTibJ321." http://blogs.orient.ox.ac.uk/kila/2011/05/08/padmasambhava-in-early-tibetan-myth-and-ritual-part-2-ioltibj321/. Accessed May 9, 2011.

———. 2012. "The Great Khu tsha zla 'od." http://blogs.orient.ox.ac.uk/kila/2012/04/27/the-great-khu-tsha-zla-od/. Accessed April 29, 2012.

———. 2013a. "Early Guru Yoga, Indigenous Ritual, and Padmasambhava." http://blogs.orient.ox.ac.uk/kila/2013/10/07/early-guru-yoga-indigenous-ritual-and-padmasambhava/. Accessed October 9, 2013.

———. 2013b. "Historical Proof by Textual Criticism?" http://blogs.orient.ox.ac.uk/kila/2013/11/08/926/. Accessed May 15, 2014.

———. 2015a. "Nyingma Tantras." In *Brill's Encyclopedia of Buddhism*, edited by Jonathan A. Silk, 1: 390–97. Leiden: Brill.

———. 2015b. "'We Swear Our Grandparents Were There!' (Or, What Can the Sex Pistols Tell Us About Padmasambhava?): The Making of Myth in 10th Century Tibet and 20th Century England." In *The Illuminating Mirror: Tibetan Studies in Honour of Per K. Sørensen on the Occasion of His 65th Birthday*, edited by Olaf Czaja and Guntram Hazod, 341–56. Weisbaden: Dr. Ludwig Reichert Verlag.

Meisezahl, R. O. 1985. *Die Große Geschichte des Tibetischen Buddhismus nach Alter Tradition*. Sankt Augustin, Germany: VGH Wissenschaftsverlag.

Nebesky-Wojkowitz, René de. 1956. *Oracles and Demons of Tibet: The Cult and Iconography of the Tibetan Protective Deities*. The Hague: Mouton and Co.

Olivelle, Patrick, trans. 2008. *Life of the Buddha by Ashva-ghosha*. Clay Sanskrit Library. New York: New York University Press & JJC Foundation.

Oesterreicher, Wulf. 1997. "Types of Orality in Text." In *Written Voices, Spoken Signs: Tradition, Performance, and the Epic Text*, edited by Egbert Bakker and Ahuvia Kahane, 190–214. Cambridge, MA: Harvard University Press.

Panglung, Jampa. 1992. "On the Narrative of the Killing of the Evil Yak and the Discovery of Salt in the Chos-'byung of Nyang-ral." In *Tibetan Studies: Language, History and Culture* 2, edited by Shoren Ihara and Zuiho Yamaguchi, 661–68. Narita: Naritasan Shinshoji.

Patrul Rinpoche. 2011. *The Words of My Perfect Teacher*, translated by the Padmakara Translation Group. New Haven, CT: Yale University Press.

Pelliot, Paul. 1961. *Histoire Ancienne du Tibet*. Paris: Adrien Maisonneuve.

Petech, Luciano. 1994. "The Disintegration of the Tibetan Kingdom." In *Tibetan Studies 6*, edited by Per Kvaerne, 649–59. Oslo: The Institute for Comparative Research in Human Culture.

Phillips, Bradford Lyman. 2004. *Consummation and Compassion in Medieval Tibet: The* Maṇi bka'-'bum chen-mo *of Guru Chos-kyi dbang-phyug*. Ph.D. dissertation at the University of Virginia.

Prats, Ramon. 1980. "Some Preliminary Considerations Arising from a Biographical Study of the Early gTer-ston." In *Tibetan Studies in Honor of Hugh Richardson*, edited by Michael Aris and Aung San Suu Kyi, 256–60. Warminster: Aris and Phillips.

Quintman, Andrew. 2013. "Life Writing as Literary Relic: Image, Inscription, and Consecration in Tibetan Biography." *Material Religion*, 9.4: 468–505.

———. 2013. *The Yogin and the Madman: Reading the Biographical Corpus of Tibet's Great Saint Milarepa*. New York: Columbia Univeristy Press.

Richardson, Hugh E. 1985. *A Corpus of Early Tibetan Inscriptions*. Hertford: Royal Asiatic Society.

———. 1998. *High Peaks, Pure Earth: Collected Writings on Tibetan History and Culture*, edited by Michael Aris. London: Serindia Publications.

Roerich, George N., trans. 1949. *The Blue Annals*, by 'Gos Lotsāwa. Delhi: Motilal Banarsidass.

Sanderson, Alexis. 2001. "History through Textual Criticism in the Study of Śaivism, the Pañcarātra and the Buddhist Yoginītantras." In *Les Sources et le Temps*, edited by François Grimal, 1–47. Pondicherry: Institut Français de Pondichery / École Française d'Extrême-Orient.

———. 2007. "The Śaiva Exegesis of Kashmir." In *Mélanges Tantriques à la Mémoire d'Hélène Brunner*, edited by Dominic Goodall and André Padoux, 231–444. Pondicherry: Institut Français de Pondichery / École Française d'Extrême-Orient.

Scherrer-Schaub, Cristina A. 2002. "Enacting Words: A Diplomatic Analysis of the Imperial Decrees (*bkas bcad*) and Their Application in the *Gra sbyor bam po gnyis pa* Tradition." *Journal of the International Association of Buddhist Studies* 25.1–2: 263–340.

Schwieger, Peter. 2013. "History as Myth: On the Appropriation of the Past in Tibetan Culture, An Essay in Cultural Studies." In *The Tibetan History Reader*, edited by Gray Tuttle and Kurtis Schaeffer, 64–85. New York: Columbia University Press.

———. 2015. *The Dalai Lama and the Emperor of China: A Political History of the Tibetan Institution of Reincarnation*. New York: Columbia University Press.

Shantideva. 2006. *The Way of the Bodhisattva*, translated by the Padmakara Translation Group. Boston: Shambhala Publications.

Sherburne, Richard. 1991. "Review of *Hidden Treasures and Secret Lives*." *Journal of the American Oriental Society* 111.1: 205–6.

Silk, Jonathan. 2003. "The Fruits of Paradox: On the Religious Architecture of the Buddha's Life Story." *Journal of the American Academy of Religion* 71.4: 863–81.

Snellgrove, David L. 1987. *Indo-Tibetan Buddhism: Indian Buddhists and Their Tibetan Successors*. Boston: Shambhala Publications.

Sørensen, Per K. 1994. *Tibetan Buddhist Historiography: The Mirror Illuminating the Royal Genealogies: An Annotated Translation of the XIVth Century Tibetan Chronicle rGyal-rabs gsal-ba'i me-long*. Weisbaden: Harrassowitz.

Sørensen, Per K. and Guntram Hazod, with Tsering Gyalbo. 2007. *Rulers on the Celestial Plain: Ecclesiastic and Secular Hegemony in Medieval Tibet. A Study of Tshal Gung-thang*. Vienna: Austrian Academy of Sciences.

Stein, R. A., ed. 1961. *Une Chronique Ancienne de bSam-yas, sBa bźed*. Paris: Institut des Hautes Études Chinoises.

———. 1972. *Tibetan Civilization*. Stanford, CA: Stanford University Press.

———. 1973. "Un ensemble sémantique tibétain: créer et procréer, être et devenir, vivre, nourrir et guérir." *Bulletin of the School of Oriental and African Studies* 36: 412–23.

Szánto, Péter-Dániel. 2013. "Before a Critical Edition of the Sampuṭa." In *Tibet After Empire: Culture, Society and Religion Between 850–1000*, edited by Christoph Cuppers,

Robert Mayer, and Michael Walter, 343–66. Lumbini: Lumbini International Research Institute.

Szerb, János. 1990. "Two Notes on the Sources of the Chos 'byung of Bu ston rin chen grub." In *Reflections on Tibetan Culture: Essays in Memory of Turrell V. Wylie*, edited by Lawrence Epstein and Richard F. Sherburne, 143–45. Lewiston, NY: The Edwin Mellen Press.

Takeuchi, Tsuguhito. 2004. "Sociolinguistic Implications of the Use of Tibetan in East Turkestan from the End of Tibetan Domination through the Tangut Period (9th–12th C.E.)." In *Turfan Revisited: The First Century of Research into the Arts and Culture of the Silk Road*, edited by Simone Christiane Raschmann, 341–48. Berlin: Dietrich Reimer.

Thondup, Tulku. 1986. *Hidden Teachings of Tibet: An Explanation of the Terma Tradition of the Nyingma School of Buddhism*. Boston: Wisdom Publications.

———. 2011. *Incarnation: The History and Mysticism of the Tulku Tradition of Tibet*. Boston: Shambhala Publications.

Thurman, Robert A. F. 1991. "Review of *Hidden Treasures and Secret Lives*." *Journal of Asian Studies* 50.2: 375–77.

———. 2003 [1976]. *The Holy Teaching of Vimalakīrti: A Mahāyāna Scripture*. University Park: Pennsylvania State University Press.

Tucci, Giuseppe. 1949. *Tibetan Painted Scrolls*, 3 vols. Rome: Librerio dello Stato.

———. 1950. *The Tombs of the Tibetan Kings*. Serie Orientale Roma 1. Rome: Instituto Italiano per l'Africa e l'Orient.

———. 1977. "On Swāt: The Dards and Connected Problems." *East and West* 27.1: 9–103.

Uray, Géza. 1968. "A Chronological Problem in the *Old Tibetan Chronicle*." *Acta Orientalia Academiae Scientiarum Hungaricae* 11: 258–69.

van Buitenen, J. A. B. 1973. *The Mahābhārata*. Chicago: University of Chicago Press.

van der Kuijp, Leonard W. J. 1984. "Miscellanea to a Recent Contribution on/to the Bsam-yas Debate." *Kailash* 11.3–4: 149–84.

———. 1991. "A Recent Contribution on the History of the Tibetan Empire." *Journal of the American Oriental Society* 111.1: 94–107.

———. 1992. "Dating the Two Lde'u Chronicles of Buddhism in India and Tibet." *Asiatische Studien* 46.1: 469–91.

———. 1994. "Review: On the Lives of Śākyaśrībhadra (?–?1225)." *Journal of the American Oriental Society* 114.4: 599–616.

———. 1995. "Tibetan Historiography." In *Tibetan Literature: Studies in Genre*, edited by José I. Cabezón and Roger R. Jackson, 39–56. Ithaca, NY: Snow Lion Publications.

———. 2005. "The Dalai Lamas and the Origins of Reincarnate Lamas." In *The Dalai Lamas: A Visual History*, edited by Martin Brauen, 14–31. Chicago: Serindia Publications.

———. 2013a. "On the Edge of Myth and History: Za hor, Its Place in the History of Early Indian Buddhist Tantra, and Dalai Lama V and the Genealogy of Its Royal Family." In *Studies on Buddhist Myths: Texts, Pictures, Traditions and History*, edited by Wang Bangwei, Chen Jinhua, and Chen Ming, 114–64. Shanghai: Zhongxi Publications.

———. 2013b. "Some Remarks on the Textual Transmission and Text of Bu ston Rin chen grub's *Chos 'byung*, a Chronicle of Buddhism in India and Tibet." *Revue d'Etudes Tibétaines* 25: 115–93.

van Schaik, Sam. 2004. "The Early Days of the Great Perfection." *Journal of the International Association of Buddhist Studies* 27.1: 165–206.

———. 2007. "Oral Teachings and Written Texts: Transmission and Transformation in Dunhuang." In *Contributions to the Cultural History of Early Tibet*, edited by Matthew T. Kapstein and Brandon Dotson, 183–208. Leiden: Brill.

van Schaik, Sam, and Kazushi Iwao. 2008. "Fragments of the *Testament of Ba* from Dunhuang." *Journal of the American Oriental Society* 128.3: 477–87.

Vitali, Robert. 1990. *Early Temples of Central Tibet*. London: Serindia Publications.

Vostrikov, A. I. 1970 [1935]. *Tibetan Historical Literature*, translated by Harish Chandra Gupta. London: Curzon Press.

Waddell, L. A. 1939 [1894]. *The Buddhism of Tibet; Or Lamaism, with Its Mystic Cults, Symbolism and Mythology, and in Its Relation to Indian Buddhism*. Cambridge, U.K.: W. Heffer & Sons.

Walters, Jonathan S. 2000. "Buddhist History: The Sri Lankan *Pāli Vaṃsas* and Their Commentary." In *Querying the Medieval: Texts and the History of Practices in South Asia*, 99–164. New York: Oxford University Press.

Wangchuk, Dorji. 2002. "An Eleventh-Century Defense of the Authenticity of the *Guhyagarbha Tantra*." In *The Many Canons of Tibetan Buddhism*, edited by Helmut Eimer and David Germano, 265–92. Leiden: Brill.

Wangdu, Pasang, and Hildegard Diemberger, eds. and trans. 2000. *dBa' bzhed: The Royal Narrative Concerning the Bringing of the Buddha's Doctrine to Tibet*. Vienna: Verlag der Österreichischen Akademie der Wissenschaften.

White, David Gordon. 2003. *Kiss of the Yoginī: "Tantric Sex" in Its South Asian Contexts*. Chicago: University of Chicago Press.

White, Hayden. 1987. *The Content of the Form: Narrative Discourse and Historical Representation*. Baltimore: Johns Hopkins University Press.

———. 2005. "Introduction: Historical Fiction, Fictional History, and Historical Reality." *Rethinking History* 9.2: 147–57.

Willis, Michael. 2012. "From World Religion to World Dominion: Trading, Translation, and Institution-Building in Tibet." In *Religions and Trade: Religious Formation, Transformation and Cross-Cultural Exchange between East and West*, edited by Peter Wick and Volker Rabens, 1–22. Leiden: Brill.

Yamaguchi, Zuiho. 1996. "The Fiction of King Dar ma's Persecution of Buddhism." In *Du Dunhuang au Japon: Etudes Chinois Michel Soymié*, edited by J. P. Drege, 230–58. Geneva: Librairie Droz.

Yamamoto, Carl Shigeo. 2009. *Vision and Violence: Lama Zhang and the Politics of Charisma in Twelfth-Century Tibet*. Leiden: Brill, 2012.

Yang Ga. 2010. *The Sources for the Writing of the Rgyud bzhi, Tibetan Medical Classic*. Ph.D. dissertation at Harvard University.

Zangpo, Ngawang. 2002. *Guru Rinpoche: His Life and Times*. Ithaca, NY: Snow Lion Publications.

Index

About the Author

DANIEL A. HIRSHBERG is Assistant Professor of Religion at the University of Mary Washington in Fredericksburg, Virginia.

Studies in Indian and Tibetan Buddhism
Titles Previously Published

Among Tibetan Texts
History and Literature of the Himalayan Plateau
E. Gene Smith

Approaching the Great Perfection
Simultaneous and Gradual Methods of Dzogchen Practice in the Longchen Nyingtig
Sam van Schaik

Authorized Lives
Biography and the Early Formation of Geluk Identity
Elijah S. Ary

Buddhism Between Tibet and China
Edited by Matthew T. Kapstein

The Buddhist Philosophy of the Middle
Essays on Indian and Tibetan Madhyamaka
David Seyfort Ruegg

Buddhist Teaching in India
Johannes Bronkhorst

A Direct Path to the Buddha Within
Gö Lotsāwa's Mahāmudrā Interpretation of the Ratnagotravibhāga
Klaus-Dieter Mathes

Foundations of Dharmakīrti's Philosophy
John D. Dunne

Freedom from Extremes
Gorampa's "Distinguishing the Views" and the Polemics of Emptiness
José Ignacio Cabezón and Geshe Lobsang Dargyay

Himalayan Passages
Tibetan and Newar Studies in Honor of Hubert Decleer
Benjamin Bogin and Andrew Quintman

How Do Mādhyamikas Think?
And Other Essays on the Buddhist Philosophy of the Middle
Tom J. F. Tillemans

Luminous Lives
The Story of the Early Masters of the Lam 'bras Tradition in Tibet
Cyrus Stearns

Mipham's Beacon of Certainty
Illuminating the View of Dzogchen, the Great Perfection
John Whitney Pettit

Omniscience and the Rhetoric of Reason
Śāntarakṣita and Kamalaśīla on Rationality, Argumentation, and Religious Authority
Sara L. McClintock

Reason's Traces
Identity and Interpretation in Indian and Tibetan Buddhist Thought
Matthew T. Kapstein

Resurrecting Candrakīrti
Disputes in the Tibetan Creation of Prāsaṅgika
Kevin A. Vose

Scripture, Logic, Language
Essays on Dharmakīrti and His Tibetan Successors
Tom J. F. Tillemans

The Svātantrika-Prāsaṅgika Distinction
What Difference Does a Difference Make?
Edited by Georges Dreyfus and Sara McClintock

Vajrayoginī
Her Visualizations, Rituals, and Forms
Elizabeth English

About Wisdom Publications

Wisdom Publications is the leading publisher of classic and contemporary Buddhist books and practical works on mindfulness. To learn more about us or to explore our other books, please visit our website at wisdompubs.org or contact us at the address below.

Wisdom Publications
199 Elm Street
Somerville, MA 02144 USA

We are a 501(c)(3) organization, and donations in support of our mission are tax deductible.

Wisdom Publications is affiliated with the Foundation for the Preservation of the Mahayana Tradition (FPMT).